Making Freedom *is a beautifully crafted five-volume sourcebook for classroom use. In its presentation of primary sources and learning strategies it has no rival in the area of African American history. This handsome, thought-provoking series belongs on the desk of every middle and high school United States history teacher who knows that without African American history there is only a partial and unbalanced United States history.*

GARY B. NASH
Director, National Center for History in the Schools
University of California, Los Angeles

The Making Freedom *Sourcebooks and CDs are a treasure trove of documents, analysis, and resources guaranteed to inspire lively classroom discussion and thoughtful student research. This original collaboration between teachers and scholars offers extraordinary access to the historical and continuing role of African Americans in the shaping of our nation.*

MARILYN RICHARDSON
Former Curator, Museum of Afro-American History and
the African Meeting House, Boston, Massachusetts

Making Freedom *offers teachers of American history a powerful and compelling teaching tool to help broaden their focus curriculum. The lessons are well crafted and provide students an opportunity to sharpen historical and critical thinking skills in a dynamic, meaningful, and relevant fashion. In the hands of teachers,* Making Freedom *will make a difference.*

JIM PERCOCO
Author, Divided We Stand: Teaching
About Conflict in U.S. History

Developed through a skillful collaboration between scholars and experienced social studies teachers and curriculum specialists—and covering a span of time from medieval Jenne-Jeno to 1970—this excellent five-volume set is built around firsthand evidence (mostly written documents but also many visual materials). Undoubtedly it will be a valuable classroom resource for students and teachers alike.

ROBERT L. HALL
Department of African-American Studies
Northeastern University, Boston, Massachusetts

For many students, the fact that the past was made up of real people who made real decisions about issues that are not far different from ones that we face today rarely comes through in the textbooks that they use. Primary Source's Making Freedom *helps open the history classroom to the lives of many different types of people. The range of documents and the* ~~~~ *been to use them creatively give a real opportunity for teachers to help th* ~~~~ *past and its relevance to today.*

COHEN
iversity

The curricula within these sourcebooks was developed by some of the most creative educators I have ever met. We are truly excited about sharing them with you.

Rachel Zucker wrote "Paul Robeson" and "The Black Press" in Sourcebook 5

I have found as both an educator and an administrator that I have learned more of my own history by being involved in this historical project. For teachers of color, it will be most helpful in the classroom where we can share the true stories of African American culture and help to correct some misinformation of the past. After all, African American history IS American history.

Deborah Ward contributed to "The Exodusters—Ho for Kansas!" in Sourcebook 4

I use primary sources in my curriculum because the students become more engaged in the process of discovering history for themselves. They are fascinated by reading and deciphering the art, documents, letters, diary entries, and law codes written in centuries past. I feel these exercises encourage students to empathize with people of the past and to better understand complex aspects of history. History comes alive!

Laurel Starks wrote "The Slave Experience: Their Words and Others" and "Slavery and Resistance" in Sourcebook 3

I recall deciding in the fourth grade that history was not for me or about me. It definitely did not make me feel connected to anything. The lessons I wrote in the Primary Source Black Yankees Seminar (subsequently a part of the series) gave me an exciting rebirth experience that forged a connection for me and turned on my search for historical truth. The Making Freedom *series empowers teachers to make history come alive for students of all ages.*

Deborah Gray wrote "Slave Literacy" and contributed to "Schooling of Free Blacks—The Roots of 'Separate But Equal'" in Sourcebook 3

I found that using these primary source materials with my students helped them understand more thoroughly the issues and complexities of the time periods being studied. Students and I use the key questions and organizing ideas to focus and guide our thinking through the many activities and assessments provided by the Sourcebooks. Students are engaged in the work and seek additional information to increase their knowledge of history.

Leslie Kramer wrote a number of lessons in Sourcebook 1, including "Sugar and Slaves," "Riverine Craft—Bringing the Skills Over," and "Resistance and Rebellions"

Writing lessons for the Making Freedom *series represented the ideal scholarly endeavor: I could use my research and analytic skills to get to the heart of the topic and then draw on my teaching experience to present the material in a meaningful way to students. I appreciate being able to give students this opportunity to immerse themselves in the richness and subtlety of history.*

Mark Meier wrote "Urban Disturbances" and "Many Roads to Freedom" in Sourcebook 5

Making Freedom

African Americans in U.S. History

SOURCEBOOK 3

Lift Ev'ry Voice

1830–1860

Making Freedom
African Americans in U.S. History

SOURCEBOOK 3

Lift Ev'ry Voice
1830–1860

COMPILED AND EDITED BY
THE CURRICULUM SPECIALISTS AT
PRIMARY SOURCE, INC.

FOREWORD BY
JAMES OLIVER HORTON

HEINEMANN
PORTSMOUTH, NH

Heinemann

A division of Reed Elsevier Inc.

361 Hanover Street

Portsmouth, NH 03801–3912

www.heinemann.com

Offices and agents throughout the world

Acknowledgments for borrowed material begin on p. 211.

Library of Congress Cataloging-in-Publication Data

Making freedom : African Americans in U.S. history / compiled and edited by the curriculum specialists at Primary Source, Inc. ; foreword by James Oliver Horton.

    p.   cm.

   Includes bibliographical references.

   ISBN 0-325-00515-X (v. 1 : acid-free paper) — ISBN 0-325-00516-8 (v. 2 : acid-free paper) — ISBN 0-325-00517-6 (v. 3 : acid-free paper) — ISBN 0-325-00518-4 (v. 4 : acid-free paper) — ISBN 0-325-00519-2 (v. 5: acid-free paper)

   1. African Americans—History—Study and teaching.   2. African Americans—History—Sources.   I. Primary Source, Inc.

E184.7.M34 2004

973'.0496073'0071—dc22   2003024628

Editor for Heinemann: Danny Miller

Editor for Primary Source: Liz Nelson

Production service: Lisa Garboski, bookworks

Production coordinator: Vicki Kasabian

CD production: Marla Berry and Nicole Guay

Interior and cover design: Catherine Hawkes, Cat & Mouse

Typesetter: TechBooks

Manufacturing: Steve Bernier

Printed in the United States of America on acid-free paper

08 07 06 05 04 VP 1 2 3 4 5

The Making Freedom *series is dedicated to the memory of*
Clara Hicks,
a former school principal in Newton, Massachusetts,
and a colleague at Primary Source.
She served briefly as a Project Administrator for this series
and has left us a legacy of wisdom and joy.

Primary Source has created the Making Freedom *Sourcebooks*
thanks to the generosity of these contributors:

National Endowment for the Humanities
Germeshausen Foundation
LEF Foundation
Massachusetts Foundation for the Humanities
Wellspring Foundation
and many individual donors

Lift Ev'ry Voice and Sing

JAMES WELDON JOHNSON

Lift ev'ry voice and sing,
Till earth and heaven ring,
Ring with the harmonies of Liberty;
Let our rejoicing rise
High as the list'ning skies,
Let it resound loud as the rolling sea.
Sing a song full of the faith that the dark past has taught us,
Sing a song full of the hope that the present has brought us;
Facing the rising sun of our new day begun,
Let us march on till victory is won.

Stony the road we trod,
Bitter the chast'ning rod,
Felt in the days when hope unborn had died;
Yet with a steady beat,
Have not our weary feet
Come to the place for which our fathers sighed?
We have come over a way that with tears has been watered,
We have come, treading our path through the blood of the slaughtered,
Out from the gloomy past,
Till now we stand at last
Where the white gleam of our bright star is cast.

God of our weary years,
God of our silent tears,
Thou who hast brought us thus far on the way;
Thou who hast by Thy might,
Led us into the light,
Keep us forever in the path, we pray.
Lest our feet stray from the places, our God, where we met Thee,
Lest our hearts, drunk with the wine of the world, we forget Thee;
Shadowed beneath Thy hand,
May we forever stand,
True to our God,
True to our native land.

Contents

Part I ✴ Slavery in the South

What were the experiences of enslaved men and women? How are their stories revealed through the eyes of black and white members of the same communities? How are the lives of free and enslaved people, black and white, constricted by the institution of slavery?

Part II ✴ The Printed Word

From Freedom's Journal *to* The North Star, *what was the role of literacy in the struggle to abolish slavery? How did the printed word fuel the cause of abolition? What impact did early black newspapers have on the development of the antislavery/ abolitionist movement?*

Part III ✳ Literacy and Schooling

How was the need for education of blacks supported and denied in northern communities? What initiatives did African Americans take to ensure their children had equal access to education? What opportunities did enslaved people take to become literate?

Part IV ✳ Leadership

Who were some of the writers and public speakers who communicated the vision and aspirations of the African American community? What was the nature of those visions? In what forms of activism did each engage? How do these visions continue to inform America's continuing struggle for democracy? What is the nature of leadership and mentoring, of leadership and equality? What caused the schism between Frederick Douglass and William Lloyd Garrison? What role did the Black Convention Movement play in the development of an agenda for change prior to the Civil War? How can the evolution of their relationship inform us about the intertwined issues of race and power in the nineteenth century?

Part V ✳ Legal Initiatives and Civil Disobedience

How did northern communities support, protect, and sequester fugitives? How widespread was the Underground Railroad? Who were its supporters? Where and how did people, still enslaved, bring suit to win their freedom? In what ways did communities and individuals respond to the Fugitive Slave Act of 1850? How and when did opponents of slavery go beyond the boundary of law? What were the effects of armed resistance? How did these acts of armed civil disobedience push the nation closer to civil war?

⁘✠⁘

Foreword

JAMES OLIVER HORTON
GEORGE WASHINGTON UNIVERSITY

The most exciting thing about history is the likelihood of discovery. Documents from the past—official papers, letters, diaries, newspapers, and maps—are windows into the public and private worlds of those who came before us, those who prepared the society that has shaped our lives.

The documents, lessons, and context essays in this book focus on the lives and experiences of African American people in the history of the United States. They make clear the importance of race in the formation of American culture and society. Through these documents and the interpretive essays that place them in historical context, *Making Freedom* illustrates a more inclusive American history, revealing the interracial, multicultural historical experience that Americans lived. It makes the critical point that African American history is American history made by Americans in America.

Every American has been—and continues to be—shaped by African and African American cultural heritage and its interaction with the multitude of other cultural heritages that have combined to form American culture. These documents help us to see the world of the past through the eyes of those who lived in that world and to understand the events of their time as they did. They enable us to appreciate the role of race in shaping American assumptions and expectations and understand the interconnection between the meaning of American freedom and the limitations Americans imposed on that freedom. If we are ever to have a successful conversation on race in today's society, it is essential that we come to terms with these issues.

Historical documents can bring history to life at a time when America needs a historical context for its contemporary concerns. Unfortunately, Americans are undereducated about their past, and our public school system has not successfully addressed this problem. If, as Thomas Jefferson believed, an educated citizenry is essential for the maintenance of democracy, America is in trouble.

Recent surveys make clear the critical need for better history education. The U.S. Department of Education reports that 60 percent of the nation's high school seniors cannot demonstrate even a fundamental knowledge of U.S. history. This ignorance is especially glaring on the subject of race. More than half of the students could not identify Africa as the continent from which people were brought to be enslaved in the Western Hemisphere. Almost two-thirds could not correctly identify the term "Jim Crow" as the set of laws that enforced racial segregation, and less than one quarter could explain the purpose of the Fifteenth Amendment as a Constitutional protection against discrimination in voting, even when the wording of the amendment was provided to them.

If there was ever a time to enhance history education, that time is now. The documents in this book do just that, and the accompanying lesson plans suggest effective teaching strategies. From first-hand accounts of the Atlantic slave trade, to descriptions of black seafaring communities after the Revolution, to the wartime experiences of black Civil War soldiers, to the emergence of the Harlem Renaissance, *Making Freedom* presents a compelling and dramatic American story. It introduces the major concerns and events of the African American experience and the significance of race in America. These documents transport students back in time and allow them to discover the past in its own words and on its own terms.

Standard history textbooks provide information about the past that is important, but too often less than engaging. These documents and lessons are as lively and interesting as the human struggles they portray. Whereas textbooks frequently separate African Americans from the general American experience, *Making Freedom* places African American history at the center of the broad sweep of national history.

Most important, it helps us to evaluate America's past through a reading of direct historical evidence. Students will come to understand history through their personal investigation. This critical component of learning can add excitement and meaning to the educational experience. Students become more than simply consumers of historical information. They move closer to being historians and begin to understand the excitement of historical discovery.

Most of us who have become professional historians remember the moment when history became something more than a list of names and events, when it became an adventurous search for meaning. At the moment when facts become not simply significant in themselves but inspiring bits of evidence to be used in building a case for historical interpretation, we started to feel like real historians, detectives on the trail of history.

When students feel like historical detectives they will have less trouble remembering the significant fundamentals of history and they will appreciate the importance of the past.

Those who understand how exciting history is and understand its meaning for the present and the future never find it boring. Instead, they become lifelong learners of history. The documents in *Making Freedom* open a new and exciting world of the past and provide a greater appreciation of the full range of American history and of the lives of the people who made it.

Project Staff

Primary Source Staff

Anna Roelofs, Project Director
Kathy Bell, Librarian
Renee Covalucci, Picture Research
Abby Detweiler, Program Associate
Jim Diskant, Curriculum Specialist
Kathleen M. Ennis, Executive Director
Betty Hillmon, Kodaly Music Consultant
Eve Lehmann, Permissions Editor
Roberta Logan, Education Director
Rachel Margolis, Program Associate
Brande Martin, Program Associate
Charles Rathbone, Board of Directors
Jesse Ruskin, Music Researcher
Kelly Scott, Program Associate
Martha Shethar, Photo Researcher
Ann Vick-Westgate, Editor

Interns

Lucia Carballo
Kendra Carpenter
Jessica Kyle Ellis
Mike Fearon
Tracey Graham, Mellon Fellow
Imani Hope
Meredith Katter
Nina Miller
Sam Schwartz

Special thanks to James Jones of Northeastern University for his musical expertise, to Marvin Karp, Benjamin Kendall, Jill Minot-Seabrook, and Anthony Parker for their advice, to The Lovejoy Society, DeKalb, Illinois; and to Pam Matz, librarian at Harvard University.

Advising Scholars

Frances Smith Foster, Emory University
V. P. Franklin, Columbia University Teachers' College (Evaluator)
Paul Gagnon, Emeritus, Boston University
Gerald Gill, Tufts University
Robert Hall, Northeastern University
Emmett Price, Northeastern University
Heather Cox Richardson, Suffolk University
John Ross, National Center of Afro-American Artists, Boston

Contributing Scholars

Robert Allison, Suffolk University
Edmund Barry Gaither, Museum of the National Center for African American Artists, Boston
Robert Hayden, Independent Scholar
Betty Hillmon, Park School
James Oliver Horton, George Washington University
Lois Horton, George Mason University
Grey Osterud, Historian
Patrick Rael, Bowdoin College
Marilyn Richardson, Independent Scholar
Julie Richter, Independent Scholar

Teacher-Authors

Wendell Bourne, Cambridge Public Schools
Phyllis Bretholtz, Teacher/Educational Consultant
Ilene Carver, Boston Public Schools
Monny Cochran, Weston Public Schools
Julie Craven, Cambridge Public Schools
Andrea Doremus Cuetara, Boston Public Schools
Inez Dover, Newton Public Schools
Kathleen Drew, Cambridge Public Schools
Sharon Fleming, Abington Public Schools
Linda Forman, Framingham Public Schools
Richard Berry Fulton, Boston Public Schools
Deborah Gray, Community Educator

Andrea Gross, Westwood Public Schools
Jennifer Hames, Boston Public Schools
Deborah Hood-Brown, Cambridge Public Schools
Leslie Kramer, Cambridge Public Schools
Roberta Logan, Boston Public Schools
Peter Lowber, Malden Public Schools
Mark Meier, University of Virginia
Nicole Miller, Westborough Public Schools
Martin Milne, Eaglebrook School, Deerfield
Edward Morrison, Winthrop Public Schools
Melisa Nasella, Lincoln-Sudbury Public Schools
Karl Netter, Boston Public Schools
Catherine O'Connor, Newton Country Day School
Alexandria Pearson, Metro Director, Natick High School
Gwynne Alexandra Sawtelle, Westborough Public Schools
Andrew Shen, Lincoln-Sudbury Public Schools
Laurel Starks, Milton Academy
Sandra Stuppard, Boston Public Schools
Deborah Ward, Wellesley Public Schools
Joseph Zellner, Concord Public Schools
Rachel Zucker, Burlington Public Schools

Introduction

Making Freedom: African Americans in U.S. History grew out of the synergy and vision of a group of Boston-area teachers, several scholars, and the program staff of Primary Source. Beginning in 1995 with a series of seminars on "Black Yankees" of the eighteenth and nineteenth centuries, the project grew and expanded to reach across the country and over time, up to the last quarter of the twentieth century.

Fortunately for all of us who see history as discovery, continuing scholarship is illuminating almost four centuries of African American thought, creativity, and activism in the social, political, and cultural development of our nation. Although work has been going on for years at the university level to understand the ways in which African American ideas and experiences influenced the development of our national culture and political ideology, little of this new thinking has yet become part of the standard school curriculum. The traditional historical narrative forming the basis of content for precollege students often relegates the study of African American history to separate units on slavery or to the struggle for civil rights. *Making Freedom* offers precollegiate teachers and their students exposure to exciting and informed scholarship on 400 years of history, thus strengthening the content and adjusting the lens through which African American history is viewed and understood.

The *Making Freedom* sourcebooks contain information and materials that demonstrate at least two important phenomena: the social agency and intellectual achievement shown throughout African American history from the colonial period forward and the inextricable relationship of African Americans to the collective history and cultural development of the United States. The primary sources contained in these sourcebooks reveal a diversity of perspectives and experiences among African Americans from their first arrival in British North America. In contemporary textbooks, slavery is often presented as a singular experience that shaped the character of all African Americans. *Making Freedom* intentionally illuminates the variety of the slave experience for African Americans, focusing both on individual ideas and actions and on collective efforts to hold America accountable to the ideals of freedom and equality.

Through the speeches and writings of scholars and activists, slave narratives, poetry, fiction, music, and fine arts, revealing agency in the face of repression,

Making Freedom illumines the ways in which Africans and African Americans have influenced American thought and cultural expression, as well as our traditions of freedom and democracy.

Making Freedom:

❖ provides teachers with multidisciplinary scholarship, primary source materials, and lesson plans concerning African American history from fourteenth-century Africa through the Civil Rights Movement of the 1970s

❖ presents this new material in ways that stimulate teachers and students to ask questions about how the intellectual history of African Americans relates to mainstream history and provokes a deeper understanding of the achievements and frustrations of African Americans in the pursuit of a lived freedom

❖ inspires teachers, who in turn inspire students, to become active learners, engaged in the process of historical research and community exploration, to tolerate both conflict and ambiguity in the historical narrative, and to learn more about themselves and others in an increasingly complex, pluralistic world

❖ addresses a variety of issues—scholarship, teaching strategies, and diverse student preparations for understanding history—and pulls them all together into a useful resource

❖ increases understanding and teaching capacity of both experienced and novice teachers for presenting the powerful and integral role of African American intellectual history in American history

The history of minorities *is* American history—to leave it out or mention it peripherally deprives students and teachers alike, giving an incomplete and often a false view of our past. Both majority and minority students gain from learning a more holistic story. Because mainstream history is often restricted to the story of one dominant group, complicating what is taught as history becomes a vital and legitimate goal for anyone seriously concerned with historical accuracy.

How This Series Was Created

In the summer of 1998, with financial support from the National Endowment for the Humanities, an enthusiastic group of teachers and scholars met to imagine and then to begin to create a multipart series of curriculum sourcebooks. We formed into working groups, each with a scholar, teachers, and a curriculum specialist.

Since its inception, the project has been informed by emerging scholarship in African American history and the growing availability of primary source materials to the general public. History has been described as a funnel—lots of stories go in, but only a few emerge to be told. Our goal is to enlarge the mainstream narrative for teachers and students, offering an inclusive history that places African Americans among the founders and shapers of our culture. *Making Freedom* uncovers stories of African American agency and intellectual vision and demonstrates how this intellectual history catalyzed movements such as abolition and civil rights and contributed to new interpretations of the Constitution. Recognizing that some of the primary source testimony of African Americans is in nonliterary form, primary source documents may be in the form of original artworks and musical scores that illustrate African American contributions to the development of American art, folk culture, and religious traditions.

Although one major thrust of this curriculum initiative is related to content, there are pedagogical objectives as well. Teachers and students need tools and strategies to enable the process of discovery and to encourage investment in learning. By using these sourcebooks, teachers can help their students become active participants in history. Through reading firsthand, authentic accounts of moments in history, looking at an engraving or listening to a piece of music, students are moved to ask questions and learn to formulate their own opinions about a person, an issue, or an event.

As we designed *Making Freedom* and began to draft materials, we drew heavily upon James Banks' paradigm for transforming curriculum. Banks' model shifts the perspective away from a conventionally focused study to reveal a more inclusive and far more interesting array of interrelated content. Offering a variety of activities and nontextbook, original source material, this approach lays the groundwork for teachers to transform their teaching goals and methods.

Who We Are

Primary Source, a teacher resource center in Watertown, Massachusetts, promotes education in the humanities that is historically accurate, culturally inclusive, and explicitly concerned with ethical issues such as racism and other forms of discrimination. Its services link university and school and combine scholarly research from original sources with practical knowledge of how adults and students learn. Through institutes, seminars, and conferences, Primary Source models an active, interdisciplinary approach to teaching. Primary Source offers educators intellectual enrichment and opportunities to participate in serious, professional dialogue with scholars and other classroom teachers.

Primary Source supports teachers' efforts to restructure their social studies teaching by serving as a conduit for primary source materials that reveal the voices of people from various ethnic, racial, and cultural groups within the United States and from countries around the world. Once these original source documents are brought to light and their intellectual and creative accomplishments are revealed, curriculum content is necessarily more inclusive of both genders and all racial and ethnic groups. Students may then see themselves in the curriculum and feel more connected to the educational process, to a cultural past, and to a civic future.

Using Primary Sources

The organization Primary Source takes its name from the same term used by historians to distinguish original, uninterpreted material from secondary or third-hand accounts. Thus a photograph, a memoir, or a letter is a primary source; an essay interpreting the photograph or memoir is usually, though not always, a secondary source. A textbook, still further removed, is a tertiary source.

In some instances, the same document or other piece of evidence may be a primary source in one investigation and secondary in another. For example, Henry Wadsworth Longfellow's poem "Paul Revere's Ride" is a primary source when it is considered as a reflection of how nineteenth-century citizens romanticized the Revolutionary War. It is not, however, a primary source that provides information about the events of April 18–19, 1775. (Paul Revere never did arrive in Concord.)

Making Freedom utilizes a range of primary sources. Included are maps, travel journals, letters, illustrations, engravings and other kinds of art, business records, diaries, wills, autobiographies, contemporary biography, advertisements (including those for the sale or recapture of slaves), music (including folk songs), and photographs of artifacts.

Although it is imperative to read secondary sources in order to understand context and background, introducing students to "the real stuff" raises student interest and curiosity and offers opportunities for students to make discoveries on their own. The closer students get to real people's lives, the better chance they have to formulate real questions and to care about people and events from another time and place. In a March 2002 speech to members of the Boston Athenaeum, historian David McCullough advised, "To understand the people of a particular historical period, you have to read what they read, not just what they wrote. You have to listen to the music, look at the paintings . . . ."

When textbooks are used as the only source of information, it is much more difficult for students to take ownership, both of their own learning and of a particular body of knowledge. It is very difficult to remember other people's generalizations or conclusions. Original source material provides students with rich opportunities for inquiry, the chance to move from concrete to abstract thinking and back again.

Teaching About Race

In the 1990s, a national dialogue about race was initiated by the Clinton administration. This endeavor was not widely covered in the media, and it is difficult to assess what was accomplished. The creators of this series believe that in order to bring about healing of a shameful national past, a dialogue about race needs to begin at the classroom level and be carried out into the world by students grounded in an honest study of history and committed to social justice.

We Are All Involved

The seeds of ignorant, biased, and racist opinions and feelings are often sown in children as they grow up, through families, the media, friendships, and even schools and religious institutions. Although students are not to blame for bringing ignorant opinions into the classroom, we must all now be accountable for attitudes and actions we take into the future. Discussions of racism often focus on blacks and other people of color as victims, essentially making it a black problem. The question of racism's cost to white people is rarely raised. Yet racism presents a serious challenge to any individual's ability to reason, make sound judgments, and develop perspective.

Individual Discovery

In studying the racial history of this country, we see that many painful things have happened in the past and continue to happen today in many communities. In general, students lack accurate information, ways to analyze this information as well as their own feelings and experiences, and an ability to articulate their analysis. Our job as teachers and students is to uncover the prejudices that exist in our institutions, our culture, and ourselves and to revisit our history in a careful, inclusive, and truthful manner. As a more accurate understanding of our complicated racial history is achieved, students can express their new knowledge in a variety of ways, as the activities in the lessons suggest. Finally, they can be encouraged to take action to address issues of unfairness in their schools and communities.

Depending on the composition of the class, there may be students who feel particularly vulnerable or targeted by the material discussed on a given day. Typically, students of color become angry and aggressive, while white students feel guilty and defensive. In addition, students who are of mixed race may feel conflicted. All students should be encouraged to express their thoughts and feelings; students learn a great deal from each other.

Giving students ample time to reflect in writing on what they have learned is a good outlet for feelings and is also a way to discover a student who may be having an especially difficult time. A piece of private reflective writing may reveal conflicts appropriate for the whole class to discuss or individual conflicts that need to be responsibly addressed by the teacher.

Class Discussion

Students seldom have the opportunity to engage in critical, analytical discussions about race. Our role as educators is to provide them with the information and tools to do so constructively. Students can be engaged in setting class guidelines for discussion of controversial subjects. Some examples follow.

1. All opinions and expressions of feelings and emotions are accepted and respected in class, whether other students share them or not.

2. Opinions and feelings expressed on sensitive topics should be kept within the confines of the classroom, not discussed elsewhere.

3. Students should speak from their own experience, using "I-statements" as much as possible. This simply means that students should start with, "I think, I heard, I believe, I feel . . . " rather than "You're wrong because . . ." The former prompts reflection, whereas the latter can feel like a direct attack on another speaker.

4. Students should know also that it is fine to choose *not* to speak.

How to Use This Book

Making Freedom is intended for use as a resource in all American history classes at the middle and high school levels. This series enables teachers to weave the African American story into and throughout the wider narrative. We have purposely emphasized individuals and events that are not often included in standard American history textbooks. Our purpose is to widen and deepen the narrative, not to repeat the few names and incidents already familiar to most teachers and students.

The five *Making Freedom* curriculum sourcebooks provide innovative, intellectually compelling curriculum materials that fit into the conventional scope and sequence. The sourcebooks specifically examine the African American intellectual tradition in the context of the following historical eras: (1) Colonial America; (2) Revolution and Forging the Nation; (3) Antebellum Reform; (4) Civil War and Reconstruction; and (5) The Gilded Age into the Twentieth Century. The five sourcebooks, with titles from "Lift Ev'ry Voice and Sing" by James Weldon Johnson, are:

True to Our Native Land: Beginnings to 1770

A Song Full of Hope: 1770–1830

Lift Ev'ry Voice: 1830–1860

Our New Day Begun: 1861–1877

March On Till Victory: 1877–1970

Each book contains the following:

❖ a table of contents for the series

❖ one or two context essays written by scholars

❖ lesson plans, including primary sources

❖ a glossary

The accompanying CD-ROM includes all primary source materials, supplementary materials, and a time line and annotated bibliography for the entire series.

Each lesson contains

❖ Introduction

❖ Organizing Idea

❖ Student Objectives

❖ Key Questions

❖ Primary Source Materials

❖ Vocabulary

❖ Student Activities

❖ Further Student and Teacher Resources

❖ Contemporary Connections

Several lessons also include music selections.

Together, the **context essays** at the beginning of each book and the **introductions** to individual lessons provide background information necessary for understanding the primary sources and engaging in the activities. Teachers can use this introductory material in a variety of ways. For example, they can have the students read the introductions in their entirety, present the information in a brief lecture, create background information sheets with key points, or ask students working in groups to research the answers to questions that create a context for the lesson.

Vocabulary lists with topical words are included, and the words are defined in the **glossary**. In many instances, given the historical period of the documents, additional vocabulary lists are provided under supplementary materials to help students better understand what they read.

Each lesson includes a variety of teaching strategies designed to engage student interest. Suggested **activities** include study and analysis of primary sources, mapping, research and writing, debating, creating graphic displays, and role-plays that involve assumption of a particular perspective, sometimes an unpopular or (in the twenty-first century) an unacceptable one. This activity needs to be understood as an attempt to see things as they were in a particular time in the past. The challenge is to try not to view all events from the perspective and values of today. When an activity calls for speculation or analysis, it is important to have verifying information available close at hand—in the classroom, the school library, or online. A speculation exercise is not a standalone activity, but, together with research to clarify information and verify a theory, it gives students the opportunity to act as historians.

Because the context essays and lessons were written by a group of scholars and teachers, they offer a variety of writing and instructional approaches. Although the format for all the lessons is the same, we have respected the authors' voices and have not edited them to a uniform length or style. The lessons vary in length and level of detail and offer a choice of activities.

We would not expect teachers to use every activity in every lesson. Rather, they should choose those lessons—and, within the lessons, those activities—that dovetail best with their instructional plan and meet the needs and learning styles of their students. We have set out a buffet—we do not intend for all of it to be consumed by each teacher.

A list of **further resources** is provided with most lessons. Although every effort has been made to ensure that references to websites are current, they do change. Teachers may wish to check URLs before giving students assignments. Students should also be cautioned to evaluate information found in a website carefully, checking who is the author and who sponsors the site.

Each lesson includes a **contemporary connection**. Our intent is to demonstrate that the issues raised by studying the primary sources do not pertain only to the past. Some remain the same; others have been transmuted a little. This feature gives resources and often asks open-ended questions for further exploration.

Some of the **primary source materials** are difficult for students to read. They have been set in type, but no changes have been made to the original language. As a result, the documents contain syntax with which students may not be familiar, as well as vocabulary no longer in active use or for which meaning has shifted. Sometimes words are spelled differently. Each teacher knows best how to adapt a lesson to students' skill levels. The books include suggestions, such as having students work in pairs or small groups, reading the documents aloud to the class, and/or providing vocabulary definitions before students tackle the documents.

The lengthier documents have been abbreviated in the sourcebooks. All **primary source materials** appear in full on the accompanying CD-ROMs and can be printed out for classroom use.

This *Adinkra* symbol represents the Akan belief that we must look at and learn from the past in order to move with wisdom into the future. It teaches people to value and protect their cultural heritage.

In Hope of Liberty

DR. JAMES O. HORTON, GEORGE WASHINGTON UNIVERSITY, AND
DR. LOIS HORTON, GEORGE MASON UNIVERSITY

Introduction

In a speech before the House of Representatives in the early spring of 1818, Henry Clay, representative from Kentucky, echoed the sentiments of the Revolutionary generation when he declared: "An oppressed people are authorized, whenever they can, to rise and break their fetters." A boy named Frederick was born into slavery early that year in Maryland, a boy who would grow up to take such words to heart. Indeed, as a man, Frederick Douglass trumpeted this message to the nation and to the world, demanding freedom for all slaves.

Most of the founding fathers who had struggled to establish a government of free men were slaveholders who did not consider African American slaves entitled to freedom. These opposing understandings of the ideals of liberty exposed a great contradiction at the heart of the early nation, a nation dedicated to freedom, whose social and economic life depended on slavery. This tension between American ideals and American reality shaped political challenges for Clay's generation. These tensions had led the founding fathers to remain silent on the question of slavery as they drew up the Constitution, never referring to it directly, so as to appease the large slaveholding states. At the same time, they increased slaveholders' political power by counting three out of five of their slaves for the purposes of state representation in Congress.

As new states were added to the Union, the issue of slavery prompted other political concessions, as when the Missouri Compromise of 1820 maintained the balance by pairing the admission of the slave state of Missouri and the free state of Maine. Congress engaged in a continual process of compromise to forestall more serious conflict between the power of southern slavery and the growing forces of antislavery reform. Clay, a slaveholder himself, played an important role, becoming known as the "Great Compromiser." In a final desperate decade, the Compromise of 1850, with its new stronger fugitive slave law, and the Kansas-Nebraska Act, with its provision for settlers themselves to decide whether a state would be slave or free, actually created more serious conflict. When compromise failed in the late 1850s,

Frederick Douglass was one of many abolitionists who believed that victory by Union troops would fulfill the promise of the American Revolution.

Slave labor and the African slave trade had been mainstays of the British economy in all thirteen American colonies. Differences in climate, landscape, and demographics gradually led the southern colonies to a greater dependence on slave labor, whereas northern shippers dominated the slave trade. Revolutionary rhetoric bolstered the strength of voices against slavery and, as new states formed out of territories, slavery was abolished or set on the road to abolition in the northern states. Vermont abolished slavery in its constitution of 1777, Massachusetts ended slavery after a decision of its Supreme Court in 1783, and slaveholding rapidly diminished in New Hampshire. Provisions for the gradual abolition of slavery were enacted by Rhode Island, Connecticut, and Pennsylvania in the 1780s, by New York in 1799, and by New Jersey in 1804.

In the South, however, slaveholders dominated state and local politics, sending to Congress advocates for an economy increasingly dominated by human bondage. A technological revolution, bringing the cotton gin that dramatically increased cotton production and made slave labor more valuable, set the stage for the expansion of slavery into the states of the Deep South carved from Thomas Jefferson's 1803 Louisiana Purchase. One of the results was the breakup of an extraordinary number of enslaved families as slave traders met the demand for labor. Profits and wealth increased as planters moved their cotton to market on new steam-powered riverboats. By the time Andrew Jackson became president in 1828, cotton was the country's most valuable export, slavery was the most important labor system in the South, and national politicians were preoccupied with balancing the interests of slave and free states as the United States expanded westward.

Freedom from slavery in northern states did not, however, bring equal rights to African Americans. Ironically, as one northern state after another freed African Americans from bondage, they restricted, often for the first time, the rights of the newly freed blacks. Historians have traditionally referred to the Jacksonian era as the era of the common man, meaning that, as states abolished property requirements for voting, elections became more open and American democracy became broader and available to more common men. Yet even as this democratization went on, free blacks—who in many northern states had the right to vote—were often removed from the voting roles as "white" became a necessary qualification for voting in states such as New Jersey and Connecticut. Most midwestern states not only restricted African American voting rights but also instituted special laws to restrict their access to the court system, keeping them off juries, and not allowing them to testify against whites. Some states restricted the rights of African Americans to hold property or even to settle in the state. Ohio required blacks to post a bond to live in the state, and Indiana and Illinois went farther, barring blacks entirely. In the West, Oregon also prohibited black settlement and California's officials placed heavy restrictions on African American rights, almost writing a black exclusion clause into its state constitution. Although slavery may have been isolated in the South, racial prejudice and injustice was very much a national phenomenon in the pre–Civil War era.

If the ideals of the Revolution did not prevent the racial restriction of American liberty, some Americans did protest the obvious inhumanity of slavery. Although the first organized antislavery efforts can be traced from the eighteenth century, the 1830s witnessed the rise of significant reform activity aimed at immediate emancipation. African Americans had led the way, protesting informally and through their churches and other institutions. Free blacks had the greatest opportunities to make their voices heard, but even slaves protested when they could, such as during the Revolution, when many slaves sent petitions to Congress and state legislatures demanding freedom for themselves and their families.

Throughout the decades before the Civil War, blacks continued to organize and protest against slavery, working through their fraternal groups, such as Boston's Prince Hall Masonic Lodge, and benevolent organizations, such as the African Societies formed in many northern cities. During the 1820s the Massachusetts General Colored Association was established specifically as an African American antislavery organization, and in 1831 blacks allied with white abolitionists to form the New England Antislavery Society. Interracial protest action often rose as part of the stunning religious revival movement known as the Second Great Awakening that burned over many of the small towns and farming communities of the North and even caught fire in many of the cities. Both African American and white preachers railed against the un-Christian injustice of slavery, raising northern white consciousness, and alerting millions to its horrors. Where the abolitionist message was strong, thousands of converts were brought to the cause of human freedom, but the political and economic power of the slaveholding South remained a formidable foe.

Even as the abolition movement grew more popular in northern society during the 1850s, it never drew the allegiance of more than a minority. During the 1830s and 1840s, antiabolitionist mobs attacked antislavery meetings and endangered abolitionist speakers. William Lloyd Garrison, white abolitionist editor of the *Liberator*, was captured by a mob in Boston in 1835 and saved only by the intervention of Boston blacks in but one example of the violence abolitionists faced. The list of such attacks is long and sometimes even deadly. In 1837 an Alton, Illinois, mob murdered abolitionist editor Elijah P. Lovejoy and destroyed his newspaper. Black abolitionists were often the special targets of mobs as they traveled though the North and Midwest spreading the antislavery message. They were singled out because they were black and because they were so effective in telling their personal stories of slavery, shocking white audiences into the realization of its horrors. Harriet Tubman, a former slave from Maryland, and Sojourner Truth, who had been a slave in New York State, held listeners spellbound with their autobiographies. The great Frederick Douglass became the most powerful antislavery speaker on both sides of the Atlantic as African Americans and their white American allies joined the grand abolitionist tours in Great Britain and on the continent of Europe. These joint efforts kept abolition alive and reformers active in what became an international movement for human freedom.

In the United States, throughout the North and in many areas of the South as well, African Americans and whites joined in an effort to aid slaves in escaping bondage in what became known as the Underground Railroad. The term was broadly used to encompass both the organized activities of abolitionist groups with elaborately structured networks of safe houses and transport routes as well as the more generalized humanitarian actions of individuals aiding human beings in need on an informal, ad hoc basis. Figures are difficult to confirm, but historians suggest that between 60,000 and 100,000 fugitive slaves were helped to freedom along the erratic lines of the Underground Railroad. They moved southward into Mexico from the plantations of the western deep South, north into the free states from the eastern and upper South, and even into the West Indies or Europe by ship from port cities such as New Orleans and Charleston.

Because fugitives were always vulnerable to recapture, especially after the 1850 Fugitive Slave Law strengthened the ability of slaveholders to regain their constitutionally protected human property, Canada became the promised land of freedom for many fugitives. Some forty thousand fugitives found shelter in free black settlements that sprang up in Canada. In Toronto, Windsor, Chatham, Wilberforce, and many other Canadian communities, African Americans supported newspapers, organized antislavery societies, and raised recruits to support antislavery action in the United States. These communities grew in importance during the 1850s as military clashes between abolitionists and proslavery forces intensified in the Kansas territory after 1854. When John Brown planned his 1859 raid on Harpers Ferry, he sought support and recruits among the blacks of Chatham in Canada.

These years during the 1850s were critical ones not only for the fate of African Americans and for the antislavery movement, but also for the nation itself. The art of political compromise that had held the United States together since the Revolution and that had been necessary to sustain a union between one society built on a commitment to slave labor and another built on free labor was no longer effective after 1850. People's determined defiance of the Fugitive Slave Law, the stubborn political protest against slavery, and the continual campaign to move northern public opinion towards opposition to the powerful proslavery influence are major themes of America history during this period. They also illustrate the intersection of African American history and national history. Interracial alliances were complex and controversial political and social issues at that time. Today they are critical to our understanding both of the society devolving in those years and of the society of our own time.

The documents in this book help to elucidate the dynamic era that led to the Civil War. While focusing directly on various aspects of the African American experience, they also help to set the context for discussing all of American history during this time. In the speeches, poems and letters of those who had experienced first hand the horrors of slavery, in the accounts of those who risked their lives and property to break slavery's grip, in the stories of those who attempted to hold families together and build lives in the midst of the United States' most chaotic era, we see the powerful impact of a determined people on the course of their society and their nation.

A Singularly American Brew
(of Attitudes and Beliefs)

MARILYN RICHARDSON, INDEPENDENT SCHOLAR

The social, political, and historical forces shaping the debates over slavery and abolition gained prodigious momentum between 1830 and 1860. During those decades the specter of possible armed conflict grew on the national horizon. Those volatile forces were a singularly American brew of attitudes and beliefs shaped by competing African American and majority white responses and claims to turning points in the nation's development.

Blacks and whites fought and died side by side in the Revolutionary War, yet the hard-won rights of citizens of a free nation were unilaterally denied all slaves in the southern states and only partially, grudgingly, and inconsistently available to free blacks in the North and in the South. The 1830s saw the rise of emphatic claims by black writers and speakers to equality under the law. Through the antislavery press, through organizations of abolitionist speakers, and with increasing debate in civic and religious forums, as well as at antislavery conventions here and abroad, the abolitionist cause gained increasing recognition and support.

Even as the very act of teaching blacks to read and write became punishable under southern law, blacks in the North and South understood that literacy and education were second only to freedom in making a better future for themselves and their children. Starting in the 1830s higher education for blacks and women changed the nature of intellectual, academic, and cultural life in America. Oberlin College in Ohio became the first in the country to admit blacks and females on an equal basis with white males, but change reached to the levels of primary and secondary education as well.

Five-year-old Sarah Roberts attended the handsome red-brick Abiel Smith School on Joy Street in Boston, Massachusetts; it was a school established in 1834 for Boston's "colored" children. In order to get there each school day, Roberts had to pass five white schools. In 1849, her father, Benjamin Roberts, a printer, filed suit against the city. Charles Sumner was his attorney, assisted by the black activist attorney Robert Morris. On December 4, 1849, Sumner appeared before the Massachusetts Supreme Judicial Court to argue for the rights of Sarah Roberts and other

African Americans in the Boston public schools. He claimed that segregated schools were unconstitutional and emotionally damaging to both black and white children. Further, he argued that separate schools could never be equal.

Although the court decided against Roberts in 1850, others, including the African American historian William Cooper Nell and the crusading white editor William Lloyd Garrison, carried the cause forward. Many black parents boycotted the segregated school and petitioned for change. Finally, in 1855, the Governor of Massachusetts signed a law that stated "[N]o distinction shall be made on account of the race, color, or religious opinions of the applicant or scholar" in the state's public schools. That September, students of both races began attending school together.

During those same decades the structure of the Underground Railroad evolved to such a level that it provided refuge to a constant and ever increasing stream of tens of thousands of fugitive men, women, and children fleeing the South and settling in northern states, Canada, Mexico, the southwest, and Europe. The Vigilance Committees organized by blacks and whites in major northern cities developed the administrative and fund-raising network necessary to assure money, food, clothing, shelter, transportation, legal assistance, and employment for the escaped slaves.

The very concept of human beings as chattel, upheld by the Fugitive Slave Act of 1850, so repelled significant numbers of black and white Americans that resistance to the arrest of fugitives led otherwise law-abiding people of all backgrounds and from all levels of society to acts of civil disobedience, public demonstrations, and often violent conflict with law enforcement agents and government troops

Those years of struggle galvanized an unprecedented interracial collaboration of political and cultural activists whose influence was both national and international. Although their views and tactics covered a spectrum wide enough to produce approaches as different as those of Nat Turner and Frederick Douglass or those of John Brown and William Lloyd Garrison, they shared the common goal of ending slavery and ensuring all Americans human and civil rights under law.

African American writers often led the charge in shaping public sentiment. The first edition of David Walker's *Appeal . . . to the Coloured Citizens of the World* appeared in 1829, followed by a second and expanded edition the next year. Hard on the heels of his mysterious and controversial death, one of his disciples, the African American Maria W. Stewart, became the first American-born woman of any race to lecture in public on political themes and leave extant copies of her texts. At the same time, *Liberator* editor William Lloyd Garrison published Stewart's first essays on human rights, women's rights, and the possibility of armed black rebellion in the United States.

A few years later, in the early 1840s, escaped slave Frederick Douglass, a "Renaissance man" in the struggle for abolition and universal human rights, began his speaking and writing career. He was a brilliant orator, prolific journalist, essayist, and autobiographer. Douglass also worked, wrote, and spoke on behalf of the temperance movement and was a vigorous supporter of women's rights.

Frances Ellen Watkins Harper (1825–1911) came into her own as a writer and antislavery lecturer following the publication of her first of many collections of poetry and prose, *Forest Leaves*, in 1845. She worked as a teacher and was much in demand as a speaker who, according to Philadelphia abolitionist William Still, "[spoke] without notes, with gestures few and fitting. Her manner [was] marked by dignity and composure."

Another writer, William Wells Brown, was born a slave near Lexington, Kentucky. Following his escape in 1834, he married and settled near Rochester, New York. His employment on a Lake Erie steamer enabled him to serve as an efficient conductor on the Underground Railroad. Later, as a speaker for the Massachusetts Antislavery Society, he moved to Boston, where he was a close associate of Garrison and Wendell Phillips. Except for the years 1849–1854 spent in Great Britain, Brown lived and wrote in New England until his death. His interests and talents were wide and deep. Among his publications were the *Narrative of William Wells Brown, A Fugitive Slave, Written by Himself* (1847); *The Antislavery Harp: A Collection of Songs for Antislavery Meetings* (1849), and *The Escape, or, A Leap for Freedom, A Drama in Five Acts* (1858). The last is possibly the first play published by a black American.

In all, Brown was the author of more than a dozen books, including *Clotel, or, the President's Daughter, A Narrative of Slave Life in the United States* one of the first novels by an African American author. Following the Civil War, Brown studied medicine privately and after serving an apprenticeship, became a practicing physician.

It is important to recognize the international dimension of the antislavery movement. Northern black activists, male and female, were a small but highly influential and quite mobile community. International conferences, lecture tours, study abroad, even at times flight to avoid capture, all took them across the Atlantic, where they argued their cause, forged political alliances, and garnered support and funds. They returned shaped by residence in European and other capitals and by having been received with honor, dignity, and a respect for their words and deeds rarely extended by whites at home.

Frederick Douglass spent most of 1845 and 1846 traveling and lecturing to great acclaim throughout Great Britain. In 1848, William Craft played the role of slave to his wife Ellen, who was disguised as a white man in order to escape from Georgia to Boston. When warrants for their arrest were issued by their former master as a result of the Fugitive Slave act of 1850, the Crafts fled first to Nova Scotia and then to England, where they remained until after the Civil War. British abolitionists arranged several speaking tours for them, sometimes on the same platform with William Wells Brown. Brown often traveled with a huge painted diorama showing vivid scenes of the evils of slavery. He had commissioned the work to counter similar artistic depictions of the pleasures of the pastoral American South. Activist and speaker Sarah Parker Remond left America in 1858 for England to argue the cause of abolition, to "breathe free air," and to further her education. These men and women, to mention just a handful, returned bearing evidence of the widest intellectual horizons, which in turn influenced and encouraged young black men and women to trust and develop their own creative and intellectual energies and aspirations in the recognition that emancipation of the spirit must accompany emancipation of the body.

Although we can imagine that the bitter historical memory of the original transatlantic journey of the Middle Passage echoed in their minds, historian James Brewer Stewart observes that black abolitionists lived their lives within "a panorama of international perspective." He remarks further that "the friendships made abroad, the gossip shared by letter, the exchange of hospitality, the monies raised and gifts given . . ." all made tangible this international experience. So too did the elaborate antislavery fairs put on annually by abolitionist women, black and white working together. Donations of items to offer for sale poured in from England, Ireland, Scotland, and France. The single most widely disseminated and recognized antislavery image, the kneeling slave imploring "Am I Not A Man And A Brother?" originated in the famed British workshop of Josiah Wedgwood.

Sourcebook 3, *Lift Ev'ry Voice: 1830–1860,* will introduce teachers and students to the lives and careers of these figures and many more. They, along with thousands of other brave, determined, creative and farsighted abolitionists, North and South, shared a vision of America's promise that led them to daily fight against brutality, corruption, and degradation even as they shaped our understanding of freedom, enlightenment, and personal fulfillment.

The Slave Experience

In the introduction to *Slave Testimony: Two Centuries of Letters, Speeches, Interviews, and Autobiographies,* John W. Blassingame writes, "If scholars want to know the hearts and secret thoughts of slaves, they must study the testimony of the blacks. But, since the slaves did not know the hearts and secret thoughts of masters, historians must also examine the testimony of whites. Neither the whites nor the blacks had a monopoly on truth, had rended the veil cloaking the life of the other, or had seen clearly the pain and joy bounded by color and caste. The perception of neither can be accepted as encapsulating the totality of plantation life. Consequently, whether we focus on the slave or the master, we must systematically examine both black and white testimony."

Hundreds of stories of slavery have been told in oral histories, autobiographical accounts, and diary entries. Both black and white authors have written compelling accounts about enslaved persons: their lives, work, families, and the treatment they received. Although there are many similarities in the accounts, each one carries its own distinct characteristics.

In *Slave Testimony: Two Centuries of Letters, Speeches, Interviews, and Autobiographies,* Blassingame seeks to compile in one volume reliable, direct evidence from slaves themselves. In his introduction to the book, Blassingame discusses the different kinds of testimony by blacks available to us and the reliability of each in trying to find out the true story of slavery in the United States. The primary sources Blassingame examines include letters—written by slaves to black relatives, by fugitive slaves, by former slaves, and by slaves to their owners; speeches by fugitive slaves; newspaper and magazine interviews of fugitive and former slaves; interviews done by the American Freedman's Inquiry Commission in 1863; interviews done by scholars; and autobiographies of fugitive and former slaves published in periodicals and books.

Harriet Beecher Stowe's fictional account *Uncle Tom's Cabin* helped educate many Americans about slavery, and this knowledge, in turn, increased abolitionist fever. Her book, first published in 1852, is considered one of the epic events of pre–Civil War history.

Solomon Northup's narrative stands out among other well-known slave narratives such as those of Frederick Douglass and William Wells Brown. Philip Foner, in his introduction to the Dover Edition of *Twelve Years a Slave*, writes: "Northup's narrative, published in 1853, is considered one of the most authentic descriptions of slavery from the viewpoint of the slave himself." After 1808, when American participation in the international slave trade became illegal, kidnapping of free black people occurred with some regularity. Northup describes his kidnapping, the brutal conditions under which he lived, and finally how he became free again through the petitions to the Governor of New York by Northup's wife, Mrs. Anne Northup.

Frances Anne (Fanny) Kemble was an actress from London who married Pierce Butler of Pennsylvania, the owner of a large plantation in Georgia. *Journal of a Residence on a Georgian Plantation 1838–1839* was published in both London and New York in 1863. Much of her story centers around her interactions with the slaves on the plantation. It is clear from her many diary entries that she encountered emotional confusion as she became engulfed in the institution of slavery. She was dismayed at the treatment of slaves; at the same time some of her descriptions and observations of black people clearly reflect the prejudice of the time.

The primary sources in this lesson have been chosen to give students a range of accounts capturing the experience of enslaved African Americans.

Organizing Idea

The experience of Africans enslaved in the United States cannot be neatly fit into one comprehensive description. Experiences differed based upon the era, region of the country in which slaves lived, the masters they served, and each person's set of familial and personal experiences.

Student Objectives

Students will:

- ❖ gain an understanding of the nature of some slaves' lives
- ❖ be introduced to different types of primary sources and explore how to extract important information from a variety of historical sources
- ❖ understand how writers, reporters, and interviewers might bring their own biases to collecting and telling history

Key Questions

- ❖ Almost all slave narratives include descriptions of extreme brutality. Why was this an integral part of the institution of slavery?
- ❖ White people included stories of slavery in their own journals and letters and wrote novels or other fiction centered around slaves' lives. How reliable is a

first-hand account of slavery written by a slave owner or his wife? How accurate is a fictional account? Why might fiction be an effective way to show the evils of slavery?

❖ What can be learned from visual images of this period?

Primary Source Materials

DOCUMENT 3.1.1: Letter to her daughter Amy Nixon from Phebe Brownrigg, Sept. 13, 1835

DOCUMENT 3.1.2: Letter to her mother from Emily Nixon, Feb. 12, 1836

DOCUMENT 3.1.3: Excerpt 1 from a speech by James Curry, reported in the *Liberator*, January 10, 1840

DOCUMENT 3.1.4: Excerpt 2 from a speech by James Curry, reported in the *Liberator*, 1840

DOCUMENT 3.1.5: Photograph of a slave cabin in Barbour County, Alabama

DOCUMENT 3.1.6: Photograph of cabins where slaves were raised in Hermitage, Savannah, Georgia

DOCUMENT 3.1.7: Pencil sketch by Edwin Forbes of slaves at work stacking wheat, Culpeper Courthouse, Virginia

DOCUMENT 3.1.8: Excerpts from *Uncle Tom's Cabin* by Harriet Beecher Stowe, 1852

DOCUMENT 3.1.9: Frontispiece from *Twelve Years a Slave* by Solomon Northrup, 1853

DOCUMENT 3.1.10: Excerpts from *Twelve Years a Slave* by Solomon Northup, 1853

DOCUMENT 3.1.11: Excerpt 1 from Frances Anne (Fanny) Kemble's *Journal of a Residence on a Georgian Plantation 1838-1839*

DOCUMENT 3.1.12: Excerpt 2 from Frances Anne (Fanny) Kemble's *Journal of a Residence on a Georgian Plantation*, Feb.14–17, 1839

Supplementary Materials

ITEM 3.1.A: Additional vocabulary lists for primary sources

Student Activities

Discussion—Letters Between Family Members

Activity 1

Students should read the two letters (3.1.1 and 3.1.2). What facts do these documents give us about the life of a slave? How much did the two writers value family relationships? Extract the sentences that tell what value a slave owner placed on the integrity of African American families. How accurately might a letter between family members reflect their lives?

Activity 2   ## Analysis—Everyday Life of a Slave

After students read the excerpts from James Curry's *Narrative* (3.1.3 and 3.1.4), ask the class to list the topics Curry mentions. Record them on the board or on a large piece of paper (for example, literacy, brutality, a woman's workday, relationships between slave owners and slaves, etc.) Divide the class into small groups and assign each group one of the topics. Ask each group to list all the details from the *Narrative* pertaining to their topic. When the groups share information with the rest of the class, record the details on the board or on paper.

Activity 3   ## Analysis of Images of Slave Life

Students should carefully examine the two photographs and the pencil drawing (3.1.5, 3.1.6, and 3.1.7). Create additional topics on slave life, and add the details to describe the topic as in Activity 2.

Activity 4   ## Fiction vs. Nonfiction—Which Gives an Accurate Portrayal of Slavery?

Students can read Chapters 1 and 2 from *Uncle Tom's Cabin* (3.1.6) aloud in class, taking the role of the narrator and characters who speak. Discuss how Stowe's—a white woman's—work of fiction compares to the first-person accounts students have read. Stowe's book sold an unprecedented 300,000 copies in its first year. Was it an effective way to show the evils of slavery? Why?

Activity 5   ## Creative Writing Extensions

Ask students to write the next chapter of *Uncle Tom's Cabin*, incorporating information about the life of a slave learned from Documents 3.1.1–3.1.7.

Activity 6   ## Discussion—Man's Inhumanity to Man

Solomon Northup's description of his experience in prison includes graphic details. First, students should examine the title page and illustration of Solomon Northup that appeared in his book (3.1.9). Discuss what we know about Northup before we have read a word of his narrative. Then read the excerpt from Chapter 3 (3.1.10). Ask students to discuss in small groups new information from this narrative. Explore why Northup reacted the way he did. Why did Burch behave so brutally? Ask the students to write a short essay putting themselves in Solomon Northup's shoes. How would they respond to the situation he found himself in?

Students may wish to reflect on all the primary sources they have examined to address the question of man's inhumanity to man.

Music Connection ✳

Juba, a traditional dance of West Africa, played a part in most major gatherings of enlaved African Americans. Although it varied by region, Juba involved foot tapping, hand clapping, and thigh and shoulder slapping in rapid and precise rhythm. Although the activity may have given the appearance of fun, the accompanying words gave people living in bondage a chance to vent their frustration and anger. As they listen to *Juba* on the accompanying CD-ROM, students should note the things that contributed to making the daily life of an enslaved person almost unbearable.

Juba this and Juba that and Juba killed a yellow cat
[the slave master]
You shift-a the meal, you give me the husk
You cook-a the break, you give me the crust
You fry the meat and give me the skin
And that's when my momma's trouble began
You just Juba, Juba, Juba, Juba.

Discussion—A Southern White Woman's Perspective

Activity 7

The excerpts from Frances Anne Kemble's journal (3.1.11 and 3.1.12) provide the students with the perspective of a white woman living on a southern plantation. Note on the developing class lists what information she corroborates. What new topics does she examine? What details does she provide? How valuable is her journal to our understanding of the life of African Americans in the nineteenth century?

Creative Extension—Reflection on the Life of a Slave

Activity 8

Ask the students to respond to what they have learned about life as a slave with a work of art. They can create, for example, a poster, a collage, an original painting, or a piece of sculpture. They may choose to express one aspect of slavery or several. When the finished art is displayed in the classroom, the students can select two or three pieces and respond to them in a short piece of writing.

Further Student and Teacher Resources

Andrews, William L., and Henry Louis Gates, Jr., eds. *Slave Narratives*. New York: Library of America, 2000.

———. *To Tell a Free Story: The First Century of Afro-American Autobiography, 1760–1865*. Illinois: University of Illinois Press, 1989.

Berlin, Ira. *Generations of Captivity: A History of African-American Slaves*. Cambridge, MA: Harvard University Press, 2003.

Berlin, Ira. *Many Thousands Gone: The First Two Centuries of Slavery in North America*. Cambridge, MA: Harvard University Press, 1998.

Blassingame, John W., ed. *Slave Testimony: Two Centuries of Letters, Speeches, Interviews, and Autobiographies*. Baton Rouge: Louisiana State University Press, 1977.

Brown, Henry Box. *Narrative of the Life of Henry Box Brown*. Introduction by Richard Newman, foreword by Henry Louis Gates, Jr. New York: Oxford University Press, 2002.

Gates, Henry Louis, ed. *Unchained Memories: Readings from the Slave Narratives*. Boston: Bulfinch, 2003.

Hamilton, Virginia, *Many Thousand Gone: African Americans from Slavery to Freedom*. New York, Alfred A. Knopf, 1993.

Hurmence, Belinda, ed. *Slavery Time When I Was Chillun*. New York: G. P. Putnam's Sons, 1997.

Jacobs, Harriet A. *Incidents in the Life of a Slave Girl, Written by Herself*. Enlarged edition. Cambridge, MA: Harvard University Press, 2000. This edition includes "A True Tale of Slavery" by Harriet's brother, John S. Jacobs.

Northrup, Solomon. *Twelve Years a Slave*. Mineola, New York: Dover Publications, 2000.

Stowe, Harriet Beecher. *Uncle Tom's Cabin*. New York: Knopf, 1994.

Websites

African American Voices. Digital History, University of Houston
www.digitalhistory. uh.edu/black_voices/black_voices.cfm
Comprehensive collection of primary and secondary source documents on slavery

Born in Slavery: Slave Narratives from the Federal Writer's Project, 1936–1938. Library of Congress, Washington, DC
http://memory.loc.gov/ammem/snhtml/ snhome.html

North American Slave Narratives. Documenting the American South, University of North Carolina
http://docsouth.unc.edu/neh/neh.html
Includes electronic texts of narratives, diaries and letters from well-known (e.g., Harriet Jacobs, http://docsouth.unc.edu/jacobs/menu.html) and less-known slaves and ex-slaves

Slave Letters in the African-American Women Online Archival Collection. Duke University
http://scriptorium.lib.duke.edu/collections/african-american-women.html

Contemporary Connection

❋

Biography, History, and Stories

Information about the historical reality of slavery has come down to us in many forms. There are first-person slave narratives such as those by Frederick Douglass, Harriet Jacobs, and Solomon Northrup. There are letters that have almost miraculously survived, such as the one to Amy Nixon. There are accounts such as Nat Turner's that were written down by white people, who often made choices of what to include or leave out. Autobiography and biography are powerful tools for helping young people identify with the lives, individuality, and critical choices of people in the past. Folktales based on truth or on flights of imagination also offer insight into the feelings and coping mechanisms of both the tellers and the listeners. Books on life during slavery written for young readers include *To Be a Slave* by Julius Lester; *The Strength in These Arms: Life in the Slave Quarters* by Raymond Bial; *Sojourner Truth: Ain't I A Woman?* by Pat McKissack; *Get On Board; The Story of the Underground Railroad* by Jim Haskins; *The People Could Fly* by Virginia Hamilton; *Her Stories: African American Folk Tales, Fairy Tales and True Tales* by Virginia Hamilton. After students have done some of this reading, ask them to make up some bedtime stories that a slave mother or father might tell to a young child.

Videos

Northrop's Odyssey. Videocassette. Monterey Movie Company, 1984.

Unchained Memories: Readings from the Slave Narratives. Videocassette. HBO Video, 2003.

Primary Source Materials
for Lesson 1

3.1.1

Letter to her daughter Amy Nixon from
Phebe Brownrigg, Sept. 13, 1835

EDENTON, NC, Sept. 13, 1835

My dear daughter—I have for some time had hope of seeing you once more in this world, but now that hope is entirely gone forever. I expect to start next month for Alabama, on the Mississippi river. Perhaps before you get this letter I may be on my way. As I have no opportunity of sending it now I shall leave it with Emily to send.

My dear daughter Amy, if we never meet in this world, I hope we shall meet in heaven where we shall part no more. Although we are absent in body, we can be present in spirit. Then let us pray for each other, and try to hold out faithful to the end.

My master, Mr. Tom Brownrigg, starts the middle of next month, with all the people, except your sister Mary, she is _____, and not able to travel. She has five children, Master Richard and family and the Doctor will go on in the spring, and Mary will come with them. Your father and myself came down to see our grand children, brother Simon and all our friends for the last time. I found your children just recovered from the measles. They all send their love to you. We shall try to send you a letter when we get settled in Alabama. Betsey sends her love to you—she expects to go with the Doctor in the spring. Your father, brothers and sisters, join me in a great deal of love to you and my dear little grand children. Kiss them for their old grand mother.

Farewell, my dear child. I hope the Lord will bless you and your children, and enable you to raise them and be comfortable in life, happy in death, and may we all meet around our Father's throne in heaven, never no more to part. Farewell, my dear child.

From your affectionate Mother, PHEBE BROWNRIGG

3.1.2

Letter to her mother from Emily Nixon,
Feb. 12, 1836

EDENTON, NC, Feb 12, 1836

My dear Mother—I heard from you by Eliza Little. The letter which you sent me gave me much pleasure to hear that you and my little sisters were well. Eliza said the letter and bundle you sent were open when she received them. I received one pair of socks, one small apron and slip, and rather more than half a yard of cotton, for which I thank you kindly. In my last letter to you I felt happy to tell you all about my wedding—but ah! mother, what have I to tell you now? A cloud has settled upon me and produced a change in my prospect, too great for words to express. My husband is torn from me, and carried away by his master. Mr. Winslow, who married Miss Little, although he was offered $800 for him that we might not be parted, he refused it. All our family sympathized with me. Miss Joyce told me to go and see Mr. Winslow myself. I went to see him—tried to prevail on him not to carry my husband away, but to suffer him to be bought for $800, that we might not be separated. But mother—all my entreaties and tears did not soften his hard heart—they availed nothing with him.—He said he would "get his own price for him." So in a few short months we had to part. O! mother, what shall I do? A time is fast approaching when I shall want my husband and mother, and both are gone! . . .

The full text of Document 3.1.2 is available on the CD-ROM.

3.1.3

Excerpt 1 from a speech by James Curry,
reported in the *Liberator*, January 10, 1840

From his Narrative given as a Speech

From my childhood until I was sixteen years old, I was brought up a domestic servant, I played with my master's children, and we loved one another like brothers. This is often the case in childhood, but when the young masters and misses get older, they are generally sent away from home to school, and they soon learn that slaves are not companions for them. . . . While I worked in the house and waited upon my mistress, she always treated me kindly, but to other slaves, who were as faithful as I was, she was very cruel. At one time there was a comb found broken in a cupboard, which was worth about twenty-five or thirty-seven and a half cents. She suspected a little girl, 9 or 10 years old, who served in the house, of having broken it. She took her in the morning, before sunrise, into a room, and calling me to wait upon her, had all the doors shut. She tied her hands, and took her frock up over her head, and gathered it up in her left hand, and with her right commenced beating her naked body with bunches of willow twigs. She would beat her until her arm was tired, and then thrash her on the floor, and stamp her with her foot, and kick her, and choke her to stop her screams. Oh! it was awful! and I was obliged to stand there and see it, and to go and bring her the sticks. She continued this torture until ten o'clock, the family waiting breakfast meanwhile. She then left whipping her; and that night, she herself was so lame that one of her daughters was obliged to undress her. The poor child never recovered. A white swelling came from the bruises on one of her legs, of which she died in two or three years. And my mistress was soon after called by her great Master to give her account. . . .

The full text of Document 3.1.3 is available on the CD-ROM.

3.1.4

Excerpt 2 from a speech by James Curry, reported in the *Liberator*, 1840

My mother's labor was very hard. She would go to the house in the morning, take her pail upon her head, and go away to the cow-pen, and milk fourteen cows. She then put on the bread for the family breakfast, and got the cream ready for churning, and set a little girl to churn it, she having the care of from ten to fifteen children, whose mothers worked in the field. After clearing away the family breakfast, she got breakfast for the slaves; which consisted of warm corn bread and buttermilk, and was taken at twelve o'clock. In the meantime, she had beds to make, rooms to sweep, &c. Then she cooked the family dinner, which was simply plain meat, vegetables, and bread. Then the slaves' dinner was to be ready at from eight o'clock in the evening. It consisted of corn bread, or potatoes, and the meat which remained of the master's dinner, or one herring apiece. At night she had cows to milk again. There was little ceremony about the master's supper, unless there was company. This was her work day by day. Then in the course of the week, she had the washing and ironing to do for her master's family, (who, however, were clothed very simply) and for her husband, seven children and herself. . . .

The full text for Document 3.1.4 is available on the CD-ROM.

3.1.5

Photograph of a slave cabin in Barbour County, Alabama

Library of Congress

3.1.6

Photograph of cabins where slaves were raised
in Hermitage, Savannah, Georgia

Library of Congress

3.1.7

Pencil sketch by Edwin Forbes of slaves at work
stacking wheat, Culpeper Courthouse, Virginia

Library of Congress

3.1.8

Excerpts from *Uncle Tom's Cabin* by
Harriet Beecher Stowe, 1852

I: "Select Incident of Lawful Trade"

Mr. Haley pulled out of his pocket sundry newspapers, and began looking over their advertisements, with absorbed interest. He was not a remarkably fluent reader, and was in the habit of reading in a sort of recitative half-aloud, by way of calling in his ears to verify the deductions of his eyes. In this tone he slowly recited the following paragraph:

"EXECUTOR'S SALE,—NEGROES!—Agreeably to order of court, will be sold, on Tuesday, February 20, before the Court-house door, in the town of Washington, Kentucky, the following negroes: Hagar, aged 60; John, aged 30; Ben, aged 21; Saul, aged 25; Albert, aged 14. Sold for the benefit of the creditors and heirs of the estate of Jesse Blutchford, Esq.

SAMUEL MORRIS,
THOMAS FLINT,
Executors."

"This yer I must look at," said he to Tom, for want of somebody else to talk to.

"Ye see, I'm going to get up a prime gang to take down with ye, Tom; it'll make it sociable and pleasant like,—good company will, ye know. We must drive right to Washington first and foremost, and then I'll clap you into jail, while I does the business.". . .

The full text of Document 3.1.8 is available on the CD-ROM.

3.1.9

Frontispiece from *Twelve Years a Slave*
by Solomon Northrup, 1853

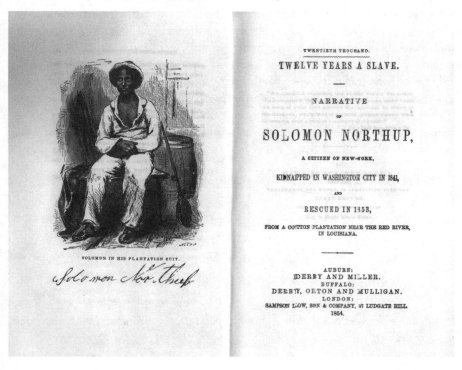

3.1.10

Excerpts from *Twelve Years a Slave*
by Solomon Northup, 1853

Born a free man in New York State in 1808, Solomon Northup was kidnapped in Washington, D.C., in 1841 and spent the following twelve years as a slave in Louisiana. After regaining his freedom in 1853, he wrote this autobiographical account of his years in captivity.

CHAPTER III

Painful meditations—James H. Burch—Williams' slave pen in Washington—The lackey, Radburn.—Assert my freedom—The anger of the trader—The paddle and cat-o'-ninetails—The whipping—New Acquaintances—Ray, Williams, and Randall—Arrival of little Emily and her mother in the pen—Maternal sorrows—The story of Eliza.

"Well, my boy, how do you feel now?" said Burch, as he entered through the open door. I replied that I was sick, and inquired the cause of my imprisonment. He answered that I was his slave—that he had bought me, and that he was about to send me to New Orleans. I asserted, aloud and boldly, that I was a free man—a resident of Saratoga, where I had a wife and children, who were also free, and that my name was Northup. I complained bitterly of the strange treatment I had received, and threatened, upon my liberation, to have satisfaction for the wrong. He denied that I was free, and with an emphatic oath, declared that I came from Georgia. Again and again I asserted I was no man's slave, and insisted upon his taking off my chains at once. He endeavored to hush me, as if he feared my voice would be overheard. But I would not be silent, and denounced the authors of my imprisonment, whoever they might be, as unmitigated villains. Finding he could not quiet me, he flew into a towering passion. With blasphemous oaths, he called me a black liar, a runaway from Georgia, and every other profane and vulgar epithet that the most indecent fancy could conceive. . . .

The full text of Document 3.1.10 is available on the CD-ROM.

3.1.11

Excerpt 1 from Frances Anne (Fanny) Kemble's *Journal of a Residence on a Georgian Plantation 1838–1839*

British actress Frances Kemble lived on a rice plantation in Georgia. Her husband was one of the richest men in the United States. Before leaving the South, she recorded her observations.

Mr. _____, in his letter, maintains that they *are* an inferior race, and, compared with the whites, "*animals*, incapable of mental culture and moral improvement": to this I can only reply, that if they are incapable of profiting by instruction, I do not see the necessity for laws inflicting heavy penalties on those who offer it to them. If they really are brutish, witless, dull, and devoid of capacity for progress, where lies the *danger* which is constantly insisted upon of offering them that of which they are incapable? We have no laws forbidding us to teach our dogs and horses as much as they can comprehend; nobody is fined or imprisoned for reasoning upon knowledge and liberty to the beasts of the field, for they are incapable of such truths. But these themes are forbidden to slaves, not because they cannot, but because they can and would seize on them with avidity—receive them gladly, comprehend them quickly; and the masters' power over them would be annihilated at once and forever. . . .

The full text of Document 3.1.11 is available on the CD-ROM.

3.1.12

Excerpt 2 from Frances Anne (Fanny) Kemble's
Journal of a Residence on a Georgian Plantation,
Feb. 14–17, 1839

Dearest E[lizabeth],

Passing the rice mill this morning in my walk, I went in to look at the machinery, the large steam mortars which shell the rice, and which work under the intelligent and reliable supervision of engineer Ned. I was much surprised, in the course of conversation with him this morning, to find how much older a man he was than he appeared. Indeed, his youthful appearance had hitherto puzzled me much in accounting for his very superior intelligence and the important duties confided to him. He is, however, a man upward of forty years old, although he looks ten years younger. He attributed his own uncommonly youthful appearance to the fact of his never having done what he called field work, or been exposed, as the common gang Negroes are, to the hardships of their all but brutish existence. He said his former master had brought him up very kindly, and he had learned to tend the engines, and had never been put to any other work, but he said this was not the case with his poor wife. He wished she was as well off as he was, but she had to work in the rice fields, and was "most broke in two" with labor, and exposure, and hard work while with child, and hard work just directly after childbearing; he said she could hardly crawl, and he urged me very much to speak a kind word for her to massa. She was almost all the time in the hospital, and he thought she could not live long. . . .

The full text of Document 3.1.12 is available on the CD-ROM.

Slavery and Resistance

Africans resisted enslavement from the moment it began and continued to resist as long as slavery existed. In their book *Runaway Slaves: Rebels on the Plantation*, John Hope Franklin and Loren Schweninger describe the ongoing resistance of slaves:

> Most of what historians have termed "day to day" resistance involved "crimes" against property. Slaves pulled down fences, sabotaged farm equipment, broke implements, damaged boats, vandalized wagons, vandalized clothing . . . They set fire to outbuildings, barns and stables; mistreated horses, mules, cattle and other livestock. They stole with impunity . . . nearly anything that was not under lock and key—and they occasionally found the key . . . Some blacks worked slowly or indifferently, took unscheduled respites, performed careless or sloppy labor when planting, hoeing, and harvesting crops . . . Slaves feigned illness, hid in outbuildings, did not complete their assigned tasks, and balked at performing dangerous work . . . Other slaves turned to whiskey or other "ardent spirits" as an expression of their frustration . . . The frequency of these acts—whether sabotage, carelessness, theft, or drinking—varied from plantation to plantation, region to region, depending on the responses of masters, proximity to towns and cities, interaction with free blacks, and control by overseers and owners. There is little doubt, however, that such expressions of displeasure were widespread (pp. 2–4).

Another persistent and pervasive form of resistance was the continuation of African cultural ways in religious practices, musical instruments and dance, work songs and spirituals, healing, cooking, and design motifs of ceramics and textiles. These "Africanisms" not only continued in lives of Africans and their descendents but also became integrated into the broader culture of the American South and eventually into that of the United States as a whole. Although there is no scholarly consensus on how widespread this practice was, some historians believe that the decorative arts were also used to send messages. In their 1999 book *Hidden in Plain View: A Secret Story of Quilts and the Underground Railroad*, Jacqueline L. Tobin and Raymond G. Dobard discuss how quilts were used by some to provide information about escape routes to fleeing slaves.

Slaves ran away and built new lives elsewhere. Protests, revolts, and rebellions also occurred. Historians James and Lois Horton write that "While an angry reaction to some specific injustice or brutal treatment may have triggered violence, rarely was the slave reacting to a single act. . . . The most radical kinds of resistance were those that struck not simply at injustice from an individual slaveholder or overseer but more consciously against the institution itself. There were fewer of these full-blown slave revolts, but they were extremely important for what they symbolized for both master and slave" (*Hard Road To Freedom: The Story of African America*, p. 109).

Organizing Idea

Slaves were treated in various ways depending on the nature of their masters as well as on the types of work they did. Physical and emotional abuse and neglect were common. From the beginning, slaves rebelled against their masters in various ways, including work slowdowns, sabotage, a continuation of African cultural ways, running away, and, occasionally, violence.

Student Objectives

Students will:

❖ begin to understand how some slaveholderss treated African Americans and why the enslaved resisted bondage from the outset

❖ know the various ways enslaved people resisted

❖ explore how current American race relations might be affected by past events in slavery and resistance

Key Questions

❖ In what ways and why did slaves resist?

❖ How did slaveholders react to acts of resistance?

❖ How might current American race relations be affected by the knowledge of slave treatment and subsequent resistance?

Primary Source Materials

DOCUMENT 3.2.1: Excerpt from American Freedmen's Inquiry Commission interview of freedman Harry McMillan, South Carolina, 1863

DOCUMENT 3.2.2: Excerpt 1 from Solomon Northup's *Twelve Years a Slave*, "Maternal Sorrows," 1853

DOCUMENT 3.2.3: Photo, Fredericksburg auction block

DOCUMENT 3.2.4: Print of wood engraving, slave auction at Richmond, Virginia

Supplementary Materials

ITEM 3.2.A: Additional vocabulary lists for primary sources

Vocabulary

betray	emancipate	insurrection	stripes—
bondage	flogging	lash	whipping
degradation	insurgent	secesh	submission

Student Activities

Activity 1

Analysis and Discussion of Documents

Divide the class in half or into workable groups for discussion. Half of them should examine the documents related to the treatment of slaves (3.2.1–3.2.5) and then discuss the answers to the following questions. Meanwhile, the other half should read the resistance excerpts (3.2.6–3.2.11) and then discuss the following questions. One person from each group should assume the role of scribe and write notes in answer to the questions so that ideas are explored further during the sharing and summarizing.

QUESTIONS ABOUT TREATMENT OF SLAVES FOR DOCUMENTS 3.2.1–3.2.5

Document 3.2.1

❖ Harry McMillan was a free man when this interview was conducted. Summarize how he felt about the ways slaves were treated.

- ❖ How might his answers have been different if he were still in slavery?
- ❖ What can you learn about the person doing the interviewing? Do his questions reveal any bias?

Documents 3.2.2–3.2.4

- ❖ What reasons are there (from a master's point of view) to separate slave families?
- ❖ What evidence is given in this document about the social standing of the mother and child?
- ❖ What thoughts come to mind as you examine the images of the slave auction block and the slave auction at Richmond, Virginia? Why would a British publication have printed this?

Document 3.2.5

- ❖ Northup had been a free black man until middle age, when slave catchers caught him. How might this have affected his reaction to being enslaved and his intention to resist?
- ❖ The institution of slavery is widely accepted to be an economic institution. What hints are given in this piece about the "business" of slavery? There should be more than one answer to this question.

GENERAL QUESTIONS FOR DOCUMENTS 3.2.1–3.2.5

- ❖ As you read about the various situations of these people, where did they have opportunities for resistance?

QUESTIONS ABOUT RESISTANCE FOR DOCUMENTS 3.2.6–3.2.10

Document 3.2.6

- ❖ How did this runaway become separated from his family initially?
- ❖ How common was this scenario of a slave being able to find his lost family members?
- ❖ What risks does this slave take in order to maintain some sense of freedom?
- ❖ Do you think he was free? What is your definition of freedom?

Document 3.2.7

- ❖ Why did James Fisher choke Mrs. Lane's brother? Was he justified in taking this action?
- ❖ How did being able to read and write enable Fisher to escape?
- ❖ Why did Fisher's boldness make people believe he could not be a runaway?

Document 3.2.8

- ❖ What risks did a runaway take?
- ❖ From Harriet Jacobs's account, what were some ways slaveowners punished captured fugitives?

Documents 3.2.9 and 3.2.10

- ❖ Compare Nat Turner's Rebellion to the other examples of resistance you have read about.
- ❖ Was the rebellion justified? Support your opinion with details.

GENERAL QUESTIONS FOR DOCUMENTS 3.2.6–3.2.10

- ❖ What are good decision-making strategies? How do you know when you have made the right decision?
- ❖ Discuss how slaves might have made the decision to openly resist slavery.

Activity 2

Sharing and Summarizing Findings from Documents

On the blackboard or a large piece of paper, each group should create a list with two columns. Each column should highlight the details that come from the documents that describe either slavery or resistance. These lists will be used to teach the other group about the details contained in the documents. Group A should summarize Documents 3.2.1–3.2.5 for Group B and then Group B should summarize Documents 3.2.6–3.2.10 for Group A. Notes taken by the scribe in each group should also be presented.

Activity 3

Discussion—Fear of Insurrection

Ask students to read Harriet Jacobs's "Fear of Insurrection," her description of the aftermath to Nat Turner's Rebellion (3.2.11). Discuss:

- ❖ What did the white mobs do?
- ❖ Nat Turner's Rebellion took place more than 50 miles away from where Harriet Jacobs lived. What do you think motivated the white people in her area?
- ❖ What reason does Jacobs give for the violence?
- ❖ Would you consider Nat Turner's Rebellion a success? Why? Do you have enough information at this time to make this determination? What else might you need to know?

Activity 4

Essay Writing—Control

Discuss the key questions in class. Encourage students to outline their ideas, with specific references to quotations from the primary sources. Then discuss the subject of control within the institution of slavery. Give examples from your primary sources that help you answer the following questions: How effectively is control used and by whom? Do the slaves have any control over particular situations? How is control exercised by the enslaved, and how does it differ from the masters' control? How does control affect the personal relationships that existed within the institution of slavery?

Music Connection

⨯⊱

Enslaved African Americans sang many songs yearning for the days when they would be free. Few of the songs survive, with the exception of spirituals. In his 1845 autobiography, Frederick Douglass recalled that slaves sang most when at their most dejected "breathing the prayer and complaint of souls boiling over with the bitterest anguish. Every tone was testimony against slavery, and a prayer to God for deliverance from chains." In "Go Down Moses" (available on the accompanying CD-ROM), enslaved people identified with Moses and the plight of the Israelites, held in bondage by Egyptians. Slaves in the United States drew hope from the story of Moses leading his people to freedom in Palestine. Words in the spiritual took on double meanings: "Egypt land" meant the South, "Pharaoh" referred to slaveowners, and "Moses" represented Underground Railroad conductor Harriet Tubman.

Writing to Extend

Activity 5

Write a sequel to any of the situations described in the documents.

Research—Resistance and Rebellion

Activity 6

Research the life of Solomon Northup. What was his life like before he was kidnapped? How did he regain his freedom? How did he live the rest of his life? Present your findings in an oral report, written paper, or a poster.

Learn more about Nat Turner. Who was he? How did the rebellion come about? What were the short-term and long-term effects?

Further Student and Teacher Resources

Blassingame, John W., ed. *Slave Testimony: Two Centuries of Letters, Speeches, Interviews, and Autobiographies*. Baton Rouge: Louisiana State University Press, 1977.

Greenberg, Kenneth S., ed. *The Confessions of Nat Turner and Related Documents*. New York: Bedford Books, 1996.

Jacobs, Harriet A. *Incidents in the Life of a Slave Girl, Written by Herself*. Enlarged edition. Cambridge, MA: Harvard University Press, 2000.

Franklin, John Hope and Loren Schweninger. *Runaway Slaves: Rebels on the Plantation*. New York: Oxford University Press, 1999.

Horton, James O., and Lois Horton. *Hard Road to Freedom: The Story of African America*. New Brunswick, NJ: Rutgers University Press, 2001.

McKissack, Patricia C., and Fredrick L. McKissack. *Rebels Against Slavery*. New York: Scholastic, 1996.

Northrup, Solomon. *Twelve Years a Slave*. Mineola, New York: Dover Publications, 1970.

Pearson, Jim, and John Robertson. *Slavery in the 19th Century: A Unit of Study for Grades 5–8*. Los Angeles: National Center for History in the Schools, 1991.

Contemporary Connection

⤝✠⤜

Resistance—Twenty-first-Century Style

History is filled with stories of resistance and agency. A contemporary example, coming from Nigeria, appeared in the *New York Times* in July 2002. A band of 150 village women from the Niger Delta, one of the poorest areas in Nigeria despite its oil wealth, shut down most of the operations of a multinational oil company for nearly a week. Seven hundred workers were trapped inside as the women, ranging in age from thirty to ninety and carrying only bundles of food, demanded, among other things, jobs for their sons and electricity for their villages. Officials of ChevronTexaco negotiated with the women and agreed to build schools, clinics, a town hall, electricity, and water systems in the villages. They also agreed to give a small number of jobs to local residents and to help build fish and chicken farms (*New York Times* on the Web, July 14, 2002). Students should look for other contemporary examples of people resisting oppression.

Rappaport, Doreen. *No More! Stories and Songs of Slave Resistance*. Cambridge, MA: Candlewick Press, 2002.

Waldstreicher, David. *The Struggle Against Slavery: A History in Documents*. New York: Oxford University Press, 2001.

White, Deborah Gray. *Let My People Go: African Americans 1804–1860*. The Young Oxford History of African Americans, 4. New York: Oxford University Press, 1996.

Websites

African American Voices. Digital History, University of Houston
www.digitalhistory.uh.edu/black_voices/black_voices.cfm
Comprehensive collection of primary and secondary source documents on slavery

Africans in America: America's Journey Through Slavery. Boston, WGBH
www.pbs.org/wgbh/aia/
A website with numerous resources for educators that accompanies the four-part video series by the same name

Black Resistance: Slavery in the United States. Compiled by Carolyn L. Bennett, Afro-America's Black History Museum
www.afro.com/history/slavery/main.html

Videos

Judgment Day, 1831–1865. Videocassette. *Africans in America: America's Journey Through Slavery*, 4. PBS Video, 1998.

Nat Turner: A Troublesome Property, 2003. Directed by Charles Burnett (58 mins.)

Northrop's Odyssey. Videocassette. Monterey Movie Company, 1984.

Unchained Memories: Readings from the Slave Narratives. Videocassette. HBO Video, 2003.

Primary Source Materials
for Lesson 2

3.2.1

Excerpt from American Freedmen's Inquiry
Commission interview of freedman
Harry McMillan, South Carolina, 1863

I am about 40 years of age, and I was born in Georgia but came to Beaufort when I was a small boy. I was owned by General Eustis and lived upon his plantation.

Q. Tell me about the tasks colored men had to do.
A. In old secesh times each man had to do two tasks, which are 42 rows or half an acre, in 'breaking' the land, and in 'listing' each person had to do a task and a half. In planting every hand had to do an acre a day; in hoeing your first hoeing where you hoe flat was two tasks, and your second hoeing, which is done across the beds, was also two tasks. After going through those two operations you had a third which was two and a half tasks, when you had to go over the cotton to thin out the plants leaving two in each hill.

Q. How many hours a day did you work?
A. Under the old secesh times every morning till night—beginning at daylight and continuing till 5 or 6 at night.

Q. But you stopped for your meals?
A. You had to get your victuals standing at your hoe; you cooked it over night yourself or else an old woman was assigned to cook for all the hands, and she or your children brought the food to the field.

The full text of Document 3.2.1 is available on the CD-ROM.

3.2.2

Excerpt 1 from Solomon Northup's *Twelve Years a Slave,* "Maternal Sorrows," 1853

As cotton production began to increase dramatically in the nineteenth century, hundreds of thousands of African America slaves were sold from their homes in Virginia and Maryland to states in the Deep South. Professor Ira Berlin of the University of Maryland in his book Generations of Captivity *refers to this as a "Second Middle Passage."*

The little fellow [Randall] was made to jump, and run across the floor, and perform many other feats, exhibiting his activity and condition. All the time the trade was going on, Eliza was crying aloud, and wringing her hands. She besought the man not to buy him, unless he also bought herself and Emily. She promised, in that case, to be the most faithful slave that ever lived. The man answered that he could not afford it, and then Eliza burst into a paroxysm of grief, weeping plaintively. Freeman turned round to her, savagely with his whip in his uplifted hand, ordering her to stop her noise, or he would flog her. He would not have such work—such sniveling; and unless she ceased that minute he would take her to the yard and give her a hundred lashes. Yes, he would take the nonsense out of her pretty quick—if he didn't he might be d–d. . . .

The full text of Document 3.2.2 is available on the CD-ROM.

3.2.3

Photo, Fredericksburg auction block

Photograph by Margaret Joan Seiter

3.2.4

Print of wood engraving, slave auction at Richmond, Virginia

This image of an African American woman being auctioned off in front of a crowd of men was published in The Illustrated London News, *Sept. 27, 1856.*

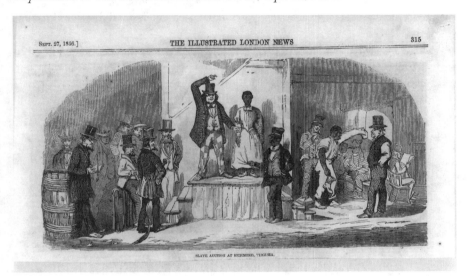

Library of Congress

3.2.5

Excerpt 2 from Solomon Northup's *Twelve Years a Slave,* "First Fight with Tibeats," 1853

As the day began to open, Tibeats came out of the house to where I was, hard at work. He seemed to be that morning even more morose and disagreeable than usual. He was my master, entitled by law to my flesh and blood, and to exercise over me such tyrannical control as his mean nature prompted; but there was no law that could prevent my looking upon him with intense contempt. I despised both his disposition and his intellect. I had just come round to the keg for a further supply of nails, as he reached the weaving-house.

"I thought I told you to commence putting on weather-boards this morning," he remarked.

"Yes, master, and I am about it," I replied.

"Where?" he demanded.

"On the other side," was my answer.

He walked round to the other side, examined my work for a while, muttering to himself in a fault-finding tone.

"Didn't I tell you last night to get a keg of nails of Chapin?" he broke forth again.

"Yes, master, and so I did; and overseer said he would get another size for you, if you wanted them, when he came back from the field."

Tibeats walked to the keg, looked a moment at the contents, then kicked it violently. Coming towards me in a great passion, he exclaimed, "G-d d-n you! I thought you knowed something."

I made answer. "I tried to do as you told me, master. I didn't mean anything wrong. Overseer said . . ." But he interrupted me with such a flood of curses that I was unable to finish the sentence. At length he ran towards the house, and going to the piazza, took down one of the overseer's whips. The whip had a short wooden stock, braided over with leather, and was loaded at the butt. The lash was three feet long, or thereabouts, and made of raw-hide strands. . . .

The full text of Document 3.2.5 is available on the CD-ROM.

3.2.6

Excerpt from John J. Audubon's *Ornithological Biography (1827–1839),* where he encounters a runaway slave

Presently a tall firmly-built Negro emerged from the bushy underwood, where, until that moment, he must have been crouched, and in a louder voice repeated his injunction. Had I pressed a trigger, his life would have instantly terminated; but observing that the gun, which he aimed at my breast, was a wretched rusty piece, from which fire could not readily be produced, I felt little fear, and therefore did not judge it necessary to proceed at once to extremities. I laid my gun at my side, tapped my dog quietly, and asked the man what he wanted.

My forbearance, and the stranger's long habit of submission, produced the most powerful effect on his mind. "Master," said he, "I am a runaway. I might perhaps shoot you down; but God forbids it, for I feel just now, as if I saw him ready to pass his judgment against me for such a foul deed, and I ask mercy at your hands. For God's sake, do not kill me, master!" . . .

The full text of Document 3.2.6 is available on the CD-ROM.

3.2.7

Excerpts from "Narrative of James Fisher," published in the *National Anti-Slavery Standard,* April 13, 1843

Twenty-six-year-old James Fisher was interviewed in Ohio after having been enslaved in Tennessee, Louisiana, and Alabama.

I was born in Nashville, Tenn. October, 1817. My mother's name was Mary Davis. Though an unmixed Cherokee Indian, she was kept in slavery all her life. My father's name was Thomas Fisher. He fled from bondage when I was a small child. They pursued, but never caught him. I have one brother, who, the last I knew, was living near Mobile, claimed as an article of property. I have two sisters in Nashville, both free women. I saw them as I came up. My mother was a very industrious woman. By washing and ironing, she earned money enough to buy herself for $500. After that, she paid $800 to the widow Stump, for my sister Ellen; and some time after, she contracted with Dick Perry for my sister Elizabeth. He asked $600 and she contrived, by hard labor and close saving, to make up the sum. This made $1,900 that she paid for the freedom of herself and children from a system of oppression and cruelty. She was extremely anxious to have all her children free. At the time of her death, she was working hard to raise money to buy me. My sisters wrote me that she talked a great deal about me during her sickness; saying she hoped to meet me in heaven, if she was never permitted to see me on earth again. . . .

The full text of Document 3.2.7 is available on the CD-ROM.

3.2.8

Excerpt from *Incidents in the Life of a Slave Girl* by Harriet A. Jacobs, 1861, describing her uncle's escape

Abolitionist Harriet A. Jacobs was born into slavery in Edenton, North Carolina in 1813. She escaped in 1842. A decade later, after her owners had made repeated attempts to capture her, abolitionists in New York purchased Jacobs and ensured her freedom. She altered names in her autobiography. "Linda" is Harriet Jacobs. "Benjamin" is her uncle Joseph.

It is not necessary to state how he made his escape. Suffice it to say, he was on his way to New York when a violent storm overtook the vessel. The captain said he must put into the nearest port. This alarmed Benjamin, who was aware that he would be advertised in every port near his own town. His embarrassment was noticed by the captain. To port they went. There the advertisement met the captain's eye. Benjamin so exactly answered its description that the captain laid hold on him, and bound him in chains. The storm passed, and they proceeded to New York. Before reaching that port Benjamin managed to get off his chains and throw them overboard. He escaped from the vessel, but was pursued, captured, and carried back to his master. . . .

The full text of Document 3.2.8 is available on the CD-ROM.

3.2.9

Illustration, "Horrid Massacre in Virginia," composite of scenes of Nat Turner's Rebellion, 1831

Library of Congress

3.2.10

Excerpt from "The Confessions of Nat Turner" by Thomas R. Gray, 1831

In his introduction to The Confessions of Nat Turner and Related Documents, *editor Kenneth S. Greenberg writes:*

> *The rebels struck the first blow before dawn on August 22 (probably about 2:00 a.m.) at Nat Turner's home farm, the Travis residence. Their basic tactic was to kill all white people at every farm they reached—men, women, and children; to move with great speed; and to gather additional recruits as they moved along. . . . However, a skirmish with the local militia and the discovery of heavily guarded bridges and roads disorganized and demoralized the insurgents. The final assault by Nat Turner's much-reduced force was repulsed at daybreak of the next morning. The militia quickly captured or killed all of the rebels, with the exception of Turner himself. Nat Turner eluded his pursuers more than two months, never leaving the immediate area, but changing hiding places several times. He was finally captured on October 30, tried one week later, and executed on November 11, 1831.*

Thomas R. Gray, an attorney but not Turner's attorney, got access to Turner's jail cell, where he interviewed him for three days and subsequently wrote the Confessions. *Over 40,000 copies were sold.*

On returning to the house, Hark went to the door with an axe, for the purpose of breaking it open, as we knew we were strong enough to murder the family, if they were awaked by the noise; but reflecting that it might create an alarm in the neighborhood, we determined to enter the house secretly, and murder them whilst sleeping. Hark got a ladder and set it against the chimney, on which I ascended, and hoisting a window, entered and came down stairs, unbarred the door, and removed the guns from their places. It was then observed that I must spill the first blood. On which, armed with a hatchet, and accompanied by Will, I entered my master's chamber, it being dark, I could not give a death blow, the hatchet glanced from his head, he sprang from the bed and called his wife, it was his last word, Will laid him dead, with a blow of his axe, and Mrs. Travis shared the same fate, as she lay in bed. The murder of this family, five in number, was the work of a moment, not one of them awoke. . .

The full text of Document 3.2.10 is available on the CD-ROM.

3.2.11

Excerpt from *Incidents in the Life of a Slave Girl*
by Harriet A. Jacobs, 1861, "Fear of Insurrection,"
describing the aftermath of Nat Turner's Rebellion

*On August 21 and 22, 1831, in Southampton County, Virginia, Nat Turner and his fol-
lowers massacred fifty-five whites. It was the bloodiest slave insurrection in American
history. Turner remained at large for more than nine weeks. Eventually he was captured,
tortured, jailed, interrogated, and tried, then executed on November 11. After the insurrection, a wave of white terror swept across the entire South. No one knows how many
blacks were murdered; historians estimate it was in the hundreds.*

It was a grand opportunity for the low whites, who had no negroes of their own to
scourge. They exulted in such a chance to exercise a little brief authority, and show
their subserviency to the slaveholders; not reflecting that the power which trampled
on the colored people also kept themselves in poverty, ignorance, and moral degradation. Those who never witnessed such scenes can hardly believe what I know was
inflicted at this time on innocent men, women, and children, against whom there
was not the slightest ground for suspicion. Colored people and slaves who lived in
remote parts of town suffered in an especial manner. In some cases the searchers
scattered powder and shot among their clothes, and then sent other parties to find
them, and bring them forward as proof that they were plotting insurrection. Every
where men, women, and children were whipped till the blood stood in puddles at
their feet. Some received five hundred lashes; others were tied hands and feet, and
tortured with a bucking paddle, which blisters the skin terribly. . . .

The full text of Document 3.2.11 is available on the CD-ROM.

David Walker's Appeal to the Coloured Citizens of the World (1829–1830)

In the introduction to his 1993 edition of *Walker's Appeal, In Four Articles; Together With A Preamble, to the Coloured Citizens of the World, but In Particular And Very Expressly, to Those of The United States Of America* (1829, 1830), historian James Turner defines David Walker's manifesto as "the most seminal expression of African American political thought to come forth in the early nineteenth century. Walker," he continues, "presents the first sustained critique of slavery and racism in the United States by an African person. David Walker's *Appeal* crystallized the universal principles against slavery, and its influence as a crucial impetus to the antislavery crusade and its coherence and organization as a movement" (p. 9).

David Walker was born in North Carolina on September 28, 1785, to a free black woman and slave father who died when Walker was a young child. North Carolina law mandated, as did the law in most southern states, that the "condition of the child follow that of the mother." A child born to a slave mother belonged to the mother's owner; a child born to a free mother, no matter if the father was enslaved, was legally free. Young Walker quickly developed a deep, lifelong anger and outrage toward the southern system. As an adult, he traveled in the South, witnessing the brutality of daily life under slavery. He later moved to Boston, where he opened a clothing shop on Brattle Street.

Although his business prospered, Walker, due to his personal generosity, lived close to the financial edge. His home, near the African Meeting House on the north slope of Beacon Hill, was well known as a refuge for those in need. "His hands were always open to contribute to the wants of the fugitive," wrote black activist clergyman Henry Highland Garnet, who described him further as "emphatically a self-made man, . . . [who] spent all his leisure moments in the cultivation of his mind" [H. H. Garnet. *Walker's Appeal with a Brief Sketch of His Life*. New York: Tobitt, 1848, p. vi]. "This little book," declared Garnet, "produced more commotion amongst slaveholders than any volume of its size that was ever issued from an American Press."

Walker's incendiary manifesto is divided into four sections:

❖ Our Wretchedness in Consequence of Slavery
❖ Our Wretchedness in Consequence of Ignorance

- ❖ Our Wretchedness in Consequence of the Preachers of the Religion of Jesus Christ
- ❖ Our Wretchedness in Consequence of the Colonizing Plan

He denounced American slavery as the most vicious form of bondage known to history. A deeply religious man, whose writings are filled with biblical references and theological reflections, he found American slavery particularly odious and hypocritical because it was supported by a supposedly Christian nation.

Education, Walker contended, would go far toward enabling blacks to decide their own fate, even if that meant violent revolt. "They want us for their slaves," he wrote, "and think nothing of murdering to subject us to that wretched condition—therefore, if there is an *attempt* made by us, kill or be killed." According to Garnet, a group of men in Georgia offered ten thousand dollars to anyone who would capture Walker alive, one thousand if he were killed. His friends and family urged him to move to Canada, but Walker stood his ground declaring, "It is not in me to falter if I can promote the work of emancipation." In 1830, soon after the publication of the second edition of his *Appeal*, David Walker was found dead. Many people believed he had been poisoned. The cause of Walker's death was investigated and debated without success and remains a mystery to this day.

Organizing Idea

David Walker's militant and inflammatory document illustrates the steady commitment to resistance and rebellion by enslaved black people in the South and their abolitionist supporters in the North.

Student Objectives

Students will:

- ❖ understand the significance of this black activist's role early in the abolitionist movement

Key Questions

- ❖ To whom is Walker talking in his *Appeal*? How do his messages to the enslaved, to free black people, and to white people differ? What actions does he ask each group to take?
- ❖ What are the similarities between the abuses by Great Britain against the colonies prior to the Revolution and those Walker describes of Americans toward black people?
- ❖ Why was Walker perceived as a threat to slaveholders?
- ❖ How effective was writing such as Walker's in bringing about change?

Primary Source Materials

DOCUMENT 3.3.1: Frontispiece from David Walker's *Appeal, In Four Articles; to the Coloured Citizens of the World*, 1830

DOCUMENT 3.3.2: Excerpts from the Preamble to David Walker's *Appeal, In Four Articles; to the Coloured Citizens of the World*, 1830

DOCUMENT 3.3.3: Excerpts from Article I of David Walker's *Appeal, In Four Articles; to the Coloured Citizens of the World*, 1830

DOCUMENT 3.3.4: Excerpts from Article II of David Walker's *Appeal, In Four Articles; to the Coloured Citizens of the World*, 1830

DOCUMENT 3.3.5: Excerpts from the Article III of David Walker's *Appeal, In Four Articles; to the Coloured Citizens of the World*, 1830

DOCUMENT 3.3.6: Excerpts from Article IV of David Walker's *Appeal, In Four Articles; to the Coloured Citizens of the World*, 1830

DOCUMENT 3.3.7: Excerpts from Dr. Martin Luther King Jr.'s "Letter from a Birmingham Jail," April 16, 1963

Supplementary Materials

ITEM 3.3.A: Additional vocabulary lists for primary sources

ITEM 3.3.B: Major themes in the *Appeal*

Vocabulary

abject	bondage	heathen	rabble-rousers
anarchy	civil	inferiority	segregationist
avarice	disobedience	oppressor	submissive
barbarous	degradation	paternalistic	tribunal
brethren	emancipate	persecute	

Student Activities

Listening to the *Appeal* and Identifying Themes

Activity 1

A few students should be assigned to read excerpts from David Walker's *Appeal* out loud in a manner similar to giving a speech. The other students in the class then write down the themes they hear in the speeches. Write a list of themes students identify on the board. In his introduction to the Black Classic Press edition of the *Appeal* (1993), Cornell University historian James Turner includes a list of the ten major themes identified by African American historian and author Vincent Harding in the *Appeal*. A list of the themes is included on the CD-ROM (Item 3.3.B). Compare this list with the one compiled by the students.

Activity 2   **Analysis of the *Appeal***

Provide everyone with a frontispiece for Walker's *Appeal* (3.3.1) and the excerpted sections from the *Appeal* (3.3.2–3.3.6). Working in small groups, students should answer the questions on the illustration and then those assigned to their group.

Frontispiece
- What is striking about the illustration? What feelings does it evoke?
- What is noteworthy about the title of Walker's work?

Document 3.3.2, "Preamble"
- What has Walker observed?
- What questions does he ask?
- What is the purpose of his writing?

Document 3.3.3, Article I
- What did Walker mean when he said in the first paragraph "*ought to be* Slaves to the American people and their children forever"?
- What analogy did he use to explain why African Americans appear to some white people to be inferior? Is it a valid analogy?
- How did Walker feel about the color of his skin?
- What does he think of people who won't stand up against slavery?
- Who are "Americans"?
- Of what does Walker accuse them?

Document 3.3.4, Article II
- Explain in your own words what Walker said about ignorance in the first paragraph.
- What African achievements did he point out?
- What was Walker's attitude toward violence?
- What did he say was the most important goal? And why was it so critical?

Document 3.3.5, Article III
- What appalled Walker about religious services?
- What did Walker mean by "little places for the reception of coloured people" in the last paragraph? How can you find out?

Document 3.3.6, Article IV
- What, according to Walker, was the intent of Colonization?

- ❖ What did he think of black men who supported Colonization?
- ❖ What is Walker's hope?
- ❖ To what important document did Walker refer? Why?

(For more information about Colonization, students can refer to Sourcebook 2, Lesson 11.)

After students have carefully studied their documents, answered questions, and shared their findings with the class, the whole group should address the following questions:

- ❖ To whom is Walker writing?
- ❖ Walker asks rhetorical questions in his writing. Why does he use this technique? Is it effective?
- ❖ What was his tone?
- ❖ Note his use of italics and punctuation. Why do you think he did this?
- ❖ Why was Walker perceived by many whites to be so threatening?

After they have answered the questions, students should discuss the implications of their answers for both the antebellum period and the early twenty-first century. Each group should report back its conclusions to the class as a whole.

Comparison of the *Appeal* to Martin Luther King Jr.'s Writing

Activity 3

For a connecting piece to the twentieth century, students should read Martin Luther King's "Letter from a Birmingham Jail" (3.3.7). Discuss and list on the board the similarities between King's message to the clergy of America and Walker's themes, referring to specific excerpts in the documents. Discuss how the two are different as well. Both David Walker and Dr. King write in a sermonlike style. Why do you think they did this and how might it have added to the power of their messages?

Creative Extensions—The Essence of Walker's *Appeal*

Activity 4

Students can articulate Walker's messages by summarizing his *Appeal* in writing or orally. Alternatively they can create a piece of art representing Walker's themes.

Essay Writing—Self-Knowledge

Activity 5

In his introduction to Walker's *Appeal*, James Turner quotes from the essay "The Basis of African Culture" by modern Caribbean scholar Timothy Callender: "What we do for ourselves depends on what we know of ourselves and what we accept about ourselves." Have students write an essay discussing how Callender's statement applies both to the life of David Walker and to their own life.

Contemporary Connection

※

From David Walker to Malcolm X

Malcolm X (1925–1965) was an outstanding and controversial twentieth-century social and political activist who studied David Walker's writing. As with Walker, many white and some black Americans found Malcolm X's angry civil rights message to be incendiary and physically threatening. Malcolm X believed that white society was committed to the systematic oppression of black people and argued that African Americans must empower themselves and resist racism "by any means necessary."

While serving a prison sentence between 1946 and 1952, the former Malcolm Little read constantly in his successful effort to become, as was Walker, a self-educated man. He studied world history, literature, the Bible, and the teachings of the Koran. In prison, he converted to Islam as it was taught by the black American self-styled cleric Elijah Muhammad and his Nation of Islam. In keeping with the practice of that group, he changed what was called his "slave name" to Malcolm X.

As a spokesman for the Nation of Islam, Malcolm X attracted a broad following with his charismatic speeches and his tireless work on behalf of his faith. Early in his public career, he argued for independence and self-sufficient African American communities. Following his 1964 pilgrimage to Mecca and his break with Elijah Muhammad, he envisioned a multiracial American and international ideal. Both David Walker and Malcolm X lived with constant death threats as a result of their activism on behalf of black human beings. Malcolm X was killed by a hail of bullets fired by three assassins while he was giving a speech at a crowded rally in New York City on February 21, 1965.

Students can learn more about him from *The Autobiography of Malcolm X* as told by Alex Haley, *Malcolm X: Make It Plain,* a Blackside Film and Video made in 1994, or by visiting *www.brother malcolm.net,* a Malcolm X research site.

Students can consider what David Walker and Malcom X had in common. What insights can we gain from understanding the connections in historical events?

Further Student and Teacher Resources

Horton, James Oliver, and Lois E. Horton. *Black Bostonians.* New York: Holmes & Meier Publishers, Inc., 1979.

Malcolm X. *The Autobiography of Malcolm X.* With the assistance of Alex Haley. Intro. by M. S. Handler. Epilogue by Alex Haley. New York: Grove Press, 1966.

Walker, David. *David Walker's Appeal, In Four Articles; Together With A Preamble, to the Coloured Citizens of the World, but In Particular, and Very Expressly, to Those of The United States Of America, Third and Last Edition, Revised and Published By David Walker, 1830.* Introduction by James Turner. Baltimore, MD: Black Classic Press, 1993.

Website

David Walker's Appeal. *Africans in America,* 4, Boston: WGBH, 1998
www.pbs.org/wgbh/aia/part4/4h2931t.html
Excerpts of the text along with educator resources

Primary Source Materials
for Lesson 3

3.3.1

Frontispiece from David Walker's *Appeal, In Four Articles; to the Coloured Citizens of the World*, 1830

The illustration in Walker's Appeal *is one of the first images showing an African American standing up. Notice the words on the tablet for which he is reaching.*

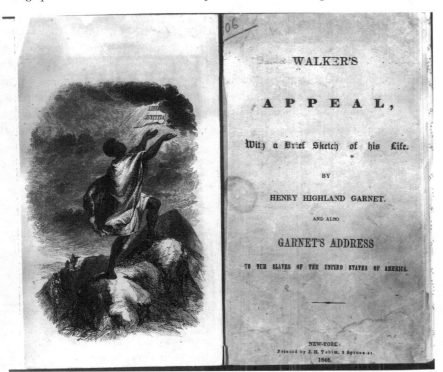

Library of Congress

3.3.2

Excerpts from the Preamble to David Walker's *Appeal, In Four Articles; to the Coloured Citizens of the World,* 1830

From the Preamble:

My dearly beloved Brethren and Fellow-Citizens:

Having travelled over a considerable portion of these United States, and having, in the course of my travels, taken the most accurate observations of things as they exist, the result of my observations has warranted the full and unshaken conviction, that we (coloured people of these United States) are the most degraded, wretched and abject set beings that ever lived since the world began; and I pray God that none like us ever may live again until time shall be no more. They tell us of the Israelites in Egypt, the Helots in Sparta, and of the Roman slaves, which last were made up from almost every nation under heaven, whose sufferings under those ancient and heathen nations were, in comparison with ours, under this enlightened and Christian nation, no more than a cypher . . .

I will ask one question here,—Can our condition be any worse?—Can it be more mean and abject? If there are any changes, will they not be for the better, though they may appear for the worse at first? Can they get us any lower? Where can they get us? They are afraid to treat us worse, for they know well, the day they do it they are gone. But against all accusations which may or can be preferred against me, I appeal to Heaven for my motive in writing—who knows that my object is, if possible, to awaken in the breasts of my afflicted, degraded and slumbering brethren, a spirit of inquiry and investigation respecting our miseries and wretchedness in this *Republican Land of Liberty! ! ! ! !*

3.3.3

Excerpts from Article I in David Walker's *Appeal, In Four Articles; to the Coloured Citizens of the World,* 1830

From Article I

OUR WRETCHEDNESS IN CONSEQUENCE OF SLAVERY

God [has made] us black—which colour, Mr. [Thomas] Jefferson calls unfortunate! ! ! ! ! ! As though we are not as thankful to our God, for having made us as it pleased himself, as they (the whites,) are for having made them white. They think because they hold us in their infernal chains of slavery, that we wish to be white, or of their color—but they are dreadfully deceived—we wish to be just as it pleased our Creator to have made us, and no avaricious and unmerciful wretches, have any business to make slaves of, or hold us in slavery . . .

The full text of Document 3.3.3 is available on the CD-ROM.

3.3.4

Excerpts from Article II of David Walker's *Appeal, In Four Articles; to the Coloured Citizens of the World*, 1830

From Article II

OUR WRETCHEDNESS IN CONSEQUENCE OF IGNORANCE

There is a great work for you to do, . . . You have to prove to the Americans and the world that we are MEN, and not *brutes*, as we have been represented, and by millions treated. Remember, to let the aim of your labours among your brethren, and particularly the youths, be the dissemination of education and religion. . .

I would crawl on my hands and knees through mud and mire, to the feet of a learned man, where I would sit and humbly supplicate him to instill into me, that which neither devils nor tyrants could remove, only with my life—for coloured people to acquire learning in this country, [would] make tyrants quake and tremble on their sandy foundation. . . . The bare name of educating the coloured people, scares our cruel oppressors almost to death.

The full text of Document 3.3.4 is available on the CD-ROM.

3.3.5

Excerpts from Article III of David Walker's *Appeal, In Four Articles; to the Coloured Citizens of the World*, 1830

From Article III

OUR WRETCHEDNESS IN CONSEQUENCE OF THE PREACHERS OF THE RELIGION OF JESUS CHRIST

Religion, my brethren, is a subject of deep consideration among all the nations of the earth. . . .

I have known tyrants or usurpers of human liberty in different parts of this country to take their fellow creatures, the coloured people, and beat them until they would scarcely leave life in them; what for? Why they say, "The black devils had the audacity to be found making prayers and supplications to the God who made them ! ! ! !" . . .

[P]ride and prejudice have got to such a pitch, that in the very houses erected to the Lord, they have built little places for the reception of coloured people, where they must sit during meeting, or keep away from the house of God, and the preachers say nothing about it.

The full text of Document 3.3.5 is available on the CD-ROM.

3.3.6

Excerpts from Article IV of David Walker's *Appeal, In Four Articles; to the Coloured Citizens of the World,* 1830

From Article IV

OUR WRETCHEDNESS IN CONSEQUENCE OF THE COLONIZING PLAN

[Colonization is] a plan to get those of the coloured people, who are said to be free, away from among those of our brethren whom they unjustly hold in bondage, so they may be enabled to keep them more secure in ignorance and wretchedness, to support them and their children, and consequently they would have the more obedient slave. For if the free are allowed to stay among the slave . . . the free will of course [teach] the slaves *bad habits*, by teaching them that they are MEN, as well as other people, and certainly *ought* and *must* be FREE. . . .

This country is as much ours as it is the whites, whether they will admit it or not, they will see it and believe it by and by. . . .

The full text of Document 3.3.6 is available on the CD-ROM.

3.3.7

Excerpts from Dr. Martin Luther King Jr.'s "Letter from a Birmingham Jail," April 16, 1963

MY DEAR FELLOW CLERGYMEN:

I am in Birmingham because injustice is here. Just as the prophets of the eighth century B.C. left their villages and carried their "thus saith the Lord" far beyond the boundaries of their home towns, and just as the Apostle Paul left his village of Tarsus and carried the gospel of Jesus Christ to the far corners of the Greco-Roman world, so am I compelled to carry the gospel of freedom beyond my own home town. Like Paul, I must constantly respond to the Macedonian call for aid.

Moreover, I am cognizant of the interrelatedness of all communities and states. I cannot sit idly by in Atlanta and not be concerned about what happens in Birmingham. Injustice anywhere is a threat to justice everywhere. . . . .

The full text of Document 3.3.7 is available on the CD-ROM.

Freedom's Journal

Newspapers shape public opinion. Sometimes they state their positions on controversial subjects openly through their editorials. But most often, they take stands through what they decide to publish and what they decide to leave out. Whose stories do they tell? Which events do they cover? Whose speeches do they put on the front page?

In the 1990s, telecommunications, including the expansion of the Internet, made vast amounts of information affordable and accessible to hundreds of millions of people around the globe. A similar communications revolution occurred in the 1830s when advances in printing and papermaking made newspaper production and purchase available to groups of people who had not had many opportunities to publish or read their side of the story previously.

At the beginning of the 1999 film *The Black Press: Soldiers Without Swords*, Victor Jarrett and Phyl Garland discuss why and how African Americans began to publish their own newspapers. Jarrett: "We didn't exist in the other papers. We were never born, we didn't get married, we didn't die, we didn't fight in any wars, we never participated in anything of a scientific achievement. We were truly invisible unless we committed a crime. And in the black press, the negro press, we did get married. They showed us our babies when they were born. They showed us graduating. They showed our PhDs." Garland: "The black press was never intended to be objective because it didn't see the white press being objective. It often took a position. It had an attitude. This was a press of advocacy. There was news, but the news had an admitted and a deliberate slant."

A newspaper by and for the black community was sorely needed. This was evidenced by the writings of the white press in the early nineteenth century. Editorials in papers such as the *New York Inquirer*, edited by Mordecai Noah, were not overly friendly towards black people. They often urged the reenslavement of those black people who had gained their freedom. "Free Negroes," one editorial said, "were raucous and rambunctious, no matter how cultured they tried to be." It went on to say, "(they were) a nuisance incomparably greater that a million slaves." The *New York Evening Post* was another strong voice for white racism. Its editor, William

Coleman, also favored slavery, and particularly praised West Indian slavery in many of his editorials.

America's first black newspaper was the brainchild of a group of prominent black men. They came together at the home of a Mr. M Boston Crummell, looking for a way to respond to the many articles in white newspapers attacking the black community. After deciding that an independent black newspaper would be the most viable answer, they selected a committee to find the most qualified men to serve as editors.

The black press was born in 1827. On March 16th of that year in New York, a Presbyterian minister named Samuel E. Cornish and one of the first college-educated black people in America, John B. Russwurm, published the first newspaper solely by and for African Americans. They named it *Freedom's Journal*.

The newspaper itself was an impressive looking, professional piece of work. Its neat 8 by 12 inches of printed matter appeared weekly in four columns on four pages, with overall dimensions of about 10 by 15 inches. Its motto, "Righteousness Exalteth a Nation," set the mood of the paper. The *Journal* was seen as an abolitionist paper by some and was filled with many writings condemning slavery. Some articles were original, whereas others were reprinted from other newspapers, an accepted practice of the time.

This first attempt in the black newspaper medium was to be the father of more than 2,800 other newspapers published to the present day. It is doubtful that Russwurm and Cornish realized that *Freedom's Journal* would be the spark that lit the flame of the black press in America, a flame that still burns today.

Organizing Idea

In *Freedom's Journal*, the first black newspaper, African Americans had an independent voice and could speak for themselves. The paper's founders and editors recognized the media as a powerful means of expression.

Student Objectives

Students will:

- ❖ know and be able to explain the origins of the African American press
- ❖ understand the role it played in the African American struggle for rights and respect
- ❖ become familiar with some of the contemporary issues and related arguments
- ❖ develop an awareness of free black people who were living, working, building, and contributing to community and agitating for an end to slavery at this time
- ❖ demonstrate an understanding of the role of the African American press, past and present

Key Questions

❖ Why was *Freedom's Journal* needed? What purposes would it serve?

❖ Where did it start? How? By whom?

❖ How was *Freedom's Journal* different from papers published by European Americans?

❖ What was the focus of the black press at the time of its origins?

❖ What is the focus of the black press today? Has it changed over time? Explain.

Primary Source Materials

DOCUMENT 3.4.1: Image of masthead from *Freedom's Journal* (includes images of the newspaper's founders)

DOCUMENT 3.4.2: "African Free Schools in the United States," *Freedom's Journal,* June 1, 1827

DOCUMENT 3.4.3: Jones, David. "The Urban Agenda: Racism Creates Bad Schools," *New York Amsterdam News,* February 3, 1999

DOCUMENT 3.4.4: Excerpt from *Freedom's Journal,* April 6, 1827

Supplementary Materials

ITEM 3.4.A: Additional vocabulary lists for primary sources

Student Activities

Activity 1

Analysis of Masthead of *Freedom's Journal*

Examine the masthead carefully (3.4.1). What does the name of the paper tell you? Why might the editors have put their images on the paper? What is the meaning of the subhead "Righteousness Exalteth a Nation"? What does it suggest about the mission of the paper?

Activity 2

Comparison of Two Articles on Education

Distribute copies of "African Free Schools in the United States" from the June 1, 1827, edition of *Freedom's Journal,* June 1, 1827 (3.4.2), and "The Urban Agenda: Racism Creates Bad Schools" from the February 3, 1999, edition of the *New York Amsterdam News* (3.4.3). Have students read the articles aloud.

Two African American newspapers, 170 years apart, speak to the critical issue of educating black youth. Each paper is a powerful voice in its own time, and each echoes across the ages carrying a message against a timeless, tenacious, and yet vulnerable foe, racism.

Once the articles are read and interpreted, students can begin to answer questions and raise new ones. Here are some questions to consider:

1. How do the *Freedom's Journal* and *Amsterdam News* articles compare? Contrast? In tone? In content?

2. Who is the intended audience?

3. What are the editors trying to accomplish?

4. What does each use to support its claims?

5. What insights into nineteenth- and twentieth-century life can you get from the education articles?

Analysis of Sample Articles

Activity 3

Read the selections from the April 6, 1827, edition of *Freedom's Journal* (3.4.4). Careful reading of the primary source materials is necessary before an engaging discussion can take place. The vocabulary and nineteenth-century style of the *Freedom's Journal* articles are challenging and instructive. Students can work individually, in pairs, or in small groups. Have the students work first with the longer selections (articles 1 and 2). They should extract phrases and sentences in their articles that make key points. When the groups have finished their analyses, the teacher can use the board, a screen, chart paper, etc., to record these short phrases. Each group should write a summary of the assigned article, incorporating quotes. They can read their summaries aloud to classmates, who compare them to the points on the board and evaluate them for accuracy.

Discussion—Beyond the Printed Word

Activity 4

Read the short excerpts (articles 3 and 4) from the paper (also Document 3.4.4). Ask the students to consider *all* the selections they have read. What topics did *Freedom's Journal* address that were likely not addressed in white mainstream papers? Who was the paper's audience? How did that affect the choice of topics? For example, why might the editors have chosen to include the Memoir of Paul Cuffe? What can students conclude were the "hot issues of the day"?

Creative Writing Extensions

Activity 5

Students can write an article, letter to the editor, or editorial or create a cartoon with appropriate caption(s) for a class-created newspaper, the local town or city paper, or the school's student newspaper. They should be mindful of the audience for whom they are writing. A discussion can follow, exploring how what they wrote might change if they were writing for a different readership.

Activity 6   **Research**

Students can research a local or regional African American newspaper—its origins, circulation, advertisers, and editorial slant. They may want to compare two articles covering the same event reported in the black newspaper and in a mainstream publication.

Students may want to discover more about the first editors of *Freedom's Journal*, the Reverend Samuel E. Cornish and John Russwurm.

Further Student and Teacher Resources

Borzendowski, Janice. *John Russwurm.* (*Black Americans of Achievement*). New York: Chelsea House Publishers, 1989.

Bullock, Penelope L. *The Afro-American Periodical Press, 1838–1909*. Baton Rouge: Louisiana State University Press, 1981.

Dann, Martin E., ed. *The Black Press, 1827–1890: The Quest for National Identity*. New York: Putnam, 1971.

Hutton, Frankie. *The Early Black Press in America, 1827–1860*. Westport, CT: Greenwood Publishing Group, 1992.

Jacobs, Donald M. *AnteBellum Black Newspapers: Indices to New York Freedom's Journal (1827–1829), Rights of All (1829), the Weekly Advocate (1837) and the Colored American (1837–1841)*. Westport, CT: Greenwood Publishing Group, Inc., 1976.

Tripp, Bernell. *Origins of the Black Press: New York 1827–1847*. Northport, AL: Vision Press, 1992.

Websites

Freedom's Journal. Wisconsin Historical Society, Madison, WI
www.wisconsinhistory.org/library/collections/digital.html
Digitized version of the complete text of the first African American periodical, published in New York, 1827–1829

Excerpts from issues of Freedom's Journal *can help spark discussion and generate questions and activities related to the role of the black press, then and now. The Wisconsin Historical Society has scanned every issue of* Freedom's Journal *and made them available online. Additional lessons using these documents can be organized around themes such as points of view and multiple perspectives on slavery, resistance, abolitionism, early nineteenth-century African American culture, the press, and intellectual and institutional racism in society, past and present.*

Time Line of the Black Press. The Black Press: Soldiers Without Swords. PBS Online, Boston
www.pbs.org/blackpress/timeline/index.html
Includes a time line and links to other resources including a bibliography

Contemporary Connection

✻

The Black Press

Following the Civil War, the number of African American newspapers grew rapidly. By 1890, there were 575 African American publications in the United States. The vast majority of these quickly went bankrupt, but a good number survived. The *Philadelphia Tribune* was founded in 1884 and is still published twice weekly. It is the oldest continuously published African American newspaper in the United States.

For a time line of black newspapers and journalism dating back to the founding of *Freedom's Journal,* see: *www.pbs.org/blackpress/film/index.html.* In 1999, PBS and Stanley Nelson produced a documentary entitled *The Black Press, Soldiers without Swords.* This film may be purchased from California Newsreel (*www.newsreel.org*).

Students can find an African American newspaper published in their region or read one online. In reading the articles, can we discover how this paper differs from other local or national newspapers?

Databases

Accessible Archives Search and Information Server. Accessible Archives, Malvern, PA, 1990–.
Freedom's Journals *is one of many eighteenth- and nineteenth-century periodicals available from this online subscription service.*

Video

The Black Press: Soldiers Without Swords. Videocassette. Dir. Stanley Nelson. Distributed by California Newsreel, 1998.

Primary Source Materials
for Lesson 4

3.4.1

Image of masthead from *Freedom's Journal*
(includes images of the newspaper's founders)

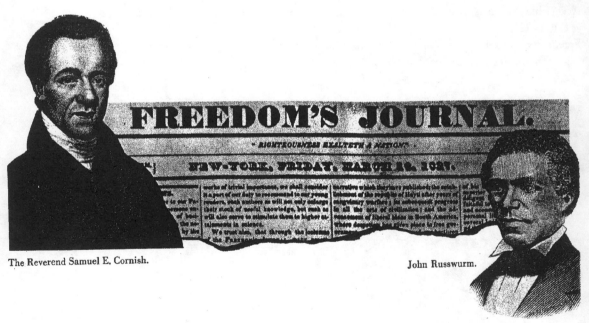

The Reverend Samuel E. Cornish.

John Russwurm.

North Wind Picture Archives

<u>3.4.2</u>

"African Free Schools in the United States,"
Freedom's Journal, June 1, 1827

Portland, ME, with coloured population of nine hundred, provides one school, for the education of their children, under the care of a mistress. Better things are in progress.

Boston, Mass. With a coloured population of two thousand, provides (assisted by the liberal donation of the late Abiel Smith, Esq.) three schools for the instruction of their children, viz. two Primary, under the care of African female teachers, and a Grammar School under a master. . . .

Salem, Mass. With a coloured population of four hundred, put a school into operation the last year, for the education of their children, but from causes unkown to us, closed it after six months.

New Haven, Conn., with a coloured population of eight hundred, provides two schools, during *three months* in the year, under the care of a master and mistress.

Providence, R.I., with a coloured population of fifteen hundred, and *Hartford, Conn.*, with five hundred provide none.

Philadelphia, with a coloured population of twenty thousand, provides *three* schools for the instruction of their children, under the care of four teachers.

New-York, with a coloured population of fifteen thousand, provides *two* schools for the instruction of their children, under the care of a master and mistress. Parents, we learn, who are able, are obliged to pay one dollar per quarter for each child.

We need not mention the names of any other places, as we know of no other schools. Seeing then, that the schools now in operation, for the education of our children, are so few and imperfect; ought *others* to wonder, that not many after arriving at manhood, are fitted to take a respectable stand in society. What are the advantages to be derived from an instruction in these schools, compared to those of a higher and more elevated nature? What are the incentives held out to a lad of colour? Are there higher schools to stimulate him to greater exertions? Is he placed, and considered, an equal with other boys in schools of the same rank? Do the committees of trustees, expect him to be as well grounded in the elementary branches? A little smattering, and a few words recommendatory from his teacher, are all they look for from a boy of colour. The very idea of his colour, is enough to elicit praise from his learned visitors, when the same exercise performed as well by another boy, would pass unnoticed, and be considered as a thing of course. . . .

The full text of Document 3.4.2 is available on the CD-ROM.

3.4.3

Jones, David. "The Urban Agenda: Racism Creates Bad Schools," *New York Amsterdam News,* February 3, 1999

Public Support Eroded

Although no one would admit it, racism is the primary reason for the [New York city] school system's decline and its failing to properly educate the next generation of New Yorkers. Earlier in the century, the schools competently educated millions of mostly white immigrants. Today, 84% of the students are children of color. The system changed from predominately white to predominately African American and Hispanic over several decades. Many white families moved to the suburbs. Those who stayed in the city often sent their children to private schools. As the racial composition of the students changed, an erosion in public support and tax dollars followed. . . .

The full text of Document 3.4.3 is available on the CD-ROM.

3.4.4

Excerpt from *Freedom's Journal,* April 6, 1827

Article 2: "People of Color" from *Freedom's Journal,* Friday, April 6, 1827, vol. I, No.4

Every attempt at a thorough discussion of this subject has always been met with a cry of danger. "You will excite the slaves to insurrection," say they. But I ask if there is now no danger? If every slave owner feels as safe when he goes to bed as if he were surrounded by a free peasantry? If not, what mean those pistols under his pillow, and that loaded rifle over it? And is there even now no small degree of danger, what will be the case when the slaves in the West Indies and the Spanish states, become all free citizens? On the subject of danger, I am happy again to avail myself of the language of Mr. Buxton. "I do not mean to say, that there are not very great perils connected with the present state of the West Indies. On the contrary, I am quite sure—as sure as it is possible for any man in the house or in the country to be—that there is imminent peril at the present moment; and that first peril will increase, unless our systems be altered. For I know wherever there is oppression, there is danger—wherever there is slavery there is great danger—danger, in proportion to the degree of suffering. But the question is, how that danger is to be avoided. I answer, that it is to be avoided by that spirit of humanity which has avoided it in other places—by doing justice to those whom we now oppress—by giving liberty for slavery, happiness for misery." . . .

The full text of Document 3.4.4 is available on the CD-ROM.

The White Abolitionist Press

No editor has ever sustained an advocacy newspaper for longer than William Lloyd Garrison, who published *The Liberator* weekly without interruption for thirty-five years. The paper did not cease publication until after ratification of the Thirteenth Amendment to the United States Constitution, which, in December 1865, abolished slavery. When twenty-five-year-old Garrison started his newspaper in 1831, Abraham Lincoln was a twenty-one-year-old sodbuster on the Illinois prairie, Jefferson Davis was a newly commissioned U.S. Army officer fighting the Sauk and Fox on the Wisconsin frontier, and Davis' West Point classmate, Robert E. Lee, was building federal fortifications on the Georgia coast. Ulysses S. Grant and William T. Sherman were still schoolboys in Ohio, and Harriet Tubman was a ten-year-old slave on a Maryland plantation. John Brown was teaching school and running a tannery in Pennsylvania, Stephen A. Douglas was reading law in western New York, Frederick Douglass was learning to read as an adolescent slave in Baltimore, and Harriet Beecher Stowe was teaching composition in her sister Catherine Beecher's Hartford Female Seminary.

Their careers a generation hence would each be profoundly shaped and, in some cases, redirected by the process Garrison and other publishers, black and white, set in motion in the 1820s and 1830s. With ferocious determination, Garrison broke the silence and made the public listen in a way that his predecessors had not. Henry Mayer in *All on Fire* writes, "He employed a writing style of extraordinary physicality—in his columns trumpets blare, statues bleed, hearts melt, apologists tremble, light blazes, nations move—that animated the moral landscape as the Romantic poets had spiritualized the natural world, and he made the moral issue of slavery so palpable that it could no longer be evaded."

The man who put the issue of slavery so dramatically before his contemporaries came from humble origins. He was a native New Englander, born in Newburyport, Massachusetts. His father, a sailor, left the family when Garrison was still a small child. His mother supported the family, at times from the distance of Baltimore, where she worked as a nurse.

Garrison attempted several apprenticeships as a shoemaker and finally completed seven years as a printer's apprentice. When his training was finished, Garrison held several newspaper jobs, where he became interested in reform movements, including one organized to oppose slavery. His writing in *Genius of Universal Emancipation*, a monthly journal that began publication in Baltimore in 1829, resulted in a libel lawsuit against Garrison by the owner of a vessel that transported slaves along the coast. Garrison had charged merchant Francis Todd of Newburyport with being connected to the slave trade. Todd sued for $5,000 for civil defamation. Garrison lost, and—when he could not pay the fine—was thrown into jail, where he served seven weeks of a six-month sentence before money was donated to free him.

While in Baltimore, Garrison had lived in a boardinghouse run by Quakers and had become friends with the African Americans staying there. He credited his black friends with his conversion to the cause of immediate emancipation. Garrison returned to New England in 1830 and on January 1, 1831, published the first issue of *The Liberator*. The majority of subscribers were free black people, who provided most of the financial support for publication of the paper; in many ways, *The Liberator* was a black community newspaper, carrying much community information useful to blacks across the North.

Mob violence in Alton, Illinois, cast a spotlight on the dangers abolitionist speakers and newspaper editors faced. Elijah P. Lovejoy, born in Maine in 1802, was a graduate of Waterville College (now Colby) and the Theological Seminary at Princeton. In 1833, he moved to St. Louis, Missouri to serve as minister of the Presbyterian Church and to launch a religious newspaper, the *Observer*. Racist violence in the city hardened Lovejoy's views on slavery. As a result of his forceful editorials calling for an end to human bondage, white mobs destroyed his press. Lovejoy moved across the Mississippi River to Alton, Illinois.

Although Illinois was a free state, Alton citizens proved no more tolerant of abolitionist views than their Missouri neighbors. Lovejoy continued to insist on his Constitutional right to publish antislavery views, but on three occasions, mobs destroyed his printing presses. The violence culminated in an armed confrontation when a mob came to destroy a replacement press sent by the Ohio Anti-Slavery Society. Elijah Lovejoy was shot dead.

Organizing Idea

Abolitionist newspapers, such as *The Liberator* or Lovejoy's *Observer*, profoundly helped to shape individual lives, and challenged and influenced national events during this time. To understand the history of this period, it is important to understand the role of the press and the men and women who defended their right to publish minority-held views.

Student Objectives

Students will:

❖ engage with the antislavery message presented in William Lloyd Garrison's *The Liberator* and will explore his use of "moral suasion" as a means for bringing about social change

❖ understand that free black people converted William Lloyd Garrison to the cause of immediate emancipation and were a majority of the subscribers to *The Liberator*

❖ evaluate the impact of the various modes of presentation: masthead, language of editorials, and calls to action

❖ understand the enormous risks faced by editors of abolitionist papers

Key Questions

❖ How was *The Liberator* different from *Freedom's Journal*?

❖ What can we learn about abolitionist views from reading *The Liberator*?

❖ How did "moral suasion" abolitionists seek to end slavery?

❖ What role did Elijah Lovejoy have in the antislavery movement?

Primary Source Materials

DOCUMENT 3.5.1: "To the Public," *The Liberator*, January 1, 1831

DOCUMENT 3.5.2A AND B: Images of *The Liberator's* mastheads

DOCUMENT 3.5.3: "The Massachusetts Antislavery Fair," *The Liberator*, December 18, 1840

DOCUMENT 3.5.4: Sketch, "A plan of Marlboro Hall, On the Days of the Massachusetts Antislavery Fair," *The Liberator*, January 1, 1841

DOCUMENT 3.5.5: Image, "Outrage," a handbill, 1837

DOCUMENT 3.5.6: Excerpt from a letter from Elijah Lovejoy to Joseph Lovejoy, January 1836

DOCUMENT 3.5.7: Excerpts from a letter from Elijah Lovejoy to Joseph Lovejoy, July 1836

DOCUMENT 3.5.8: Final public speech made by Elijah Lovejoy, November 3, 1837

DOCUMENT 3.5.9: Image of the proslavery riot of November 7, 1837

Supplementary Materials

ITEM 3.5.A: Additional vocabulary lists for primary sources

Student Activities

Activity 1   **Surveying the Documents**

Visiting workstations, small groups of students view each of the primary source documents. For example, copies of "To the Public" (3.5.1) should be placed in an area of the room where small groups can comfortably read and discuss the article.

At intervals of about thirty minutes, students should be asked to move to the next workstation until they have read and discussed each of the primary sources. One station with two documents deals with antislavery fairs (3.5.3 and 3.5.4) that were organized both to educate the public about the evils of slavery and to raise money for abolitionist activities. A dictionary should be available to look up unfamiliar words (Item 3.5.A).

Questions to begin or fuel the discussion should be posted at each workstation. These questions should be written on a piece of poster paper with room left for students to record their own questions or observations to help following groups. Advise students that later they will be asked to write a story, a letter, or an essay that reflects on their experience with the primary source documents.

The following questions should be recorded at each workstation (others can be added):

"To the Public" (3.5.1)

❖ Whom did Garrison have in mind as the "public" addressed in his editorial?

❖ What language did Garrison use to describe the public?

❖ Quote phrases or passages that show the effect Garrison wanted to have on the public.

The Mastheads of The Liberator *(3.5.2a and b)*

❖ What are the settings for the figures in the illustrations?

❖ Observe the characters depicted in the scenes.

❖ What is going on in each scene?

❖ What kind of messages did the mastheads send to readers?

❖ Compare the two. How did they change over time? Which do you find more effective?

The Liberator *"Massachusetts Antislavery Fair" (3.5.3) and "Marlboro Hall, On the Days of the Massachusetts Antislavery Fair" (3.5.4)*

❖ Who were the managers of the fair?

❖ Which communities are involved?

❖ What was sold at the fair?

❖ In addition to making purchases at the fair, what other participation was possible?

❖ Was the fair considered a success? Why or why not?

"Outrage" (3.5.5)

❖ What risks did abolitionists take? Revisit this question after reading about Elijah Lovejoy.

❖ Identify the words in the handbill that would be likely to inflame emotions.

Activity 2   **Essay Writing—Lovejoy: A Martyr?**

Elijah P. Lovejoy is sometimes referred to as the first martyr to freedom of the press. After reading Documents 3.5.6, 3.5.7, and 3.5.8, students should

- ❖ discuss whether the description of Lovejoy as a martyr fits
- ❖ consider what additional information would be helpful
- ❖ debate the following: Does a community have the right to encourage an editor, who publishes minority viewpoints, to leave?
- ❖ consider how the Bill of Rights, Article 1, fits into the debate

Following a class discussion, students should write an essay presenting their point of view.

Activity 3   **Class Discussion—Going Beyond the Documents**

What did students make of all these documents? What was clear and what was confusing? What further questions do students have, and where might they find answers? What would they like to ask Garrison and Lovejoy if they could? What qualities in a piece of writing help an audience to think more deeply about history?

Activity 4   **Writing to Extend—A Call to Action**

After the class discussion, ask students to write a story, letter, or essay addressing what they have discovered about the time period 1830–1850 and the abolitionist newspapers. Ask students to choose a point of view, or "voice," that allows them to step inside this historical time period.

Encourage students to include questions and/or proposals for action in their writing. In other words, they should consider themselves participants in the time they are writing about rather than observers. Explain to students that their writing will be shared and should help others in the class to think more deeply about the issue.

When the letters and essays are complete, have students share them in groups or with the entire class. Allow time for students to respond to one another's work. Bring attention to writing that encourages deeper reflection. Finally, ask students again to respond to this question: What qualities in stories, letters, or essays help an audience to think more deeply about history?

Activity 5   **Persuasive Writing—A Conversation with Elijah Lovejoy**

Students should imagine a conversation between Elijah and his wife, mother, brother, or close friend. Write the script for a scene in a play. The setting is immediately after a mob has destroyed one of his printing presses. Choose exactly which event has occurred. Find out what preceded the mob action. The person talking with Elijah will try to persuade him to either soften his stance on abolition or cease publication altogether or will support his stand.

Extended Research—Who Were They?

Activity 6

WILLIAM LLOYD GARRISON

William Lloyd Garrison was a very controversial figure in his time. Students can work in small groups and assume responsibility for exploring various aspects of Garrison's life, his tactics, writing, speeches, etc. After each group presents its findings, the class can debate the effectiveness of Garrison's approach.

THE LOVEJOY BROTHERS

Working in groups, students can explore Elijah Lovejoy's life and work in more detail. Others can conduct research on Owen Lovejoy, Elijah's brother. An outspoken abolitionist, he was elected as a representative from Illinois to the United States Congress in 1856.

WILLIAM WELLS BROWN

Students may wish to explore the connections between William Wells Brown, who worked for Lovejoy in St. Louis, and Brown's later work with William Lloyd Garrison.

Further Student and Teacher Resources

Brown, William Wells. *Narrative of William W. Brown, A Fugitive Slave.* Boston: The Anti-slavery Office, 1847.

Cain, William E., ed. *William Lloyd Garrison and the Fight against Slavery: Selections from The Liberator.* New York: Bedford Books of St. Martin's Press, 1995.

Currie, Stephen. *The Liberator: Voice of the Abolitionist Movement.* San Diego, CA: Lucent Books, 2000.

Garrison, William Lloyd. *The Letters of William Lloyd Garrison.* 6 vols. Cambridge, MA: The Belknap Press of Harvard University, 1971–1981.

Harrold, Stanley. *American Abolitionists.* Harlow, England: Pearson Education, 2001.

Hutton, Frankie, and Barbara Straus Reed, eds. *Outsiders in 19th Century Press History: Multicultural Perspectives.* Bowling Green, OH: Bowling Green University Popular Press, 1995.

Jacobs, Donald. M., ed. *Courage and Conscience: Black and White Abolitionists in Boston.* Bloomington: Indiana University Press, 1993.

Mayer, Henry. *All on Fire: William Lloyd Garrison and the Abolition of Slavery.* New York: St. Martin's Press, 1998.

Websites

Elijah Lovejoy, 1802–1837. Illinois Historic Preservation Agency
www.state.il.us/hpa/lovejoy/table.htm

Contemporary
Connection
✠

Lovejoy's Legacy

In memory of the great work of Elijah Lovejoy, Colby College in Maine established the Elijah Parish Lovejoy Award in 1952, and it continues today. This award recognizes a member of the newspaper profession who continues Lovejoy's legacy of fearlessness and freedom and who has contributed to this nation's journalistic achievement. As quoted on the Colby site, "The purpose of the award is threefold: to honor and preserve the memory of Elijah Parish Lovejoy; to stimulate and honor the kind of achievement embodied in Lovejoy's own courageous actions; and to promote a sense of mutual responsibility and cooperation between a journalistic world devoted to freedom of the press and a liberal arts college devoted to academic freedom." Students should consider the role of journalists and publishers today in advocating unpopular causes. Are there any contemporary examples of journalists actually being in danger as a result of what they write?

Owen Lovejoy House. National Park Service, Aboard the Underground Railroad
www.cr.nps.gov/NR/travel/underground/il1.htm

William Lloyd Garrison. *Africans in America*, PBS Online
www.pbs.org/wgbh/aia/part4/4p1561.html

Lovejoy Society
www.lovejoysociety.org

Primary Source Materials
for Lesson 5

3.5.1

"To the Public," *The Liberator,*
January 1, 1831

During my recent tour for the purpose of exciting the minds of the people by a series of discourses on the subject of slavery, every place that I visited gave fresh evidence of the fact, that a greater revolution in public sentiment was to be effected in the free States—and particularly in New-England—than at the South. I found contempt more bitter, opposition more active, detraction more relentless, prejudice more stubborn, and apathy more frozen, than among slave owners themselves. Of course, there were individual exceptions to the contrary. This state of things afflicted, but did not dishearten me. I determined, at every hazard, to lift up the standard of emancipation in the eyes of the nation, within sight of Bunker Hill and in the birth place of liberty. That standard is now unfurled; and long may it float, unhurt by the spoliations of time or the missiles of a desperate foe—yea, till every chain be broken, and every bondman set free! Let southern oppressors tremble—let their secret abettors tremble—let their northern apologists tremble—let all the enemies of the persecuted blacks tremble. . . .

The full text of Document 3.5.1 is available on the CD-ROM.

3.5.2A AND B

Images of *The Liberator's* mastheads

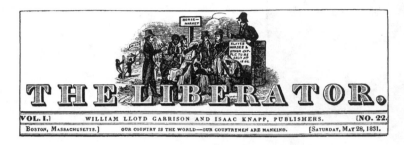

By 1850, the masthead had become far more elaborate.

North Wind Picture Archives

3.5.3

"The Massachusetts Antislavery Fair,"
The Liberator, December 18, 1840

The Massachusetts Anti-Slavery Fair
Will Open

On Tuesday, December 22,
In the Marlborough Hall,
At 9 o'clock in the morning.

The collection of articles, both useful and ornamental, already surpasses that of any former year, though not more than half the towns engaged in preparing for it are yet heard from.

In addition to the rare and beautiful foreign articles, Greek and Etruscan vases, work baskets, paper folders, salad spoons and forks, silk winders, bell pulls, carved and painted with the costumes and scenery of the Swiss Cantons—French box and bakery work, of the richest silk, and embossed and painted paper in very great variety, the American articles are desirable and beautiful in an unexampled degree. Probably so great and various a selection for Christmas and New Year's presents have never been offered in the city.

It comprises German Worsted Work, of every description—gentlemen's, ladies, and children's slippers—reticular, cabas and travelling bags—ladies' opera hoods—children's caps, tippets and neck-ties, of all colors and styles—mittens, muffatees and hose—sabourets and lamp mats—splendid double shawls, etc. . . .

The full text of Document 3.5.3 is available on the CD-ROM.

3.5.4

Sketch, "A plan of Marlboro Hall, On the Days of the Massachusetts Antislavery Fair," *The Liberator*, January 1, 1841

During the 1840s and 1850s, antislavery fairs were chiefly the work of vast numbers of women active in the abolitionist movement.

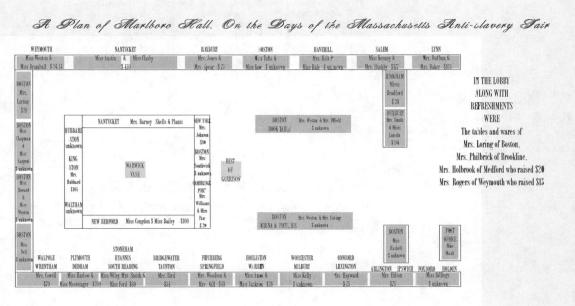

3.5.5

Image, "Outrage," a handbill, 1837

This handbill is typical of the kind that sometimes appeared when abolitionists were scheduled to speak. An emotion-laden handbill is believed to have been a factor in the well-known Boston riot of October 21, 1835. A mob broke into the hall where the Boston Female Anti-Slavery Society was meeting and threatened William Lloyd Garrison's life.

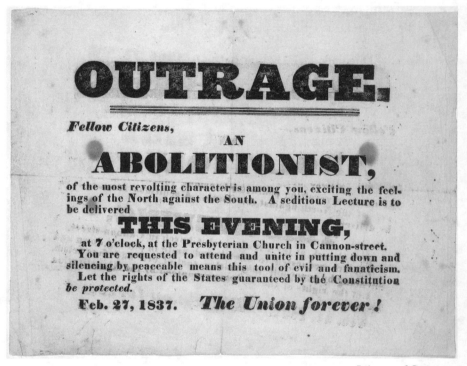

Library of Congress

3.5.6

Excerpt from a letter from Elijah Lovejoy to Joseph Lovejoy, January 1836

St. Louis   January, 1836

My Dear Brother

The mobs in Boston, Philadelphia, and New York gave them this fore text. During the summer an elder in the First Presbyterian Church was frequently coming to me and telling me to beware—that I was in danger, that the constant talk was about mobbing me. [To] this I paid no heed. The first of last week, I went to Poiosi, a town about sixty miles southwest of this, to attend a camp meeting. On my way back I heard that two men had waited in that village for half a day for the purpose of tarring and feathering me. Providentially, I did not come into town till the next morning, and these men tired of waiting went home. On my return into the city I found the excitement getting up, and I was informed by the elder above mentioned, that a hand-bill had been printed to circulate throughout the city, for the purpose of establishing a mob to tear down the office of the Observer . . .

3.5.7

Excerpts from a letter from Elijah Lovejoy to Joseph Lovejoy, July 1836

Alton, (Illinois,) July 30th, 1836

Dear Brother Joseph,

By the Alton Telegraph, which I send you today, you will learn that I have had the honour of being *mobbed* at last. I have been expecting the catastrophe for some time, and now it has come.

The "Observer" will have informed you of the immediate cause of the outrage. Because I dared to comment upon the charge of Judge Lawless—an article so fraught with mischief and falsehood; the mob, which I chose to call his *officials*, tore down my office. What a comment upon the freedom of our institutions! . . .

Though cast down, I am not destroyed, nor in the least discouraged; and am now busily engaged in endeavouring to make arrangements for starting the "Observer" again. I think I shall succeed. I do believe the Lord has yet a work for me to do in contending with his enemies, and the enemies of humanity. I have got the harness on, and I do not intend to lay it off, except at His command. . . .

Your affectionate brother,
Elijah P. Lovejoy

The full text of Document 3.5.7 is available on the CD-ROM.

3.5.8

Final public speech made by Elijah Lovejoy, November 3, 1837

Mr. Chairman—it is not true, as has been charged upon me, that I hold in contempt the feelings and sentiments of this community, in reference to the question which is now agitating it. I respect and appreciate the feelings and opinions of my fellow-citizens, and it is one of the most painful and unpleasant duties of my life, that I am called upon to act in opposition to them. If you suppose, sir, that I have published sentiments contrary to those generally held in this community, because I delighted in differing from them, or in occasioning a disturbance, you have entirely misapprehended me. But, sir, while I value the good opinion of my fellow-citizens, as highly as any one, I may be permitted to say, that I am governed by higher considerations than either the favour or the fear of man. I am impelled to the course I have taken, because I fear God. As I shall answer it to my God in the great day, I dare not abandon my sentiments, or cease in all proper ways to propagate them. . . .

The full text of Document 3.5.8 is available on the CD-ROM.

3.5.9

Image of the proslavery riot of November 7, 1837

On November 7, 1837, a large crowd gathered at the offices of the Observer *with the intent of destroying Elijah Lovejoy's press and razing the building. In the violence that ensued, Lovejoy was shot dead.*

Illinois State Historical Library

Frederick Douglass and The North Star

Frederick Douglass' thoughtful and literate "presence" as an abolitionist lecturer led some observers to speculate that he had never been a slave. In May of 1845, Douglass published his first autobiography, *Narrative of the Life of Frederick Douglass, An American Slave, Written by Himself* to answer any who doubted his past experiences. The stories in the *Narrative* set the record straight; Douglass had indeed suffered the abuse and indignities of being a slave. Douglass' work was so convincing and detailed that it put him at risk of being captured by his former master. For reasons of security, as well as for the opportunity to spread the abolitionist cause, Douglass left for Great Britain, arriving in the late summer of 1845.

During twenty-one months abroad, Douglass gained great recognition and support, including funds for his personal needs or to start a newspaper. In his third autobiograhy, *The Life and Times of Frederick Douglass* (1881), he wrote, " Prepared as I was to meet with many trials and perplexities on reaching home, one of which I little dreamed was awaiting me. My plans for future usefulness, as indicated in the last chapter, were all settled, and in imagination, I already saw myself wielding my pen as well as my voice in the great work of renovating the public mind, and building up a public sentiment, which should send slavery to the grave, and restore to 'liberty and the pursuit of happiness' the people with whom I had suffered."

His literary step in "sending slavery to the grave" was met with reservations and opposition from some of those closest to him in the abolitionist cause. They feared that if Douglass undertook publication of an abolitionist newspaper (of which there were many), the cause would lose one of its most effective speakers. Douglass weighed his decision for months and then went on to make the idea of "wielding his pen" a reality. On December 3, 1847, he published the first edition of his newspaper, *The North Star*.

Organizing Idea

After returning from a successful and acclaimed trip to England, Douglass made plans to publish his own abolitionist newspaper, *The North Star*. Understanding the story of its founding gives us a fuller picture of Frederick Douglass, who began life as a slave and went on to become a powerful voice for freedom—a voice that still speaks to us today.

Student Objectives

Students will:

- ❖ learn how and why Douglass came to create *The North Star* by "listening" to his own words
- ❖ consider how such goal setting and determination in their own lives has led to a decisive action

Key Questions

- ❖ Why did Frederick Douglass begin his own antislavery newspaper in 1847?
- ❖ In Douglass' own writings, what does he tell us about the reaction of his colleagues, including William Lloyd Garrison, to the formation of this new journal?
- ❖ What does William Lloyd Garrison give as his reasons for opposing Frederick Douglass' proposed venture?

Primary Source Materials

DOCUMENT 3.6.1: Excerpt from "Our Mind is Made Up," *The North Star*, by Frederick Douglass, December 3, 1847

DOCUMENT 3.6.2: Excerpt from *The Life and Times of Frederick Douglass*, "Triumphs and Trials," by Frederick Douglass, 1881

DOCUMENT 3.6.3: Excerpt from *The Liberator*, July 23, 1847

DOCUMENT 3.6.4: Excerpt from a letter from William Lloyd Garrison to his wife, Helen, October 20, 1847

DOCUMENT 3.6.5: Image, masthead for *The North Star*

DOCUMENT 3.6.6: Image of Frederick Douglass

Supplementary Materials

ITEM 3.6.A: Additional vocabulary lists for primary sources

Vocabulary

advocate	orator	redress
disparagement	persevere	vindication

Student Activities

Engaging the Students—Taking a Stand

Activity 1

Write on the board, "My mind is made up. I know that I may make mistakes but I am going to try this on my own." Ask students to think about situations in their own lives where this quotation applies and why they took the stand that they did. Students should describe the situation in a short piece of writing, which they may wish to share with the class.

Analysis of "Our Mind is Made Up"

Activity 2

Pass out "Our Mind is Made Up" (3.6.1). Discuss the thoughts on Douglass' mind at the time he wrote this article. What reasons does he give for wanting to launch *The North Star*? What challenges does he anticipate?

Discussion of *The North Star* Venture

Activity 3

Working in pairs or small groups, students should read the excerpt from Frederick Douglass' autobiography, "Triumph and Trials" (3.6.2). They can choose to address the following questions as they read or after they have finished. They may mark the document where they find relevant information and should jot down their answers.

- ❖ Why did fellow abolitionists oppose Douglass' plans for a newspaper?
- ❖ What is your reaction to this opposition?
- ❖ What concerns did Frederick Douglass express concerning his new venture?
- ❖ How and why did Douglass' views shift regarding which strategies should be pursued to abolish slavery?
- ❖ What were the results of this shift?
- ❖ What opposition did Douglass face in Rochester?
- ❖ How else did Frederick Douglass spread his message?
- ❖ What benefits does Frederick Douglass attribute to his having undertaken this project?
- ❖ Beyond what Douglass writes, what do you think might have been the effects of his publishing the paper?

When students have carefully addressed the questions, they can discuss their responses as a class.

Discussion—Garrison's Voice

Activity 4

Students should read William Lloyd Garrison's writing in *The Liberator* (3.6.3) and the excerpt from a letter to his wife (3.6.4). Why did Garrison oppose Frederick Douglass' plans to begin a newspaper? Is there a difference between how Douglass perceived the reasons for Garrison's opposition and the reasons Garrison gives? What is the tone in each of the Garrison excerpts?

Activity 5

Creative Extensions—*The North Star's* Masthead

Working in pairs or small groups, students should examine the original masthead of *The North Star* and the slogan (3.6.3) as well as the image of Frederick Douglass (3.6.4).

- ❖ Discuss why Frederick Douglass may have chosen this illustration for his masthead.
- ❖ What is the significance of the name he chose for his paper?
- ❖ What does each segment of the slogan mean?

Students may choose from several options: (1) Create a masthead for an abolitionist paper; (2) create a masthead for a paper that captures the student's core beliefs; (3) create a poster in which the student shows all he or she has learned about Frederick Douglass.

Activity 6

Compare and Contrast Two Publications

By searching on various websites and skimming books about Douglass and Garrison, students can access copies of *The Liberator* and *North Star*. Compare and contrast the first issues of each. Alternatively, pick a major event of the times and look at how each paper reported it. (*Note:* Students may need help from a resource librarian to conduct the research.)

Activity 7

Further Research—Frederick Douglass

Frederick Douglass had a significant impact on the abolitionist movement and U.S. history. Students can explore his lifework by reading his autobiographies, his speeches, and other writing and/or subsequent biographies written about him.

Further Student and Teacher Resources

Blassingame, John W., ed. *The Frederick Douglass Papers, Series One: Speeches, Debates, and Interviews.* 5 vol. New Haven, CT: Yale University Press, 1979–1992.

Blassingame, John W. ed. *The Frederick Douglass Papers, Series Two: Autobiographical Writings, Narrative of the Life of Frederick Douglass, An American Slave, Written by Himself.* New Haven, CT: Yale University Press, 1999 and 2001.

Bullock, Penelope L. *The Afro-American Periodical Press, 1838–1909.* Baton Rouge: Louisiana State University Press, 1981.

Dann, Martin E., ed. *The Black Press, 1827–1890: The Quest for National Identity.* New York: Putnam, 1971.

Contemporary Connection

⟶❉⟵

The Black Press Today

In 1955 there were only thirty-one African Americans working in mainstream papers (newspapers read by all races). A breakthrough for the African American community came in 1962 when Mal Goode joined ABC, becoming the first African American correspondent hired by a national network. However, change came slowly. A 1985 study found that 95 percent of the journalists at daily newspapers were white (4 percent were black), 92 percent of U.S. newspapers had no African American in news executive positions, and 54 percent had no African American employees. Five years later, the number of African Americans working in mainstream papers had risen to 4,000. For an informative survey of the Black Press from *Freedom's Journal* up to the 1990s, see *www.africana.com*. Click on *topics*, then *media*; then press *black in the U.S.* For up-to-date information on black journalism in the United States, students should go the website for the National Association of Black Journalists (*www.nabj.org*). There are many topics from which to choose to bring this topic up to date for the twenty-first century.

Douglass, Frederick. *Life and Times of Frederick Douglass,* 1881. Reprinted in New York: Collier Books, 1962.

———. *My Bondage and My Freedom,* 1885. Reprinted in Cambridge, MA: Belknap Press of Harvard University, 1960.

———. *Narrative of the Life of Frederick Douglass: An American Slave. Written by Himself.* 1845. Reprinted in Cambridge, MA: Belknap Press of Harvard University, 1960.

Jacobs, Donald M. *AnteBellum Black Newspapers: Indices to New York Freedom's Journal (1827–1829), Rights of All (1829), the Weekly Advocate (1837) and the Colored American (1837–1841).* Westport, CT: Greenwood Publishing Group, Inc., 1976.

Mayer, Henry. *All on Fire.* New York: St. Martin's Press, 1998.

Tripp, Bernell. *Origins of the Black Press: New York 1827–1847.* Northport, AL: Vision Press, 1992.

Websites

The Frederick Douglass Papers at the Library of Congress. American Memory Project, Library of Congress, Washington, DC
http://memory.loc.gov/ammem/doughtml/doughome.html

The Frederick Douglass Papers Project. Indiana University–Purdue University, Indianapolis
www.iupui.edu/~douglass/

University of Rochester Frederick Douglass Project. University of Rochester Libraries, Rochester, NY
www.lib.rochester.edu/rbk/douglass/home.stm

Primary Source Materials
for Lesson 6

3.6.1

Excerpt from "Our Mind is Made Up," *The North Star*, by Frederick Douglass, December 3, 1847

It is neither a reflection on the fidelity, or a disparagement of the ability of our friends and fellow laborers to assert what "common sense affirms and only folly denies," that the man who has suffered the wrong is the man to demand redress—that the man struck is the man to cry out—and that he who has endured the cruel pangs of slavery is the man to advocate liberty. It is evident we must be our own representatives and advocates, not exclusively, but peculiarly—not distant from but in connection with our white friends. In the grand struggle for liberty and equality now waging, it is meet, right, and essential that there should arise in our ranks authors and editors, as well as orators, for it is in these capacities that the most permanent good can be rendered to our cause. . . .

We are not wholly unaware of the duties, hardships, and responsibilities of our position. We have easily imagined some, and friends have not hesitated to inform us of others. Many doubtless are yet to be revealed by that infallible teacher, experience. A view of them solemnize but do not appall us. We have counted the cost. Our mind is made up, and we are resolved to go forward.

The full text of Document 3.6.1 is available on the CD-ROM.

3.6.2

Excerpt from *The Life and Times of Frederick Douglass*, "Triumphs and Trials," by Frederick Douglass, 1881

My friends in Boston had been informed of what I was intending and I expected to find them favourably disposed towards my cherished enterprise. In this I was mistaken.

They had many reasons against it. First, no such paper was needed; secondly, it would interfere with my usefulness as a lecturer; thirdly, I was better fitted to speak than to write; fourthly, the paper would not succeed. . . .

I can easily pardon those who saw in my persistence, an unwarrantable ambition and presumption. I was but nine years escaped from slavery. In many phases of mental experience I was but nine years old. That one under such circumstances should aspire to establish a printing press, surrounded by an educated people, might well be considered unpractical if not ambitious. My American friends looked at me with astonishment. 'A wood-sawyer' offering himself to the public as an editor! A slave, brought up in the depths of ignorance, assuming to instruct the highly civilised people of the North in the principles of liberty, justice, and humanity! The thing looked absurd. . . .

The full text of Document 3.6.2 is available on the CD-ROM.

3.6.3

Excerpt from *The Liberator,* July 23, 1847

Of one thing, we and his friends are certain: as a lecturer, his power over a public assembly is very great, and it is manifestly his gift to address the people en masse. With such powers of oratory, and so few lecturers in the field where so many are needed, it seems to us as clear as the noon-day sun, that it would be no gain, but rather a loss, to the anti-slavery cause, to have him withdrawn to any considerable extent from the work of popular agitation, by assuming the cares, drudgery and perplexities of a publishing life. It is quite impracticable to combine the editor with the lecturer, without either causing the paper to be more or less neglected, or the sphere of lecturing to be severely circumscribed.

3.6.4

Excerpt from a letter from William Lloyd Garrison
to his wife, Helen, October 20, 1847

It is not strange that [Frederick] Douglass has not written a single line to me, or to any one, in this place, inquiring after my health, since he left me on a bed of illness? It will also greatly surprise our friends in Boston to hear, that, in regard to his project for establishing a paper here, to be called "The North Star," he never opened to me his lips on the subject, nor asked my advice in any particular whatever. Such conduct grieves me to the heart. His conduct[. . . *] paper has been impulsive, inconsiderate, and highly inconsistent with his decision in Boston. What will his English friends say of such a strange somerset? I am sorry that friend [Edmund] Quincy did not express himself more strongly against this project in the *Liberator*. It is a delicate matter, I know, but it must be met with firmness. I am sorry to add, that our friend Saml. Brooke is at the bottom of all of this, and has influenced Douglass to take this extraordinary step, as he thinks the *Bugle* might as well be discontinued, or merged in Douglass's paper! Strange want of forecast and judgment!—But, no more now.

*Letter is torn here.

3.6.5

Image, masthead for *The North Star*

FREDERICK DOUGLASS, Editor.   RIGHT IS OF NO SEX—TRUTH IS OF NO COLOR—   GOD IS THE FATHER OF US ALL, AND ALL MEN ARE BRETHREN.   JOHN DICK, Printer.

VOL. III. NO. 9.   ROCHESTER, N. Y., FRIDAY, FEBRUARY 22, 1850.   WHOLE NO. 113

Lavery Library, St. John Fisher College

3.6.6

Image of Frederick Douglass

This photograph of Frederick Douglass was taken between 1847 and 1860.

The Granger Collection

Schooling of Free Blacks — The Roots of "Separate But Equal"

In the case of *Roberts v. The City of Boston*, the African American community in the city turned to the courts to help ensure equal educational opportunities for their children. However, the arguments presented in the case and the decision handed down in 1850 had national ramifications.

In their book, *In Hope of Liberty: Culture, Community and Protest Among Northern Free Blacks, 1700–1860*, James and Lois Horton write about the function of education for free black people:

> Better education for free blacks was intrinsically valuable and would enhance the prospects for the independence of individuals and community institutions, but it also served the antislavery cause. More successful free black relatives and friends would give the slaves' most committed and tenacious allies more power. Black leaders also believed that black progress would refute allegations of black inferiority and colonizationists' contentions that African Americans could never be incorporated into American society. Lorenzo de Zavala, who toured the United States in the late 1820s, observed that the degraded condition of free blacks was frequently used as "an argument that discouraged antislavery's most ardent [white] supporters" and was "the great argument against the emancipation of the slaves." Thus, many white reformers were convinced that the progress of free blacks was an argument for antislavery. Frances Wright, an English writer and reformer who came to America in the 1830s to establish a Utopian settlement and educational experiment in Tennessee, was motivated by this belief. Wright hoped to educate black children and white children on an equal basis in order to prove that race was no barrier to intellectual ability, working against both slavery and racial prejudice (p. 219).

Frances Wright's Utopia was not, however, the reality for most free black children. The Hortons write of the difficulties they faced, "black children were engaged in the struggle for equality partly because they could not be sheltered from it. In freedom, they were often the targets of racial prejudice, and it was common for children to be harassed on their way to school" (p. 216).

In 1840, there were 161 primary schools in the City of Boston—160 of these were reserved exclusively for white children. On the surface, the 161st, the Smith

School, was the same as other schools in Boston. For example, students used the same textbooks, and black children were permitted to continue their studies in the Latin or High School if they were advanced enough. Over the years, a few black students were admitted to Boston's prestigious Latin School. However, the Smith School had poor funding and oversight by the school committee as well as unequal treatment in terms of the emphasis placed on academic achievement.

The first petition against the Smith School was presented to the Boston Grammar School Committee in 1840. Signatories included such noted abolitionists as William Lloyd Garrison and Wendell Phillips. Later petitions were submitted in 1844, 1845, 1846, and 1849. In every case, the school committee refused to change its policy even though visiting committee members reported extensively on the Smith School's weaknesses and failures. There were a couple of school committee members who agreed with the petitioners and published their own minority report on Boston's segregated schools.

In 1844, William Cooper Nell headed a movement, the Equal School Association, which led a boycott of the school that lasted eleven years. Attendance fell from 263 in 1840 to 51 in 1849. The boycott also caused increased tensions within the black community between those participating in the boycott and those who chose to send their children to school despite any reservations or dissatisfactions they might have had. Some members of the black community, including Nell, wanted the school committee to close the Smith School and allow black students to go to their neighborhood "white" school. Others, including Reverend James Simmons and Thomas P. Smith, petitioned the committee to maintain the separate "colored" school with reforms, such as appointing a black headmaster with a college degree.

In 1846, five-year-old Sarah Roberts had to walk directly past five primary schools to get to the Smith Grammar School in the west end of Boston. Her father Benjamin Roberts, a printer, was prominent in antislavery and social reform groups. He had tried on four separate occasions to enter Sarah in one of the public schools closer to her home, but each time her application for admission was rejected. This segregation was not in response to any state or city law; it was simply mandated by the Boston School Committee.

Mr. Roberts brought suit against the City of Boston to compel Sarah's admission to one of the white primary schools closer to her home. He based his suit on a statute that provided that any child illegally excluded from a city's public school might recover damages from the city.

The case of *Roberts v. The City of Boston* (1849), argued for the plaintiff by Charles Sumner with the assistance of black lawyer Robert Morris, would have a significant impact on the lives of African Americans. Judge Lemuel Shaw ruled against the plaintiff. In Massachusetts, the legislature quickly repaired the damage. In 1855, they passed a law stating that "no person shall be excluded from a Public School on account of race, color, or religion opinions." However, ironically, in 1897 U.S. Supreme Court justices used the decision of Judge Shaw of the Supreme Judicial Court of Massachusetts as a basis for their ruling in *Plessy v. Ferguson*, which established the "separate by equal" standard that formally legalized segregation in the United States.

A century after the Roberts case, Thurgood Marshall relied in part on Charles Sumner's argument to urge the United States Supreme Court to reconsider the "separate but equal" doctrine. In 1954, when the court ruled on *Brown v. Board of Education of Topeka*, the nation finally witnessed the beginning of the end. Reversing its decision of 1897, separate, the court declared, is not equal.

Organizing Idea

Schooling for black students has been a keen issue for African Americans and their allies at least since the late 1700s. The case of *Roberts v. The City of Boston* in 1849 reflects the efforts of the African American community. It included groundbreaking arguments and resulted in a far-reaching decision.

Student Objectives

Students will:

❖ know the positive and negative forces affecting the schooling of free black students in the first half of the nineteenth century

❖ understand how the case *Roberts v. the City of Boston* challenged segregation in the Boston Public Schools. Although the state legislature addressed the issue in Boston, the Roberts court case set the precedent for separate but equal schools and led to the creation of segregated facilities all over the country.

Key Questions

❖ What forms of activism were used to promote educational opportunities for black students in Boston?

❖ What were the obstacles in Boston that prevented black children from obtaining the best possible education?

❖ How did the decision in *Roberts v. the City of Boston* affect schooling for black children nationally?

Primary Source Materials

DOCUMENT 3.7.1: A description of Smith School from the *Boston Almanac of 1849*

DOCUMENT 3.7.2: Report of the Boston School Committee visit to Smith School, 1849

DOCUMENT 3.7.3: Report of the Boston School Committee visit to Wells School, 1849

DOCUMENT 3.7.4: Excerpt from article "Smith School," *The Liberator*, August 27, 1841

DOCUMENT 3.7.5: Letter to the Editor, "School for Young Ladies," *The Liberator,* October 15, 1841

DOCUMENT 3.7.6: Letter to the Editor from an African American parent, "The Smith School," *The Liberator,* February 15, 1850

DOCUMENT 3.7.7: Petition from colored citizens of Boston to the Primary School Committee of the City of Boston, 1846

DOCUMENT 3.7.8: Excerpts from the June 15, 1846, *Report* of the Primary School Committee of the City of Boston responding to the parents' petition

DOCUMENT 3.7.9: Image (and transcription) of the original petition sent by African American parents to the Boston School Committee, entered in the record July 1849

DOCUMENT 3.7.10: Excerpts from the argument by Charles Sumner, "Equality Before the Law: Unconstitutionality of Separate Colored Schools in Massachusetts," delivered to the Supreme Judicial Court of Massachusetts in the case of *Sarah C. Roberts v. The City of Boston,* 1849

DOCUMENT 3.7.11: Ruling of Justice Lemuel Shaw in the case *Sarah C. Roberts v. The City of Boston,* 1850

Supplementary Materials

ITEM 3.7.A: Additional vocabulary lists for primary sources

Vocabulary

abolition	deficient	oppression	physiology
benefactor	incumbent	perpetuate	plaintiff
caste	macrocosm	petitioners	precedent

Student Activities

Activity 1

Reading and Analysis—Black Students–Only School

Introduce students to the primary source documents (3.7.1–3.7.6) that uncover some of the positive and negative forces affecting the education of free black students in Boston in the first half of the nineteenth century. Organize the students into groups of four to six, giving each group three or four documents to review.

Suggest that they read the material as if they are trying to solve a puzzle. Their questions about missing pieces should be considered as valuable as the information they do find in the documents.

What do these documents tell them about schooling for black students in Boston in the years before the Civil War? What resources did they have and what barriers did they face? What facts can they learn from the documents? What information is missing?

Ask each group to report back what they learned and what is missing to the class as a whole.

Letter to the Editor—Segregated Education

Activity 2

Tell students to write a letter to the editor of *The Liberator* expressing a point of view based on documents that they have read and analyzed. This letter should be dated around the middle of the nineteenth century, in line with the source documents. Explain that the letter may include questions they would like answered about the environment for educating free black students as well as statements of opinion about what they gathered from the reading material.

Encourage students to use one or more documents as the background for their writing. Invite students to brainstorm together the point of view for a "model" letter, recording the central point of view and supporting ideas or facts on the board.

Display the completed letters on the wall. Students should read the letters and then discuss how effective they are as opinion pieces in shedding light on facts or questions about the educational environment for free black students in Boston in the 1840s and 1850s. Encourage discussion among the students as they read the letters. When the reading is complete, bring the students together to share examples of effective writing found in the letters to the editor.

Finally, ask students to reflect on their letters. Ask them to consider their writing in relation to what they consider to be effective presentation of opinions and questions on the topic presented in class. Tell them to write a critique of their letters to the editor in which they evaluate their own writing and state goals for writing strategies on a similar assignment in the future.

Discussion of Petitions

Activity 3

Ask students to read the two petitions from black parents (3.7.7 and 3.7.9). Working in small groups, students should discuss the approaches taken by the parents. What tactics did they use to press their points? Which tactic does each group of students think would be most persuasive in getting the school committee to give the parents what they wanted?

Analysis of School Committee Response

Activity 4

Students should read excerpts from the school committee's response to the petitions (3.7.8) and identify the main arguments used by the committee to justify keeping the schools segregated. They can also identify racist language and attitudes. Students should then compare the committee's response with their own responses to the petitions (Activity 3).

Activity 5

Analysis of Legal Argument

After reading excerpts from arguments by the Roberts' lawyer, Charles Sumner (3.7.10), and the ruling of Justice Lemuel Shaw (3.7.11), students should identify the main arguments of both men and the supporting evidence given by each. Which of Sumner's arguments are the strongest and which are the least convincing? Ask students, working in small groups, to discuss whether they agree with Shaw's statements that the law cannot force a change in attitudes such as racism and that forced integration will not make people want to integrate or be less racist.

Activity 6

Research—Beyond *Roberts v. The City of Boston*

Students should research the case of *Plessy v. Ferguson* (1896) and *Brown v. the Board of Education of Topeka* (1954). In the Plessy case, which argument did the Supreme Court agree with, the one presented by Sumner or Judge Shaw's? Answer the same question for the Brown case. Read Thurgood Marshall's argument before the U.S. Supreme Court and compare it to Sumner's of 1849.

Research—Beyond the Segregation Case

Activity 7

The cause of desegregation in Boston in the 1840s and 1850s involved a number of individuals who played significant roles in African Americans' long road to justice. William Cooper Nell went on to become the first published black historian in the United States. Abolitionist Charles Sumner became a U.S. senator and was also active in the reconstruction of the South. Robert Morris, the second African American to practice law in the country, was appointed by the governor in 1852 as the first black magistrate in Massachusetts. The class can be divided into small groups, with each group responsible for researching the life of one of the men. The groups can present their findings to the class in the form of a short video, a formal lecture, or a skit.

Further Student and Teacher Resources

Bell, Derrick, ed. *Race, Racism, and American Law,* 3d ed. Boston: Little, Brown & Co., 1992.

"Desegregation." *Magazine of History* 15:2 (2001).

Horton, James, and Lois Horton. *In Hope of Liberty: Culture, Community and Protest Among Northern Free Blacks, 1700–1860.* New York: Oxford University Press, 1997.

King, Wilma. *Stolen Childhood: Slave Youth in Nineteenth-Century America.* Bloomington: Indiana University Press, 1995.

Levy, Leonard, ed. *Jim Crow in Boston: The Origin of the Separate but Equal Doctrine.* New York: Da Capo Press, 1974.

Parson, William S., and Margaret A. Drew. *The African Meeting House in Boston: A Sourcebook.* Boston: Museum of Afro American History, 1990.

Sumner, Charles. *Equality before the law, unconstitutionality of separate coloured schools in Massachusetts: argument of Charles Sumner, Esq., before the Supreme Court of Massachusetts, in the case of Sarah C. Roberts vs. the city of Boston, December 4, 1849.*

Websites

The Black Heritage Trail. Boston African American National Historic Site, National Park Service, Washington, DC
www.nps.gov/boaf/blackheritagetrail.htm
Provides information about the Abiel Smith School, which is part of the Black Heritage Trail in Boston and open to the public, and William Cooper Nell, who led the desegregation efforts

Equality before Law. Charles Sumner before the Supreme Court of Massachusetts, in the case of Sarah C. Roberts v. the city of Boston, December 4, 1849; The African American Pamphlet Collection, American Memory Project, Library of Congress, Washington, DC
http://memory.loc.gov

In Pursuit of Freedom and Equality: Brown v. Board of Education of Topeka. Washburn University School of Law, Topeka, KS
www.brownvboard.org

Sarah Roberts v. Boston. Long Road to Justice, Boston, MA
www.atsweb.neu.edu/longroad/02education/roberts.htm

Contemporary Connection

✠

So What Has Changed?

The issue of school desegregation in Boston has not been resolved with any permanence. In 1974, under court order, the schools were desegregated through the busing of children from one neighborhood to another. In 1999, the Boston School Committee dropped race as a factor in school placement, putting in place instead a policy that reserves half the seats in elementary and middle schools for children who live close enough to walk. The other half may enroll from any neighborhood.

In 2002, this 1999 policy was challenged in court by parents whose children did not get into their neighborhood schools and who, therefore, are bused to another part of the city. The attorney for the ten families in the lawsuit says the policy is unconstitutional because "it is an effort by government to manipulate the racial makeup of schools by pushing some children out of the way to make room for another group of children of a different race." The Boston school department sees it differently. If the policy were to be changed, children would be required to attend the closest school with no options to go elsewhere. That would greatly diminish parental choice.

The underlying issue, of course, has to do with housing patterns. In these early years of the twenty-first century, it is still the case that neighborhoods are often segregated, not only in Boston but in other communities across the country as well. If integrated schools are to occur naturally, with children going to school in their own neighborhoods, housing patterns will have to be different.

Students may wish to explore the issues of integrated schools in their own community or a nearby location. Were the schools ever segregated? When and for how long? How did integration come about?

Primary Source Materials for Lesson 7

3.7.1

A description of Smith School from the
Boston Almanac of 1849

This school is for colored children of both sexes. A school for Africans was commenced by themselves, in 1798, the Selectman having first granted permission; and was kept in the house of Primus Hall. The yellow fever broke it up, and three years afterwards it was revived by Rev. Drs. Morse of Charlestown, Kirkland of Harvard College, Channing, and Lowell, and Rev. Mr. [William] Emerson of Boston. They provided for its entire support two years. It was then proposed to have the colored people hire a building, and a carpenter's shop was selected adjoining to the old church, and this continued three years. The site of the meeting-house was then selected, and purchased by subscription, and the African Baptist Church erected a house, of which the school occupied the basement. The room was completed in 1808, and immediately occupied by the school, and the reverend gentleman mentioned supported the school, with aid from subscriptions, until 1812, when the town first took notice of it, granting $200 annually. In 1815 Abiel Smith, Esq., died and left a legacy of about $5000, the income of which is to be appropriated "for the free instruction of colored children in reading, writing and arithmetic." The city then took the school under its entire charge, and in 1833 the ill-condition of the room attracted attention, and Committee, of which D.L. Child was Chairman, reported in favor of a new house. The present house was built in the next two years, and on the 10th of February 1835, the school was named for its benefactor. Its masters have been Prince Saunders, James Waldach, John B. Russwarm, William Bascom, Abner Forbes, and the present incumbent, since 1836. Latest attendance show only 18 pupils; attendance, 53.

<u>3.7.2</u>

Report of the Boston School Committee
visit to Smith School, 1849

SMITH SCHOOL

BELKNAP STREET.

A. Wellington, Master.

This School was visited and examined May 7, P.M. by the Chairman and Messrs. Winkley and Palmer.

We regret to say that in almost all respects it is in a very low condition. In most of the studies the best scholars were deplorably deficient, considering the time, expense, and care that have been bestowed upon them. The reading of three or four (all who were called on) was pretty good, but we were surprised at the ignorance of Grammar. The best scholar in the class was called on to parse the word " is," and she called or guessed it to be a preposition, and two or three other parts of speech before it occurred to her that it might be a verb.

The result of the oral examination in Arithmetic was to show a very limited and imperfect acquaintance with the rules, but in working out a single problem in vulgar fractions, on the blackboard, a little more readiness was manifested, though nothing more than would be found in much younger classes in the other Schools. . . .

The full text of Document 3.7.2 is available on the CD-ROM.

<u>3.7.3</u>

Report of the Boston School Committee
visit to Wells School, 1849

WELLS SCHOOL,

MCLEAN STREET.

Cornelius Walker, Grammar Master.
Reuben Swan, Jr, Writing Master.

This School was visited May 11th, A.M., by the Chairman and Messrs. Winkley and Palmer.

It fully maintains the character it has acquired in former years, for the thoroughness of the instruction. The pupils appeared very well in all the studies of the course. There appears to be an extraordinary development of the powers of thought and perception in this School, and maturity of intellect and of knowledge such as is seldom met with in children of the age of the pupils here assembled. The masters have great advantages from the character of the population of the School district, and as far as could be judged from the examination, they have been most faithful in improving them.

3.7.4

Excerpt from article "Smith School," *The Liberator*, August 27, 1841

The annual examination of the Smith School in Belknap street, under the direction of Mr. Abner Forbes, passed off in a manner lightly creditable to the pupils, and greatly to the satisfaction of their parents and friends who were present. Where all the performances were praiseworthy, it is difficult to make a distinction, though if it would not appear invidious, we might allude to several of the youthful performers by name, as those who were decidedly *superior*. The exercises in general and selected reading, and the correctness and ability manifested during the recital of lessons in grammar, geography, and other branches, gave evidence of close application, and was worthy of all praise. . . .

The full text of Document 3.7.4 is available on the CD-ROM.

3.7.5

Letter to the Editor, "School for Young Ladies," *The Liberator*, October 15, 1841

Mr. Editor,

It has long been a source of regret to many residents of this city that there has been no opportunity afforded, through the medium of which their daughters could obtain a knowledge of those branches deemed so necessary to the completion of a young lady's education. The baneful prejudice in active exercise against a large number of our citizens, merely because of complexional difference, has presented a barrier which has shut them out of from those facilities so richly enjoyed by the more *favored* classes.

But it is our pleasure to inform your readers, that a school has lately been opened in this city by Miss Susannah Bradshaw (a colored young lady,) where the accomplished branches are taught. Judging from the exercises to which we have listened, and the specimens of painting, sketching, rug-work, &c together with penmanship, composition, etc., with an examination of which we were favored, we feel justified in recommending the school to the attention of the public.

The terms are favorable and will be made known on application to the precep-tress, at the school room in the basement story of the Baptist Church, Belknap Street.

N.

3.7.6

Letter to the Editor from an African American parent, "The Smith School," *The Liberator*, February 15, 1850

Mr. Editor,—Dear Sir, In perusing the last number of the Liberator, I was exceed-ingly amused by a strain of characteristic allusions and a certain resolution in a com-munication signed by one W.C.N.; and that fairness may prevail, you will, I know, allow me a word in defence of those who have not favored the abolition of colored schools in Boston. It is most untrue and unphilosophical, that we should oppose the abolition of colored schools in order to degrade ourselves or our posterity. We are colored men, exposed alike to oppression and prejudice; our interests are all identi-cal—we rise or fall together. We believe colored schools to be institutions, when properly conducted, of great advantage to the colored people. We believe society imperatively requires their existence among us. . . .

Yours, with highest respect,
THOMAS PAUL SMITH.

3.7.7

Petition from colored citizens of Boston to the Primary School Committee of the City of Boston, 1846

To the Primary School Committee of the City of Boston:

The undersigned colored citizens of Boston, parents and guardians of children *now* attending the exclusive Primary Schools for colored children in this City, respectfully represent:—that the establishment of exclusive schools for our children is a great injury to us, and deprives us of those equal privileges and advantages in the public schools to which we are entitled as citizens. These separate schools cost more and do less for the children than other schools, since all experience teaches that where a small and despised class are shut out from the common benefit of any pub-lic institutions of learning and confined to separate schools, few or none interest themselves about the schools,—neglect ensues, abuses creep in, the standard of scholarship degenerates, and the teachers and the scholars are soon considered and of course become an inferior class.

But to say nothing of any other reasons for this change, it is sufficient to say that the establishment of separate schools for our children is believed to be unlawful, and it is felt to be if not in intention, in fact, insulting. If, as seeks to be admitted, you are violating our rights, we simply ask you to cease doing so.

We therefore earnestly request that such exclusive schools be abolished, and that our children be allowed to attend the Primary Schools established in the respective Districts in which we live.

George Putnam,
And Eighty-five Others

3.7.8

Excerpts from the June 15, 1846, *Report* of the
Primary School Committee of the City of Boston
responding to the parents' petition

We maintain, that the true interests of both races require, that they should be kept distinct. Amalgamation is degradation. We would urge on our brethren of the African race, the duty of cultivating the genuine virtues, peculiar to that race. Is it degrading to them to be unmingled with their pale-faced neighbors? Confound the tongue that would utter such slander upon them! Let them not lean upon, nor look up to, the whites; but trust, under God, to their own native energies, unmingled and uncorrupted. Let them cultivate a respect for themselves, for their own race, their own blood, aye, and for their own *color*. Let them not come to us with the humiliating confession, that they cannot make their separate schools as good as those for the white children and tell us that their children, if put by themselves, even under the best instruction, must sink, unless they have the white children to pull them up. We will not believe this, we pronounce it a slander on the colored people; but we do say, that this course of policy will never elevate them, nor cause them to be respected. . . .

The full text of Document 3.7.8 is available on the CD-ROM.

3.7.9

Image (and transcription) of the original petition sent by
African American parents to the Boston School Committee,
entered in the record July 1849

Boston Public Library

The transcribed text of Document 3.7.9 is available on the CD-ROM.

3.7.10

Excerpts from the argument by Charles Sumner, "Equality Before the Law: Unconstitutionality of Separate Colored Schools in Massachusetts," delivered to the Supreme Judicial Court of Massachusetts in the case of *Sarah C. Roberts v. The City of Boston,* 1849

Charles Sumner (1811–1874) was a lawyer from Boston and a United States Senator from 1851 until his death. Renowned as an active abolitionist, it is noteworthy that he also was very sensitive to racism. He is profiled in John F. Kennedy's Profiles in Courage. *In the Roberts case, Sumner worked with Robert Morris, a young black abolitionist and activist lawyer.*

In this rule—without the unfortunate exception—is part of the beauty so conspicuous in our Common Schools. It is the boast of England, that, through the multitude of schools, education in Boston is brought to every *white* man's door. But it is not brought to every black man's door. He is obliged to go for it, to travel for it, to walk for it—often a great distance. The facts in the present case are not so strong as those of other cases within my knowledge. But here the little child, only five years old, is compelled, if attending the nearest African School, to go a distance of two thousand one hundred feet from her home, while the nearest Primary School is only nine hundred feet, and, in doing this, she passes by no less than five different Primary Schools, forming part of our Common Schools, and open to white children, all of which are closed to her. Surely, this is not Equality before the Law. . . .

Still further, and this consideration cannot be neglected, the matters taught in the two schools may be precisely the same, but a school exclusively devoted to one class must differ essentially in spirit and character from that Common School known to the law, where all classes meet together in Equality. It is a mockery to call it an equivalent.

The full text of Document 3.7.10 is available on the CD-ROM.

3.7.11

Ruling of Justice Lemuel Shaw in the case *Sarah C. Roberts v. The City of Boston,* 1850

The plaintiff had access to a school, set apart for colored children, as well conducted in all respects, and as well fitted, in point of capacity and qualification of the instructors, to advance the education of children under seven years old, as the other primary schools; the objection is, that the schools thus open to the plaintiff are exclusively appropriated to colored children, and are at a greater distance from her home. Under these circumstances, has the plaintiff been unlawfully excluded from public school instruction? Upon the best consideration we have been able to give the subject, the court are all of opinion that she has not. . . .

The full text of Document 3.7.11 is available on the CD-ROM.

Slave Literacy

In her book *When I Can Read My Title Clear*, Janet Duitsman Cornelius explains that in the aftermath of publications such as David Walker's *Appeal* (see Lesson 3), Nat Turner's Rebellion (Lesson 2), a rebellion in Jamaica, and the 1833 emancipation of West Indies by the British, slaveholders in the South passed repressive slavery codes. These contained provisions against teaching slaves or free blacks to read or write. In Georgia, the penalty could be a fine, whipping, or a jail term. Louisiana law stated, "all persons who shall teach, or permit or cause to be taught, any slave in this State to read or write, shall be imprisoned not less than one or more than twelve months."

Although only four states (Virginia, North Carolina, South Carolina, and Georgia) kept the laws on the books until the end of the Civil War and cases rarely came before courts, the intent of the laws succeeded. Enslaved African Americans throughout the South understood that literacy was forbidden to them. Slave owners and /or patrollers meted out brutal punishment, including whippings and dismemberment of digits.

Beyond the fear of widespread revolt, many slaveholders did not want slaves to become literate for fear of their reading about freedom and wanting to go North. They didn't want slaves to be able to write passes, which they could use to leave the plantation and move around from place to place. However, some slaveholders taught their slaves to read the Bible to them as a comfort. Others read the Bible to their slaves as a means of moral instruction.

Despite the risks, attaining literacy was of such importance to some enslaved African Americans that they pursued it by whatever means possible. Many literate slaves taught others to read and write in secrecy. Some used creative means to get literate whites to teach them. And some found ways to teach themselves.

For her article "We Slipped and Learned to Read: Slave Accounts of the Literacy Process, 1830–1865" in the September 1983 issue of *Phylon, the Atlanta University Review of Race and Culture*, Janet Cornelius drew slaves' stories of becoming literate from narratives gathered by the Federal Writers Project of the Works Progress Administration. In 3,428 interviews with former slaves done during the Federal Writers Project, 179 people mentioned personal experiences of learning to read and write while they were being held in bondage.

For example, Belle Caruthers said, "The baby had alphabet blocks to play with, and I learned my letters while she learned hers." Moses Slaughter's mother, who was a housekeeper, would tell the owner's daughter, "Come here Emily, Mamma will keep your place for you" and, while little Emily read, Mamma Emalina followed each line until she too was a fluent reader and could teach her own children. Many of the former slaves attributed their learning to white sons and daughters of slaveholders, mistresses, or teachers hired by their owners. Washington Curry recalled, "There were so many folks that came to see the doctor and wanted to leave numbers and addresses that he had to have someone to 'tend to that, and he taught my father to read and write so that he could do it." Adeline Willis' mistress taught her the letters on the newspapers and what they spelled so she could bring the papers the whites wanted. Simpson Campbell's "Marse Bill" taught some of his slaves reading and writing so he could use them "booking cotton in the field and such like."

The freedmen and women talked about teaching themselves to read. Elijah P. Marrs said, "Very early in life I took up the ideal that I wanted to learn to read and write . . . I availed myself of every opportunity, daily I carried my book in my pocket, and every chance that offered would be learning my ABCs." Families taught each other or made ways to get lessons for someone who would teach the others. Henry Bruce's family was an example: "The older one would teach the younger, and while mother had no education at all, she used to make the younger study the lessons given by the older sister or brother, and in that way we all learned to read and some to write."

The measures that the former slaves used to gain literacy illustrate their determination and drive to attain knowledge that would lead to freedom. The study reports that slaves borrowed books from their owners or bought them when it wouldn't raise any suspicion. They made their own writing materials and used planks to write on, or they practiced in the sand. They studied late at night or on Sundays. Preachers who could read from the Bible were respected leaders of the community both during and after slavery. Those who could read taught others and kept the rest of the population up-to-date on the war and the coming of freedom. Milla Granson established a midnight school in Natchez, where she taught hundreds of fellow slaves to read. A number of literate slaves opened schools immediately after the Civil War, including Sally Johnson, who learned to read and write at the academy run by her owners where she served as a nurse.

Forty-five of the former slaves in the study became ministers, either during or after slavery. They served congregations or traveled circuits, were appointed as bishops or to other positions in church hierarchies, or became missionaries like Thomas Johnson, evangelist to Africa and the British Isles. Literate slaves opened schools immediately after the war, including Sally Johnson, mentioned above, and Celia Singleton, who established her own school in Georgia two years after freedom.

Included in this lesson are first-person accounts of how enslaved people learned to read and write. Literacy was viewed as the pathway to success. It was a means of developing a deep sense of accomplishment and self-worth. In a nation where the decision makers had a general sense of superiority over people of color, it became important to many black people to "prove themselves." Literacy was seen as a measure of intelligence and a route to power; the more one knew, the better one's chances to progress in life. Education was the key to opening the door to a career, profession, business or occupation.

Organizing Idea

Freedom was the major prize to be attained by enslaved African Americans, but literacy was also of significant importance to many enslaved people. Freedom and literacy appeared to go hand in hand. In many cases, literacy was the ticket to freedom. For others, freedom afforded the opportunity to attain literacy.

Student Objectives

Students will:

- ❖ understand why many slaves wanted to become literate
- ❖ learn the many creative ways enslaved people employed to learn to read and write
- ❖ understand how literacy and education is a gateway to expanded opportunities

Key Questions

- ❖ What is literacy?
- ❖ Why would an enslaved person want to learn to read and write?
- ❖ Why were many owners opposed to slaves becoming literate?

Primary Source Materials

DOCUMENT 3.8.1: Extract from Alabama Slavery Code, 1833

DOCUMENT 3.8.2: Excerpts from *His Promised Land: The Autobiography of John P. Parker, Former Slave and Conductor on the Underground Railroad*, 1880s

DOCUMENT 3.8.3: Excerpt 1 from *Narrative of the Life of Frederick Douglass: An American Slave By Himself*, 1845

DOCUMENT 3.8.4: Excerpt 2 from *Narrative of the Life of Frederick Douglass: An American Slave By Himself*, 1845

DOCUMENT 3.8.5: Excerpt from *The Interesting Narrative of the Life of Olaudah Equiano or Gustavus Vassa, The African. Written By Himself*, 1789

DOCUMENT 3.8.6: Excerpt from *Running a Thousand Miles for Freedom; or the Escape of William and Ellen Craft from Slavery* by William and Ellen Craft, 1860

DOCUMENT 3.8.7: Excerpt from an interview with C. H. Hall, 1863

DOCUMENT 3.8.8: Excerpt from the 1867 autobiography of the Reverend John Sella Martin

Supplementary Materials

ITEM 3.8.A: Vocabulary lists for primary sources

Student Activities

Discussion of Literacy

Activity 1

Ask each student to write a definition of *literacy*. Then define the term as a class and display the definition prominently in the classroom. Students who have visited a country where a different language is spoken, especially if it is written in a different alphabet, and students who have come to the United States not speaking English may wish to share with the class or in writing what that experience is like. How are these experiences similar to being illiterate?

Understanding Southern Slave Codes

Activity 2

Students should read Document 3.8.1, an extract from the slavery codes of Alabama. What is their reaction to the law? Explore why students are reacting like this. Do documents exist in the United States that would seem to make such codes illegal? After sharing information from the introduction with students and referring back to Documents 3.2.10, 3.2.11, and 3.3.2–3.3.6, discuss why white people in southern states placed such laws on the books.

Reading and Discussion of First-Person Accounts

Activity 3

Divide the class into small groups and assign each group one or two of the first-person accounts (3.8.2–3.8.8) to read aloud. Then have students answer the questions. Each group should report back to the entire class on what they learned.

- ❖ Who is the author?
- ❖ What did the individual think about reading and writing?
- ❖ What were some misconceptions?
- ❖ Why was it so important to him or her to become literate?
- ❖ How did he or she achieve the goal of literacy?

Research on the Ultimate Impact of Literacy

Activity 4

The Janet Cornelius study, based on interviews with former slaves, credits the literacy of the black people who had learned to read and write during slavery for their leadership positions after Emancipation. Have students research the life of a literate leader who was formerly enslaved. Options include founders and presidents of black colleges, such as Isaac Lane and Isaac Burgan; scholars and writers like W. S. Scarborough and N. W. Harlee; businessmen like Edward Walker of Windsor, Ontario;

Blanche K. Bruce, a U.S. Senator from Mississippi; and Isaiah Montgomery, who with his family founded the black colony of Mount Bayou, Mississippi.

While doing their research, students should decide how important literacy was to the person's success. How did that person learn to read and write? Could he or she have assumed a leadership position without being able to read and write? How did literacy help them to succeed? Students should report their findings in a short paper or an oral report to the class.

Further Student and Teacher Resources

Blassingame, John. W., ed. *Slave Testimony: Two Centuries of Letters, Speeches, Interviews, and Autobiographies.* Baton Rouge: Louisiana State University Press, 1977.

Cornelius, Janet Duitsman. *When I Can Read My Title Clear: Literacy, Slavery and Religion in the Antebellum South.* Columbia, SC: University of South Carolina, 1991.

Curry, Barbara K., and James Michael Brodie. *Sweet Words So Brave: The Story of African American Literature.* Madison, WI: Zino Press, 1996.

Douglass, Frederick. *Autobiographies: Narrative of the Life of Frederick Douglass: An American Slave by Himself; My Bondage and My Freedom; Life and Times of Frederick Douglass.* New York: Penguin Books, 1994.

McHenry, Elizabeth. *Forgotten Readers: Rediscovering the Lost History of African American Literary Societies.* Durham, NC.: Duke University Press, 2002.

Parker, John P. *His Promised Land: The Autobiography of John P. Parker.* Ed. Stuart Seely Sprague. New York: W. W. Norton & Company, 1996.

Video

Nightjohn. Hallmark Home Entertainment, Los Angeles, CA, 1996. (PG13) is the story of slave life on a plantation when a new slave arrives who knows both how to read and to teach.

Contemporary Connection

→※←

Literary Retrospective

A thirst for learning to read is apparent in most stories written by or about slaves. Many did not have the opportunity until after the Civil War when schools were opened in some places in the South for black children. In the urban North, from the beginning of the nineteenth century, literary societies were formed to promote the development of a literate black population. Scholar and author Elizabeth McHenry tells us that literary societies not only became places of refuge for "the self-improvement of their members," but also represented "acts of resistance to a hostile racial climate that made the United States an uncomfortable and unequal place for all black Americans, regardless of their social or economic condition" (*Forgotten Readers: Recovering the Lost History of African American Literary Societies*).

These early societies considered newspapers such as *Freedom's Journal*, the *Colored American*, and the *North Star* to be vehicles for reading and discussion. In including these, the literary societies "fur-thered the evolution of a black public sphere and a politically conscious society" (*Forgotten Readers*).

In 1922, one Kathryn Johnson made a decision that black people needed to see in print all the ways in which their place in society is reflected. She loaded her car with books by W. E. B. Du Bois, Carter Woodson, James Weldon Johnson, Paul Lawrence Dunbar, and others, and she drove throughout the North and Southeast, selling the books from her automobile. In $2^{1}/_{2}$ years, she sold over 5,000 books to, by, and about African Americans.

Literary societies play important roles in African American communities today. The Go On Girl! Book Club, which began in New York, has recreated itself into many chapters. Once a year, the entire membership gathers to choose books for the coming year and to give awards to noteworthy authors and publishers. Finally, Oprah's Book Club, launched in 1996, has inspired many Americans to read more books. Students could consider how a popular television star can affect our culture. Are there book groups in their school? In the community? Students can consider initiating such a group if none exists.

Primary Source Materials
for Lesson 8

3.8.1

Extract from Alabama Slavery Code, 1833

S31. Any person who shall attempt to teach any free person of color, or slave, to spell, read or write, shall, upon conviction thereof by indictment, be fined in a sum not less than two hundred fifty dollars, nor more than five hundred dollars.

3.8.2

Excerpts from *His Promised Land: The Autobiography of John P. Parker, Former Slave and Conductor on the Underground Railroad,* 1880s

John P. Parker was born in Norfolk, Virginia in 1827. He was the son of a black woman and a white man. Parker was eight years old when he was chained to another slave and walked to Richmond. There he was sold and walked as part of a long chain of slaves from Richmond to Mobile, Alabama. The doctor who bought him had two sons who became very close to Parker.

My education was carried out secretly; even the good doctor, who was truly my friend, did not know what was going on. Though there was a law, which was strictly enforced, against slaves being taught to read or write or have books, from that time forward, I always had several books at hand. The boys were faithful in their task of supplying me with books from the home library, which were excellent. I read the Bible, Shakespeare, and the English poets in the hayloft at odd times, when I was not driving the doctor to see his patients. . . .

The full text of Document 3.8.2 is available on the CD-ROM.

3.8.3

Excerpt 1 from *Narrative of the Life of Frederick Douglass: An American Slave By Himself,* 1845

Douglass was born about 1818. His mother was a slave and his father a white man, rumored to have been her owner. Douglass was sent to Baltimore at about the age of seven or eight where his education began with the discovery of what he called "the pathway from slavery to freedom."

Very soon after I went to live with Mr. and Mrs. Auld, she very kindly commenced to teach me the A, B, C. After I had learned this, she assisted me in learning to spell words of three or four letters. Just at this point of my progress, Mr. Auld found out what was going on, and at once forbade Mrs. Auld to instruct me, telling her, among other things, that it was unlawful, as well as unsafe, to teach a slave to read. To use his own words, further, he said, "If you give a nigger an inch, he will take an ell. A nigger should know nothing but to obey his master—to do as he is told to do. Learning would *spoil* the best nigger in the world. Now," said he, "if you teach that nigger (speaking of myself) how to read, there would be no keeping him. It would forever unfit him to be a slave. He would at once become unmanageable, and of no value to his master. As to himself, it could do him no good, but a great deal of harm. It would make him discontented and unhappy.". . .

The full text of Document 3.8.3 is available on the CD-ROM.

3.8.4

Excerpt 2 from *Narrative of the Life of Frederick Douglass: An American Slave By Himself,* 1845

At twelve years old, Douglass realized he might be a slave for life and this placed a heavy burden on him. He was reading the book The Colombian Orator, *one part of which was a dialogue between a master and his slave. The arguments posed by the slave resulted in his emancipation.*

The more I read, the more I was led to abhor and detest my enslavers . . . I would at times feel that learning to read had been a curse rather than a blessing. It had given me a view of my wretched condition, without the remedy. It opened my eyes to the horrible pit, but to no ladder upon which to get out . . .

I looked forward to a time when it would be safe for me to escape. I was too young to think of doing so immediately; besides, I wished to learn how to write, as I might have occasion to write my own pass. I consoled myself with the hope that I should one day find a good chance. Meanwhile, I would learn to write. . . .

The full text of Document 3.8.4 is available on the CD-ROM.

3.8.5

Excerpt from *The Interesting Narrative of the Life of Olaudah Equiano or Gustavus Vassa, The African. Written By Himself,* 1789

Olaudah Equiano was born in 1745 in the Kingdom of Benin in what is now the eastern part of the African nation of Nigeria. When Equiano was 11, he and his sister were captured and sold into slavery in Africa. He was then sold into transatlantic slavery and enslaved by a Philadelphia owner who put him to work on small trading vessels where he received his education and traveled the seas. In 1766, Equiano purchased his own freedom. The last part of his life was devoted to antislavery work in England.

From Chapter III

I had often seen my master and Dick employed in reading: and I had a great curiosity to talk to the books as I thought they did, and so to learn how all things had a beginning. For that purpose I have often taken up a book, and have talked to it, and then put my ears to it, when alone, in hopes it would answer me; and I have been very much concerned when I found it remained silent. . . .

From Chapter IV

While I was in the Ætna particularly, the captain's clerk taught me to write and gave me a smattering of arithmetic, as far as the rule of three. There was also one Daniel Queen, about forty years of age, a man very well educated, who messed [ate meals] with me on board this ship, and took very great pains to instruct me in many things. He taught me to shave and dress hair a little, and also to read in the Bible, explaining many passages to me, which I did not comprehend. I was wonderfully surprised to see the laws and rules of my country written almost exactly here; a circumstance which I believe tended to impress our manners and customs more deeply on my memory. I used to tell him of this resemblance; and many a time we have sat up the whole night together in this employment. . . .

3.8.6

Excerpt from *Running a Thousand Miles for Freedom; or the Escape of William and Ellen Craft from Slavery* by William and Ellen Craft, 1860

William and Ellen Craft were born in different towns in Georgia. Ellen, the daughter of a black woman and her master, was nearly white in complexion. They succeeded in escaping slavery when Ellen disguised herself as a young white "master" and William as her slave. When they successfully arrived in Philadelphia, a Quaker family took them in and immediately taught them to write and spell their names before they moved on to Boston.

The ladies and their good brother brought out the spelling and copy books and slates, &c., and commenced with their new and green pupils. We had, by stratagem, learned the alphabet while in slavery, but not the writing characters; and as we had been such a time learning so little, we at first felt that it was a waste of time for anyone at our ages to undertake to learn to read and write. But, as the ladies were so anxious that we should learn, and so willing to teach us, we concluded to give our whole minds to the work, and see what could be done. By doing so, at the end of the three weeks we remained with the good family we could spell and write our names quite legibly. . . .

3.8.7

Excerpt from an interview with C. H. Hall, 1863

The following is from an interview conducted in Canada by the American Freedman's Inquiry Commission in 1863. At the time of the interview, C. H. Hall was 52 years of age.

I was born in Maryland. My mother was the mother of fifteen children, I being the seventh child. I was born a slave and came up a slave until I was about 12 years old, and at that time my oldest brother was sold to Georgia. That first opened my eyes against slavery. I took into consideration how it was that my mother's children were sold, and other children were not sold. I got uneasy, and began to think over these things. It was a rule in that country, that a slave must not be seen with a book of any kind; but old madam Bean, my mistress, belonged to the Baptist Church, and she said we might all learn to spell and read the Bible. The old man fought against it for some time, but found it prevailed nothing. After she got to work pretty well, she used to teach me with the children, I learned how to spell considerable, and afterwards I got so I could read a little. . . .

Hall's first attempt to escape did not succeed, but he did make it North a few years later.

The full text of Document 3.8.7 is available on the CD-ROM.

3.8.8

Excerpt from the 1867 autobiography of the Reverend John Sella Martin

The Reverend John Sella Martin was born into slavery in 1832 in North Carolina. After escaping, he became a pastor of churches in Boston and Washington, D.C., and Superintendent of Schools in a Louisiana School District. He was a poet, orator and abolitionist and led campaigns against segregation in schools and public accommodations.

I learned that there were coloured people in some far off place called Canada who were free. I learned, too, from seeing them reading and writing, that they could make paper and the little black marks on it talk. It is difficult for children who see this from their earliest years to realise the incredulity with which a slave-boy ten year of age regards the achievement of reading when he notices it for the first time. For a long time I could not get it out of my head that the readers were talking to the paper, rather then the paper talking to them. When, however, it became a reality to me, I made up my mind that I would accomplish the feat myself. But when I asked the white boys with whom I played marbles to teach me how to read, they told me that the law would not allow it. Now the law was a sort of hobgoblin who had not stood very high in my opinion ever since he had torn my mother and sister from me, and me from my home; and as I hoped to get back to my old home, where I was certain my mother and sister would join me after awhile, I had no disposition to provoke the law to tear me away from where I then was. So, for a time, I abandoned the idea of learning to read.

But though the white boys would not teach me to read, they could not control or prevent the acquisition of a quick and retentive memory with which I was blessed, and by their bantering one another at spelling, and betting each on his proficiency over the other, I learned to spell by sound before I knew by sight a single letter in the alphabet. . . .

The full text of Document 3.8.8 is available on the CD-ROM.

Maria W. Stewart—An African American Woman Speaks

In her first publication, an 1831 religious and political pamphlet printed in Boston by William Lloyd Garrison and titled *Religion and the Pure Principles of Morality, The Sure Foundation on Which We Must Build,* Maria W. Stewart (1803–1879), born Maria Miller, introduced herself to her readers:

> I was born in Hartford, Connecticut, in 1803; was left an Orphan at five years of age; was bound out in a clergyman's family; had the seeds of piety and virtue early sown in my mind, but was deprived of the advantages of education, though my soul thirsted for knowledge. Left them at fifteen years of age; attended Sabbath schools until I was twenty; in 1826 was Married to James W. Stewart; was left a widow in 1829 . . .

These few words are all we know about the early life of the extraordinary African American woman who became the first American-born woman of any race to lecture in public on political themes and leave published copies of her speeches. As a young orphan, she was "bound out," which means that in exchange for room and board she lived as an unpaid household servant in the home of a Methodist minister until her midteens.

After that, on her own and earning her living as a paid domestic worker, she sought an education at Sabbath schools. These schools, which used the King James Bible as a primary but not exclusive text, provided valuable basic academic skills to thousands of black and white workers, such as young Maria Miller, who commonly labored ten and twelve hours a day, six days a week.

Miller arrived in Boston in the 1820s. She married James W. Stewart, a veteran of the War of 1812, and a successful merchant who outfitted sailors and ships leaving and entering the busy port of Boston. Boston was the center of a strong New England abolitionist movement, although far from a majority of white New Englanders actively supported an end to southern slavery. Nonetheless, black and white Bostonians, in separate organizations and together, worked against slavery and on behalf of the steady stream of fugitives who made their way north settling in the free states or continuing on to Canada.

Stewart was widowed after barely three years of marriage. She was cheated out of most of her inheritance by white colleagues of her husband and was thrown, once again, upon her own resources. At this low point in her life, Maria Stewart underwent a religious conversion, what we would call today a "born-again" experience. She believed that God called her to speak out on behalf of abolition and women's rights. This was at a time when it was generally considered scandalous for a woman to undertake such a public-speaking career.

Starting in 1831, Maria W. Stewart became a controversial writer and lecturer who raised the issues of black rights and self-determination later taken up by Frederick Douglass, Sojourner Truth, the Grimke sisters, and the many influential champions of human rights throughout the nineteenth century.

Maria W. Stewart read widely. She studied history, enjoyed poetry, and read the major newspapers of her day to stay informed about national and international events. She declared her major influences to be the Bible, the work of radical black abolitionist David Walker (1785–1830), author of *Walker's Appeal . . . to the Coloured Citizens of the World* 1829, and studies of women's lives such as the 1790 volume, *Woman, Sketches of the History, Genius, Disposition, Accomplishments. . . of the Fair Sex in all Parts of the World . . .* by the British historian John Adams (1750–1814).

In her lectures, Stewart urged black men and women in the North to fight against political and economic exploitation by developing strong institutions within their communities, including businesses, banks, and schools along with churches. In response to slavery, she followed Walker's call for armed uprising in the South if all other attempts at emancipation failed. Although Stewart's speeches drew large audiences, her activist "social gospel"—a mix of religion and politics, often delivered in a scolding tone—was not always well received. Decades after she left Boston feeling unappreciated, black historian William Cooper Nell recalled in a letter to William Lloyd Garrison that "in the perilous years of '33–'35, a colored woman—Mrs. Maria W. Stewart—fired with a holy zeal to speak her sentiments on the improvement of colored Americans, encountered an opposition even from her Boston circle of friends, that would have dampened the ardor of most women" (Richardson, p. 26).

During her public career in Boston, Stewart published a political pamphlet (1831) and a collection of religious meditations (1832), delivered four advertised public lectures (1832–1833) and saw her speeches printed in whole or in part in *The Liberator*. After moving to New York, where she became a school teacher in Brooklyn, Stewart published a volume of her collected works in 1835. She continued a life of activism, writing for African American publications, participating in antislavery organizations and women's rights groups and advancing the cause of black education in New York and later, during and after the Civil War, in Baltimore and Washington, D.C. There she published an expanded edition of her collected works just prior to her death in 1879.

Organizing Idea

During the 1830s, Maria W. Stewart felt called by God to write, lecture, and teach for the benefit of her race. Her major concerns were the abolition of slavery in the

South and the end of discrimination in the North; education; women's rights; religion; and black unity.

Student Objectives

Students will:

❖ become familiar with Maria W. Stewart's work and the unique role she played

❖ understand the issues she raised

❖ relate her writing and speaking to the work of like-minded activists such as David Walker and William Lloyd Garrison

Key Questions

❖ How did Maria Stewart view whites?

❖ What did she believe was the role of black women?

❖ What did she urge all African Americans to do?

Primary Source Materials

DOCUMENT 3.9.1: Selections from "Religion and the Pure Principles of Morality, the Sure Foundation on Which We Must Build," by Maria Stewart, 1831 with a notice from *The Liberator*, October 3, 1831

DOCUMENT 3.9.2: Selections from a "Lecture Delivered at The Franklin Hall, Boston," September 21, 1832

DOCUMENT 3.9.3: Selections from "An Address Delivered At The African Masonic Hall," Boston, by Maria Stewart, February 27, 1833, with a notice from *The Liberator*, March 2, 1833

DOCUMENT 3.9.4: Selections from Mrs. Stewart's "Farewell Address To Her Friends in The City Of Boston." Delivered September 21, 1833, with a report from *The Liberator*, September 28, 1833

Supplementary Materials

ITEM 3.9.A: Additional vocabulary lists for primary sources

Student Activities

Reading and Discussion—Maria Stewart's Views

Activity 1

The class can be divided into small groups, with each group responsible for reading all or a part of a selection, answering the questions and summarizing the document for the rest of the class.

Document 3.9.1

❖ What is Maria Stewart's tone?

❖ What topics does she address in this document?

❖ Whom does Stewart mean by American people?

❖ Why does she make that distinction? Were African Americans "American"? Why or why not?

❖ What accusations does Stewart aim at white people?

❖ What solutions does she suggest?

❖ What does she say are a mother's responsibilities?

❖ What are her goals for girls and women?

❖ Why does she write one phrase in capital letters? Is it a warning? A threat?

Documents 3.9.2 and 3.9.4

❖ What topic(s) does Maria Stewart address in these documents?

❖ Who is her audience?

❖ What obstacles stand in the way of young black women working as anything but a servant?

❖ On what basis should men take women seriously?

Document 3.9.3

❖ What is Maria Stewart's tone?

❖ What have white people done and what are they doing?

❖ What does Stewart think of Colonization?

Activity 2

Letter to the Editor of *The Liberator*

Maria W. Stewart's primary audience was African American, although there are some passages where, at least rhetorically, she addresses white people. Her speeches were printed whole or in part by William Lloyd Garrison in *The Liberator*, which was read by black and white people throughout the country. So, even people who did not attend her lectures knew of Stewart's opinions.

Write a letter to the editor of *The Liberator* in response to a selected argument of Stewart's. Whether you are writing to agree or disagree, be specific and build a case for your views based upon her actual words. Choose to write from the perspective of

❖ a nineteenth-century African American man

❖ a nineteenth-century African American woman

❖ a nineteenth-century white man

❖ a nineteenth-century white woman

❖ a twenty-first-century reader

Creative Extensions—Maria Stewart's Views

Activity 3

Students can create a poster or collage representing Maria Stewart's views on the role and responsibilities of black women. Alternatively, they can create a poster with quotes from Maria Stewart's writing that they find most powerful and that reflect Stewart's strong views on multiple subjects.

Finding Connections—Walker and Stewart

Activity 4

Maria Stewart was significantly influenced by David Walker and his *Appeal* (see Lesson 3). Have students find passages in his work that show his influence on Stewart's ideas. What similarities do students find in their writing and views? Both David Walker and Maria Stewart had little formal education. How do students account for the broad range of information they drew upon to build their arguments? Have students write an essay in which they address the connections between Walker and Stewart.

Further Student and Teacher Resources

Houchins, Susan, ed. *Spiritual Narratives*. New York: Oxford University Press, 1988.

Jeffrey, Julie Roy. *The Great Silent Army of Abolitionism*. Chapel Hill: The University of North Carolina Press, 1998.

Richardson, Marilyn, ed. *Maria W. Stewart, America's First Black Woman Political Writer: Essays and Speeches*. Bloomington, IN: Indiana University Press, 1987.

Sterling, Dorothy, ed. *We Are Your Sisters: Black Women in the Nineteenth Century*. New York: W. W. Norton & Company, 1989.

Contemporary Connection

⇥✳⇤

Linking Past and Present

Alice Walker (1944–) stands as a contemporary figure very much in the line of Maria W. Stewart. Prolific in many areas of expression, poetry, fiction, essays, and speeches, Walker's themes often echo those central to Stewart's life and work: human rights, African American civil rights, black women's empowerment, and the relationship of the black woman to the larger contexts of race, class, and nation.

Pulitzer Prize–winner Walker has brought attention to the voices of black women through novels and collections of short stories. Her youth in a family of Georgia sharecroppers and her work in the Civil Rights Movement in Mississippi in the 1960s are reflected in her distinctive merging of the personal and the political. Further, in her effort to revive the reputation of novelist, anthropologist, and pioneering African American folklorist Zora Neale Hurston (1891–1960) and to bring her work back into print, she restored an important writer to the American literary canon.

As was Stewart, Alice Walker has been a controversial figure at times. In her commitment to the vivid presentation of generations of black struggle, Walker's characters display flaws, virtues, and considerable complexity. As a consequence, she has been accused by some critics of a feminist, or—to use her term—"womanist" bias against black men. Others see her compromising the ideals of black family life with sympathetic portrayals of same-sex relationships.

Walker's landmark 1972 essay "In Search of Our Mothers' Gardens" is regarded as a classic introduction to the creative legacy of African American women. By acknowledging and drawing upon the power and persistence of both the formal traditions and the folk culture of the black past, Alice Walker argues, as did Maria W. Stewart, for the continuing process of individual and collective redefinition and self-invention.

At a 1989 book signing at the African Meeting House on Beacon Hill in Boston, Massachusetts, where Maria Stewart had delivered her 1833 "Farewell Address To Her Friends in The City Of Boston," Walker remarked that in that building she could feel "the spirit of the ancestors who struggled so hard and so long for the things they believed in." "When I think of Frederick Douglass," she continued, "when I think of Maria Stewart, I think of people who had great love and great passion, and who left us that legacy of speaking out and standing up —in the belief that honesty is a sign of love" (*The Museum-Smith Court News*, Vol. 2, No. 1, June 1989, p. 3. The Museum of Afro-American History). Students should find statues, plaques, or other memorials in their area honoring minority women and men. If there are none, they may wish to design a memorial.

Primary Source Materials for Lesson 9

3.9.1

Selections from "Religion and the Pure Principles of Morality, the Sure Foundation on Which We Must Build," by Maria Stewart, 1831 with a notice from *The Liberator*, October 3, 1831

All the nations of the earth are crying out for liberty and equality. Away, away with tyranny and oppression! And shall Afric's sons be silent any longer? . . .

This is a land of freedom. The press is at liberty. Every man has a right to express his opinion. Many think, because your skins are tinged with a sable hue, that you are an inferior race of beings; but God does not consider you as such. He hath formed and fashioned you in his own glorious image, and hath bestowed upon you reason and strong powers of intellect. He hath made you to have dominion over the beasts of the field, the fowls of the air, and the fish of the sea [Genesis 1:26]. He hath crowned you with glory and honor; hath made you but a little lower than the angels; and according to the Constitution of the United States, he hath made all men free and equal. . . It is not the color of the skin that makes the man, but it is the principles formed within the soul. . . .

The full text of Document 3.9.1 is available on the CD-ROM.

3.9.2

Selections from a "Lecture Delivered at The Franklin Hall, Boston," September 21, 1832

Before Maria Stewart began her speaking career, and during it, there were a few women, black and white, who were well-known preachers. Their right to deliver sermons was sometimes challenged, but they established a precedent in churches that helped Stewart take to the secular platform. She drew on that history by declaring that she was following the will of God in her own public work.

Why sit ye here and die? If we say we will go to a foreign land, the famine and the pestilence are there, and there we shall die. If we sit here we shall die. . . .

I have asked several individuals of my sex, who transact business for themselves, if providing our girls were to give them the most satisfactory references, they would not be willing to grant them an equal opportunity with others? Their reply has been—for their own part, they had no objection; but it was not the custom, were they to take them into their employ, they would be in danger of losing the public patronage.

And such is the power of prejudice. Let our girls possess whatever amiable qualities of soul they may; let their characters be fair and spotless as innocence itself; let their natural taste and ingenuity be what they may; it is impossible for scarce an individual of them to rise above the condition of servants.

The full text of Document 3.9.1 is available on the CD-ROM.

3.9.3

Selections from "An Address Delivered at The African Masonic Hall," Boston, by Maria Stewart, February 27, 1833, with a notice from *The Liberator*, March 2, 1833

The term "African" was commonly used to describe themselves by black Americans whose families had been here for generations; it did not generally refer to people born in Africa. Place names such as the African Meeting House or the African Masonic Hall referred to members' shared African ancestry.

Boston's African Masonic Lodge, founded in 1787 by Prince Hall, a Methodist minister, had a distinguished history as a forum for agitation against slavery and discrimination.

The unfriendly whites first drove the native American from his much loved home. Then they stole our fathers from their peaceful and quiet dwellings, and brought them hither, and made bond-men and bond-women of them and their little ones. They have obliged our brethren to labor, kept them in utter ignorance, nourished them in vice, and raised them in degradation; and now that we have enriched their soil, and filled their coffers, they say that we are not capable of becoming like white men, and that we can never rise to respectability in this country. They would drive us to a strange land. But before I go, the bayonet shall pierce me through. African rights and liberty is a subject that ought to fire the breast of every free man of color in these United States, and excite in his bosom a lively, deep, decided, and heartfelt interest.

The full text of Document 3.9.3 is available on the CD-ROM.

3.9.4

Selections from Mrs. Stewart's "Farewell Address To Her
Friends in The City Of Boston." Delivered
September 21, 1833, with a report from
The Liberator, September 28, 1833

This speech, Stewart's last in Boston, was delivered in the basement school room of the African Meeting House on Beacon Hill. Just a few years earlier, Stewart and her late husband had been married by the Rev. Thomas Paul, the pastor of the Meeting House which was a Baptist church.

[B]e no longer astonished then, my brethren and friends, that God at this eventual period should raise up your own females to strive, by their example both in public and private, to assist those who are endeavoring to stop the strong current of prejudice that flows so profusely against us at present. . . .

What if such women as are here described should rise among our sable race? And it is not impossible. For it is not the color of the skin that makes the man or woman, but the principle formed in the soul. Brilliant wit will shine. Come from whence it will; and genius and talent will not hide the brightness of its lustre.

The full text of Document 3.9.4 is available on the CD-ROM.

Frederick Douglass, An Agent for the Massachusetts Anti-Slavery Society 1838–1843

Frederick Douglass' autobiographical writing offers students of the antislavery movement an opportunity to view the Abolitionists from the point of view of an escaped slave. It also sheds light on how Douglass changed, developing his own skills and opinions, which altered his relationship with his white sponsors and, sometimes, created conflict with them.

Douglass had escaped slavery in September 1838, and within a fortnight he was in New Bedford, Massachusetts, seeking an opportunity to work at his trade, caulking ships. Douglass quickly learned the limits to his freedom when he was denied work in his trade. As he wrote in *The Life and Times of Frederick Douglass,* "[I] prepared myself to do any kind of work that came to hand. I sawed wood, shoveled coal, dug cellars, moved rubbish from backyards, worked on the wharves, loaded and unloaded vessels, and scoured their cabins" (p. 159).

Some five months into his New Bedford experience, he continued, "there came a young man to me with a copy of *The Liberator,* the paper edited by William Lloyd Garrision, and published by Isaac Knapp, and asked me to subscribe for it. I told him I had but just escaped from slavery and was of course very poor, and had no money then to pay for it. He was very willing to take me as a subscriber, notwithstanding, and from this time I was brought into contact with the mind of Mr. Garrison, and his paper took a place in my heart, second only to the Bible" (p. 160).

In the summer of 1841, Douglass left his work in New Bedford to attend an antislavery convention held on Nantucket Island under the direction of Garrison. For Frederick Douglass, this evening was a watershed. For the first time in his life, he spoke to a white audience. In addition, he was tremendously impressed by Garrison and credited him with "swaying a thousand heads and hearts at once."

Later that evening, John Collins, general agent of the Massachusetts Anti-Slavery Society, encouraged Douglass to accept a position as an agent of the Society. Agents were paid just over $400 a year to lecture extensively and to collect money for the abolitionist cause. In addition, they helped others form local and state auxiliary societies. Thus began Frederick Douglass' extraordinary career as an advocate for African Americans, free or enslaved.

Organizing Idea

Antislavery organizations had both black and white leaders, and members who at times disagreed on the tactics to be used in reaching the same goal.

Student Objectives

Students will:

❖ learn how Frederick Douglass' skills, political views, and social consciousness changed over time and how those changes sometimes caused conflict

❖ understand the range of views held by individuals dedicated to a single cause

❖ understand the risks abolitionists faced

Key Questions

❖ What was Frederick Douglass' experience as an agent for the Massachusetts Anti-Slavery Society from 1841 to 1844?

❖ According to Douglass, what did some of the key abolitionists seem to expect of him as an agent?

❖ What did Douglass' black friends expect of him?

❖ What dangers did Douglass face?

Primary Source Materials

DOCUMENT 3.10.1: "Introduced to the Abolitionists," Chapter III in *The Life and Times of Frederick Douglass,* 1881

DOCUMENT 3.10.2: "Recollections of Old Friends," Chapter IV in *The Life and Times of Frederick Douglass,* 1881

DOCUMENT 3.10.3: "One Hundred Conventions," Chapter V in *The Life and Times of Frederick Douglass,* 1881

DOCUMENT 3.10.4: Excerpts from "Antislavery Convention," *The Vermont Observer,* July 18, 1843

DOCUMENT 3.10.5: "Mob in Middlebury," *The Observer,* July 25, 1843

DOCUMENT 3.10.6: Excerpt from *Pendleton Republic* signed by "Old Settler," March 5, 1896

Supplementary Materials

ITEM 3.10.A: Additional vocabulary lists for primary sources

ITEM 3.10.B: A partial speaking itinerary for Frederick Douglass in 1843

ITEM 3.10.C: An outline map of northern United States

Vocabulary

agent	eloquent	melee	orator
chattel	Jim Crow	mob-ocratic	perpetrator

Student Activities

Activity 1   **Reading and Analysis of Douglass' Writing**

Divide students into small groups, giving each group the responsibility for one of the chapters. Distribute copies of the assigned chapters (3.10.1 and 3.10.2) as well as the questions and vocabulary (Item 3.10.A) to each student. Ask one student in each group to be the secretary, who records answers to the questions.

Document 3.10.1

❖ Describe in your own words what Douglass felt about the way Garrison spoke to the crowd.

❖ When Douglass began to give speeches, why was it a very risky undertaking, so that "overcoming one difficulty only opened the way for another"?

❖ What were some of the ways Douglass felt that he changed as he spent time away from slavery?

❖ What does Douglass realize when his abolitionist friends suggest that he be sure to "include a little plantation speech" in his presentations?

❖ Why would they ask this of him? What is your reaction?

Document 3.10.2

❖ In what ways did the Thomas W. Dorr proposal for a new Constitution want to *expand* suffrage, and in what way did it want to *limit* suffrage? Did Douglass and his abolitionist colleagues win this political battle, the "Dorr war"?

❖ Despite being in the North, the railways, steamboats, and public houses had many regulations that discriminated against people of color. What was the choice faced by Douglass' "white friends" that had an impact on the way he felt about them?

❖ How did Douglass sometimes get around the problem of not being allowed to speak in public buildings?

❖ How did Stephen A. Chase, "supt. of the road," use a comparison between the Evangelical Church and the railroads to justify discriminatory practices? What happened as a result of Douglass refusing to give up his first-class ticket? Did the "barbarous practices" come to an end?

After completing the reading and answering the questions, each team should create a brief summary of the selection, highlighting key points. A member of the group will share the summary with the class.

Creative Extensions—Douglass' Shifting Views

Activity 2

The Frederick Douglass papers (speeches, debates, and interviews) can be found online. Working in groups, students can study these primary sources and collect quotes demonstrating the progression of Douglass' thinking. Use the findings to design an exhibit for the class and/or school.

Mapping—On the Road with Frederick Douglass

Activity 3

Distribute Douglass' speaking itinerary (Item 3.10 B) to all students. Using the map (Item 3.10.C) and an atlas for guidance, students should draw lines between the cities and towns where Frederick Douglass spoke in 1843. Ask the students to estimate how far he traveled that year. How would he have traveled?

Reading and Analysis—"One Hundred Conventions"

Activity 4

Divide the class into groups. Document 3.10.3, "One Hundred Conventions," can be split in two parts (the first ending after Douglass' Rochester appearance.) Other groups will read Documents 3.10.5 and 3.10.6. Students should also keep Douglass' itinerary (3.10.B) on hand. Each group is responsible for answering the questions and reporting to the class.

Document 3.10.3

❖ What was the one thing that Douglass felt was "all that the American people needed"?

❖ What kinds of problems did Douglass and other agents have to solve when they went into a new town to conduct an antislavery convention?

❖ What dangers did they face?

❖ What kinds of activities went on at an antislavery convention?

Document 3.10.5

❖ What happened when Frederick Douglass spoke?

❖ What is the tone of this article?

❖ Is the reporting impartial? If you think not, highlight the words that you consider biased.

Document 3.10.6

❖ How accurate do you think the description is? Explain your reasoning.

❖ Do you think "Old Settler" was an eyewitness?

❖ Who is he?

❖ Is this report impartial? If you think not, highlight the words that you consider biased.

Activity 5   **Reading for Bias**

Ask students to read "Antislavery Convention" (3.10.4). What dividing issues within the abolitionist movement does the writer raise? Is the article impartial? Identify words you consider biased.

Activity 6   **The Means to an End**

Ask the students to consider all the documents they have read. As a class, list the ways in which leaders and members of the antislavery movement differed in opinion and tactics.

Further Student and Teacher Resources

Blassingame, John W., ed. *The Frederick Douglass Papers, Series One: Speeches, Debates, and Interviews.* 5 vol. New Haven, CT: Yale University Press, 1979–1992.

Blassingame, John W., ed. *The Frederick Douglass Papers, Series Two: Autobiographical Writings, Narrative of the Life of Frederick Douglass, An American Slave, Written by Himself.* New Haven, CT: Yale University Press, 1999 and 2001.

Brockmann, Carolee. *Frederick Douglass, Incorporating the Words of Frederick Douglass from the Life and Times of Frederick Douglass, Written by Himself.* Carlisle, MA: Discovery Enterprises, 1996.

Brown, Wesley, ed. *The Teachers and Writers Guide to Frederick Douglass.* New York: Teachers and Writers Collaborative, 1996.

Douglass, Frederick. *Life and Times of Frederick Douglass,* 1881. Reprinted in New York: Collier Books, 1962.

———. *My Bondage and My Freedom,* 1885. Reprinted in Cambridge, MA: Belknap Press of Harvard University, 1960.

———. *Narrative of the Life of Frederick Douglass: An American Slave. Written by Himself.* 1845. Reprinted in Cambridge, MA: Belknap Press of Harvard University, 1960.

Foner, Phillip S. *The Life and Writings of Frederick Douglass.* 4 vols. New York: International Publishers, 1950–1955.

Hansen, Debra Gold. *Strained Sisterhood: Gender and Class in the Boston Female Antislavery Society.* Amherst: University of Massachusetts Press, 1993.

Horton, James Oliver, and Lois E. Horton. *In Hope of Liberty.* New York: Oxford University Press, 1997.

Huggins, Nathan Irvin. *Slave and Citizen: The Life of Frederick Douglass.* Glenview, IL: Scott, Foresman and Co., 1980.

Khan, Lurey. *One Day, Levin . . . He Be Free.* New York: E.P. Dutton, 1972.

Meltzer, Milton., ed. *Frederick Douglass, in His Own Words.* San Diego: Harcourt Brace, 1995.

Contemporary Connection
—※—

Frederick Douglass Today

Far from being a dusty figure from the past, Frederick Douglass continues to excite interest because of the immense influence he has had on the course of American history. The Frederick Douglass National Historic Site in Washington, D.C., is run by the National Park Service and serves many visitors each year. The site sponsors yearly oratorical contests for elementary and secondary students from D.C., Maryland, and Virginia. Students memorize and deliver the speeches of Frederick Douglass; winners receive cash prizes. The Rokeby Museum in Vermont helped to erect a state historic marker on the site of one of the "Great Convention" speeches given by Douglass in 1843. In July 2003, at the unveiling ceremony, an actor gave the very speech delivered there by Douglass in 1843.

There are many sites about Douglass on the Internet. One of the most informative has been created by the Frederick Douglass Papers Project based at Indiana University. Project staff work to organize the systematic publication of Douglass' speeches, correspondence, and memoirs. Originals of these papers are housed in several repositories—Library of Congress, Boston Public Library, University of Rochester, and Syracuse University. The Project website also offers links to related websites, including the American Abolitionist Project.

Using on-site visits where possible, plus internet resources, students have many opportunities for in-depth research projects on Frederick Douglass' life and his continuing importance in U.S. history.

Voss, Frederick S. *Majestic in His Wrath: A Pictorial life of Frederick Douglass.* Washington, DC: Smithsonian Institution Press, 1995.

Winch, Julie. *A Gentleman of Color: The Life of James Forten.* Oxford, UK: Oxford University Press, 2002.

Websites

The Frederick Douglass Museum and Cultural Center, Rochester, NY
www.ggw.org/freenet/f/fdm/index.html

Frederick Douglass National Historic Site; National Park Service, Washington, DC
www.nps.gov/frdo/freddoug.html

The Frederick Douglass Papers at the Library of Congress; American Memory Project, Library of Congress, Washington, DC
http://memory.loc.gov/ammem/ doughtml/doughome.html

The Frederick Douglass Papers Project. Indiana University–Purdue University, Indianapolis
www.iupui.edu/~douglass/

University of Rochester Frederick Douglass Project. Rochester, NY
www.lib.rochester.edu/rbk/douglass/home.stm

Video

Frederick Douglass. Videocassette. New York: A&E Home Video, 1996.

Primary Source Materials for Lesson 10

3.10.1

"Introduced to the Abolitionists," Chapter III in
The Life and Times of Frederick Douglass, 1881

In the summer of 1841, a grand anti-slavery convention was held in Nantucket, under the auspices of Mr. Garrison and his friends. I had taken no holiday since establishing myself in New Bedford, and feeling the need of a little rest, I determined on attending the meeting, though I had no thought of taking part in any of its proceedings. Indeed, I was not aware that anyone connected with the convention so much as knew my name. Mr. William C. Coffin, a prominent abolitionist in those days of trial, had heard me speaking to my coloured friends in the little schoolhouse on Second Street, where we worshipped. He sought me out in the crowd and invited me to say a few words to the convention. Thus sought out, and thus invited, I was induced to express the feelings inspired by the occasion, and the fresh recollection of the scenes through which I had passed as a slave. It was with utmost difficulty that I could stand erect, or that I could command and articulate two words without hesitation or stammering. I trembled in every limb. I am not sure that my embarrassment was not the most effective part of my speech, if speech it could be called. At any rate, this is about the only part of my performance that I now distinctly remember. The audience sympathised with me at once, and from having been remarkably quiet, became much excited. . . .

The full text of Document 3.10.1 is available on the CD-ROM.

3.10.2

"Recollections of Old Friends," Chapter IV in
The Life and Times of Frederick Douglass, 1881

While thus remembering the noble anti-slavery men and women of Rhode Island, I do not forget that I suffered much rough usage within her borders. It was, like all the Northern States at that time, under the influence of slave power, and often showed a proscription and persecuting spirit, especially upon its railways, steamboats and public houses. The Stonington route was a 'hard road' for a coloured man to travel in that day. I was several times dragged from the cars for the crime of being coloured. On the Sound, between New York and Stonington, there were the same proscriptions which I have before named, as enforced on the steamboats running between New York and Newport. No coloured man was allowed abaft the wheel, and in all seasons of the year, in heat or cold, wet or dry, the deck was his only place. If I would lie down at night, I must do so upon the freight on a deck, and this in cold weather was not a very comfortable bed. . . .

The full text of Document 3.10.2 is available on the CD-ROM.

3.10.3

"One Hundred Conventions," Chapter V in
The Life and Times of Frederick Douglass, 1881

As soon as we began to speak, a mob of about sixty of the roughest characters I ever looked upon ordered us, through its leaders, to be 'silent,' threatening us if we were not with violence. We attempted to dissuade them, but they had not come to parley, but to fight, and were well armed. They tore down the platform on which we stood, assaulted Mr. White, knocking out several of his teeth; dealt a heavy blow on William A. White, striking him on the back part of the head badly cutting his scalp and felling him to the ground. Undertaking to fight my way through the crowd with a stick which I caught up in the melee, I attracted the fury of the mob, which laid me prostrate on the ground under a torrent of blows. Leaving me thus, with my right hand broken, and in a state of unconsciousness, the mob-ocrats hastily mounted their horses and rod to Andersonville, where most of them resided. . . .

The full text of Document 3.10.3 is available on the CD-ROM.

3.10.4

Excerpts from "Antislavery Convention,"
The Vermont Observer, July 18, 1843

Before proceeding to our sketch we wish to say a word or so in regard to the speakers. Mr. Douglas, the fugitive slave is an eloquent and effective speaker. He is possessed of intellectual power sufficient to supply half a dozen pale faces that we have heard declaiming upon the inferiority of the colored race, and placing them as a connecting link between men and monkeys. As was playfully remarked by Mr. Bradburn of the Mass. Legislature, speaking of the intellectual powers of himself and Daniel Webster, "he is" said he "as much superior to me, as I am superior to an oyster lying quietly in its shell on the shore," so is Mr. D. as much superior to some white faces who prate about the inferiority of negro intellect. His heart is in the work of abolition, he feels for the slave and for our common humanity. Had he fallen among some other class of abolitionists, and other influences than those which have excited within him such a prejudice against the church he might, under God, have been a powerful instrument for good. But we say it with all honesty and sincerity, that unless he will divest himself of the denunciatory style, unless he will cease to brand the whole American nation as "a nation of liars, a nation of thieves, a nation of scoundrels," unless he will cease his indiscriminate and wholesale denunciations of the clergy and the church, as an abolitionist he is shorn of his strength. . . .

The full text of Document 3.10.4 is available on the CD-ROM.

3.10.5

"Mob in Middlebury," *The Observer,* July 25, 1843

Mob in Middlebury

Mob in Middlebury.—We find one or two papers attempting to make capital out of what they call a mob in Middlebury. The facts are simply these—Mr. Douglas, the fugitive slave, gave notice the first day, that during the Convention he would give an account how he learned to read and write. At the close of the afternoon session of the last day, Mr. D. said that in the evening he would give this narrative. The evening came, and the Town-room was filled with those who came to hear Mr. D. Instead of D., Mr. Bradburn arose and commenced an attack upon the church and clergy, after which they called for Douglas. Mr. Bradburn still kept on until about half-past nine. Some looked upon the notice given as a trap, and a number of the boys in the back seats began to shout and throw shot and gravel; and among the rest three eggs were thrown. This disturbance continued until Mr. B. closed and Mr. D. commenced, when the house was perfectly still. . . . As it was, we hazard the opinion that there would have been no disturbance, had not the speakers pursued a course *apparently designed to produce it!*

The full text of Document 3.10.5 is available on CD-ROM.

3.10.6

Excerpt from *Pendleton Republic* signed by "Old Settler," March 5, 1896

Several histories of Madison County, Indiana, written in the late nineteenth century and early twentieth century refer to the "mob at Pendleton" when Frederick Douglass tried to speak there. The 1897 Historical Sketches and Reminiscence of Madison County, Indiana *refers to "a stain. . . cast upon Madison county because of this outrage." It is unclear whether the piece written by "Old Settler" is an eyewitness report or a retelling of the incident; however, it is consistent with the descriptions given in the Madison County histories.*

After Mr. Douglas began speaking, a mob from the country, southeast of town a few miles, came and attacked Mr. Douglas and the crowd. They knocked Mr. Douglas down with a stone, striking him on the back of the head, cutting quite a gash and making him insensible. Then attacking the crowd, the melle [sic] was an exciting and dangerous one for a time, but no one was seriously hurt but Mr. Douglas. The mob was soon dispersed with a struggle.

Mr. M. G. Walker, Theodore Walker, Neal Hardy and many others took part in the fray. There was a man named Robert Graham here at the time, visiting his sister, Mrs. David Bowsman. He was from New Paris, Ohio. A man of large build and herculean strength. A number of the mob attacked him, and in quick succession he knocked down six men, piling them across a slab seat until their combined weigth [sic] broke the slab into two pieces. He came away with but a little scratch on the chin.

Mr. Douglas was brought over to the residence of Dr. Fussell, and after dark was taken east of town in a wagon to the residence of Neal Hardy, where he was kindly cared for.

[signed]
Old Settler

The full text of Document 3.10.6 is available on the CD-ROM.

Spreading the Abolitionist Message

Although abolitionists often addressed educated audiences through published essays or public speaking engagements, they also used many other venues to issue their calls for action against slavery. Antislavery activists published books and pamphlets for general audiences, posted handbills, popularized antislavery songs, and even used children's rhymes to garner public support. Readers, people who read aloud to groups in barbershops, churches, and other places, reached those who could not read. These types of tactics were successful in the abolition movement and utilized in other causes because of the wider audiences they attract.

In addition to reading David Walker's *Appeal* (Lesson 3) and the speeches and writings of Maria Stewart (Lesson 9), Frederick Douglass, and William Lloyd Garrison, it is important to study some of the popular initiatives that helped further the antislavery movement. In contrast to potentially dangerous actions such as sheltering people escaping from slavery, these publications and popularized songs could easily be incorporated into a person's private life. Although it took courage to actively speak out against any part of slavery, it did not involve the same risks as helping someone flee the South.

Organizing Idea

Through study of broadsides, songs, pamphlets, and other abolitionist propaganda, students explore how these materials might have been used and whether or not they think these methods might have helped spread the abolitionist message.

Student Objectives

Students will:

❖ become familiar with various techniques used to popularize the abolitionist message

❖ discuss and discover attributes common to these documents

❖ critique the relative success of each technique and example

❖ begin to identify with the abolitionists' message by learning and singing songs that have already been set to familiar tunes and rhymes

❖ explore the positive and negative purposes of propaganda and its use today to popularize social issues

Key Questions

❖ What is propaganda?

❖ How did antislavery activists use propaganda to make people sympathetic to their cause?

❖ How is propaganda used today to support social change?

Primary Source Materials

DOCUMENT 3.11.1: Lyrics for "I am an Abolitionist," "Spirit of Freemen, Wake," "Ye Sons of Freemen"

DOCUMENT 3.11.2: Map of Slavery in the United States, late 1850s

DOCUMENT 3.11.3: Declaration of Sentiments of the American Anti-Slavery Society, 1833

DOCUMENT 3.11.4: Illustrations of the American Anti-Slavery Almanac for 1840

DOCUMENT 3.11.5A AND B: Cover illustration of *New England Anti-Slavery Almanac for 1841;* "Things for the Abolitionist to Do"

DOCUMENT 3.11.6: *The Anti-Slavery Alphabet* printed for the Anti-Slavery Fair in Philadelphia, 1847

DOCUMENT 3.11.7: *The Slave's Friend*, 1836, an antislavery publication for children

DOCUMENT 3.11.8: Broadside for Illinois Antislavery Convention, 1837

DOCUMENT 3.11.9: Broadside "Slave Market of America," Washington, D.C., 1836

Supplementary Materials

ITEM 3.11.A: Additional vocabulary lists for primary sources

Vocabulary

abolitionist	fugitive	infringement	oppression
expatriation	inalienable rights	insurrection	

Student Activities

Activity 1 ### Discussion of "Propaganda"

Ask the students to define "propaganda." Write a definition that most agree to on the board. Give present-day examples.

- ❖ Why do groups, governments, and political parties use propaganda?
- ❖ How is propaganda different from newspaper and TV reporting?
- ❖ Is it always different?

Have students survey different news outlets for several days and report to the class examples of propaganda they saw or heard.

Activity 2 ### Antislavery Songs

Read the lyrics to the songs out loud and discuss them.

- ❖ How does it make you feel?
- ❖ To whom would it appeal?
- ❖ Why would it be important in a struggle against slavery to use popular songs or short rhymes to gather support from the general public?
- ❖ Can you think of songs that could be considered propaganda?

Activity 3 ### Analysis of Propaganda Methods

Display Documents 3.11.2–3.11.9 at workstations around the room. (Some documents can be combined; for example, 3.11.2 with 3.11.3, and 3.11.6 with 3.11.7.)

Students work in pairs or small groups and move from one station to the next. They should consider the following questions as they analyze the documents:

- ❖ Does this document fit the definition of propaganda that the class wrote?
- ❖ As a propaganda tool, what is most compelling to you about this document? What do you find most powerful—the words, the drawing, the idea, the visual impact, or something else?
- ❖ In what ways could this document be disseminated? Who would use it and in what ways? Is it unique? How? Think in terms of design and content.
- ❖ How does this document differ from a speech given to a group at an antislavery meeting? How might the audience differ?
- ❖ How is the document different from other documents you've examined?
- ❖ Why would someone create these? Think of more than one reason.

Essay Writing—"The Most Effective Tool"   *Activity 4*

Students should write an essay describing the document they feel was likely most effective in bringing about an end to slavery. The essay needs to include details from the document and reasons for the opinion. The teacher may wish to have students share various opinions with the class.

Creative Extensions   *Activity 5*

Students are assigned or choose a particular event in African American history and create their own propaganda tools in a similar fashion to the ones in this lesson. Alternatively, students choose a current issue and create a broadside, a poster, a song, etc. to state their views.

Further Teacher and Student Resources

Douglass, Frederick. *Autobiographies: Narrative of the Life of Frederick Douglass: An American Slave by Himself; My Bondage and My Freedom; Life and Times of Frederick Douglass.* New York: Penguin Books, 1994

Harrold, Stanley. *American Abolitionists.* Harlow, UK: Longman, 2001.

Jeffrey, Julie Joy. *The Great Silent Army of Abolitionism: Ordinary Women in the Antislavery Movement.* Chapel Hill: The University of North Carolina Press, 1998.

Kraditor, Aileen S. *Means and Ends in American Abolitionism: Garrison and His Critics on Strategy and Tactics, 1834–1850.* New York: Random House, 1969.

Lowance, Mason, ed. *Against Slavery: An Abolitionist Reader.* New York: Penguin Books, 2000.

Mayer, Henry. *All on Fire: William Lloyd Garrison and the Abolition of Slavery.* New York: St. Martin's Press, 1998.

Stowe, Harriet Beecher. *Uncle Tom's Cabin.* New York: Signet Classic, 1998.

Websites

Abolition. African American Mosaic. American Memory Collection. Library of Congress, Washington, DC
www.loc.gov/exhibits/african/afam005.html

From Slavery to Freedom: the African American Pamphlet Collection, 1824–1909. American Memory Collection, Library of Congress, Washington, DC
http://memory.loc.gov/ammem/aapchtml/aapchome.html

http://hdl.loc.gov/loc.rbc/rbpe.11801100
For a full text of the American Anti-Slavery pamphlet, excerpted in Document 3.11.3

Contemporary Connection
※

Advocacy and Censorship Today

Advocacy messages are spread by many means in the twenty-first century. Examples range from vigils, marches, Internet essays, and protest songs during recent wars to antismoking posters and antiabortion and pro-choice ads on TV. Advocacy messages are also found in rap music and in books written to make real a powerful perspective. For example, students may wish to read books such as *Black Boy* (Richard Wright), *Blues for Mr. Charlie* (James Baldwin), *The Color Purple* (Alice Walker), and *Still I Rise* (Maya Angelou). The writers advocate by informing. There are often differences of opinion in the United States about what can be defined as *protected speech* and what is not. Attempts are made from time to time to censor certain messages. The National Coalition Against Censorship exists to address such attempts. For more information see *http://www.ncac.org*.

Students can be asked to notice all the many different kinds of advocacy in our society today and consider the means by which these messages reach us. Ask, When does censorship become a freedom of speech issue? When is it not?

Primary Source Materials for Lesson 11

3.11.1

Lyrics for "I am an Abolitionist," "Spirit of Freemen, Wake,"
"Ye Sons of Freemen"

I am an Abolitionist (sung to "Auld Lang Syne")

I am an Abolitionist!
I glory in the name
Through now by Slavery's minions hiss'd
And covered o'er with shame
It is a spell of light and power—
The watchword of the free:—
Who spurns it in the trial hour,
A craven soul is he!

I am an Abolitionist!
Then urge me not to pause
For joyfully I do enlist
In FREEDOM'S sacred cause
A nobler strife the world ne'er saw,
Th'enslaved to disenthrall;
I am a soldier for the war,
Whatever may befall!

The full text of Document 3.11.1 with additional song lyrics is available on the
CD-ROM.

3.11.2

Map of Slavery in the United States, late 1850s

This map, published in London, is an example of how involved the British were in the antislavery movement. It was based on data "collected during a personal tour in the years 1853 and 1854." The mapmaker further notes in his subheading that "the depth of its shade represents the degree of Slavery in the Several States." Virginia leads with 472,528 slaves and is stained black.

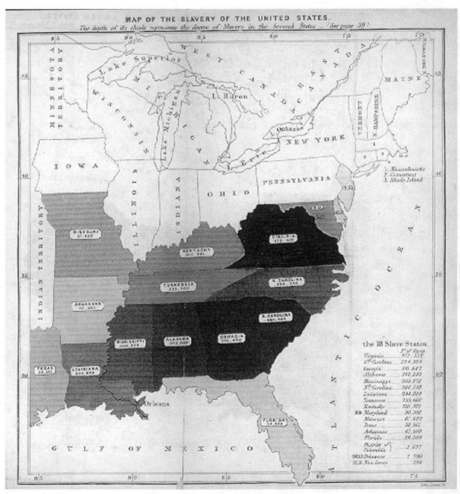

Special Collections Library, University of Virginia

3.11.3

Declaration of Sentiments of the American Anti-Slavery Society, 1833

In 1845, the American Anti-Slavery Society published a thirty-six-page pamphlet, which included, among other things, its declaration of sentiments, excerpted here, its platform, a discussion of immediate abolition, and a piece titled, "The Influence of Slavery."

These are our views and principles—these our designs and measures. With entire confidence in the overruling justice of God, we plant ourselves upon the Declaration of our Independence and the truths of Divine Revelation, as upon the Everlasting Rock.

We shall organize Anti-Slavery Societies, if possible, in every city, town, and village in our land.

We shall send forth agents to lift up the voice of remonstrance, of warning, of entreaty, and rebuke.

We shall circulate, unsparingly and extensively, anti-slavery tracts and periodicals.

We shall enlist the pulpit and the press in the cause of the suffering and the dumb. . . .

The full text of Document 3.11.3 is available on the CD-ROM.

3.11.4

Illustrations of the American Anti-Slavery Almanac for 1840

Library of Congress

Transcription of the captions is available on the CD-ROM.

3.11.5A AND B

Cover illustration of *New England Anti-Slavery Almanac for 1841;*
"Things for the Abolitionist to Do"

THE

NEW ENGLAND ANTI-SLAVERY

ALMANAC,

FOR

1841.

BEING THE 65TH YEAR OF AMERICAN INDEPENDENCE.
CALCULATED FOR BOSTON AND THE
EASTERN STATES.

"They can't take care of themselves."

BOSTON:
PUBLISHED BY J. A. COLLINS,
NO. 25 CORNHILL.
1841.

THINGS FOR ABOLITIONISTS TO DO.

1. *Speak for the slave*; plead his cause everywhere, and make every body feel that you are in earnest. Get up anti-slavery discussions in debating societies, lyceums, and wherever you can get an opening, abroad and at home, in social circles and in public conveyances, wherever you find mind to be influenced, *speak for the slave*. Get others to speak for him, enlist as many as you can to take his part. Words from a full heart *sink deep*.

2. *Write for the slave*. Do you take a religious or a political paper? write a short article for it, a fact, an argument, an appeal, a slave law, testimony as to the condition of slaves, with the name of the witness, an appeal, copy from anti-slavery papers and tracts something short and pithy, a brief statement of abolition sentiments, answers to objections, anti-slavery poetry—in short, *something*, if not more than five lines, *full of liberty*, and get them into your newspaper. If every abolitionist were to do what he might in this way, our principles would be spread before more minds in three months than they have reached from the beginning of our enterprise up to now.

3. *Petition for the slave*. Begin at once to circulate petitions for the immediate abolition of slavery in the District of Columbia, and in Florida, against the admission of Florida into the Union as a slave state, for the prohibition of the internal slave trade, for the recognition of Hayti as an independent nation, for a repeal of the unconstitutional act of 1793, and for the abrogation of that unconstitutional standing rule of the U. S. House of Representatives, adopted at the last session, which lays upon the table, without debate, all petitions, &c., on the subject of slavery. Instead of relaxing effort on account of this rule, let petitions be poured into congress a hundred-fold more than ever. Let every abolitionist bestir himself also in circulating petitions to the legislature of the state in which he lives, praying the repeal of all laws graduating rights by the *skin*.

4. *Work for the slave*. Distribute anti-slavery publications, circulate them in your neighborhood, take them with you on journeys, take them as you go to meetings, to the polls, to the stores, to mill, to school, and every where; establish an anti-slavery library; get subscribers for anti-slavery newspapers, and collect money for anti-slavery societies; gather facts illustrating the condition of slaves; search out all who have lived in slave states, get them to write out their testimony as to the food, clothing, lodging, shelter, labor, and punishments of slaves, their moral condition, the licentiousness of slave-holders, &c., &c., and forward them to some anti-slavery paper for publication; also gather and forward all the facts in your power exhibiting the *pro-slavery* of the free states; for *remember* that just in proportion as the pro-slavery of ministers, churches, lawyers, literary institutions, merchants, mechanics, and all classes in the free states, is exposed, light breaks on the path of freedom.

5. *Work for the free people of color*; see that your schools are open to their children, and that they enjoy in every respect all the rights to which as human beings they are entitled. Get merchants to take them as clerks, mechanics as apprentices, physicians and lawyers as students: if the place of worship which you attend has a negro seat, *go and sit in it*, and testify against the impiety which thus prostitutes the temples and worship of Him who has said, "If ye have respect of persons ye commit sin."

A WORD TO ABOLITION VOTERS.

Remember, that by voting for a man to fill an office you make him *your agent*, and if you vote for him *knowing* that his principles are wrong, when he puts forth those principles in his official acts, those acts are *your* acts, you are just as guilty as if you had performed them yourself. By voting for him, *with the knowledge you have*, you assume the responsibility of his acts; you become a partner in his sin, and shall be partaker of his plagues. President Van Buren and General Harrison have both publicly taken the side of the

American Antiquarian Society

3.11.6

The Anti-Slavery Alphabet printed for the Anti-Slavery
Fair in Philadelphia, 1847

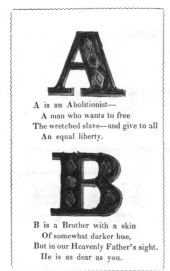

A is an Abolitionist—
A man who wants to free
The wretched slave—and give to all
An equal liberty.

B is a Brother with a skin
Of somewhat darker hue,
But in our Heavenly Father's sight,
He is as dear as you.

C is the Cotton-field, to which
This injured brother's driven,
When, as the white man's *slave*, he toils
From early morn till even.

D is the Driver, cold and stern,
Who follows, whip in hand,
To punish those who dare to rest,
Or disobey command.

Boston Athenaeum

A sample page and the full text are on the CD-ROM.

3.11.7

The Slave's Friend, 1836,
an antislavery publication
for children

*The American Anti-Slavery Society pro-
duced this pamphlet for children every
month. It included abolitionist poems,
songs, and stories.*

American Antiquarian Society

THE
SLAVE'S FRIEND.

VOL. II. No. VIII.   WHOLE No. 20

THE EMANCIPATED FAMILY.
The above picture has been in the
Slave's Friend before, but there was no
story with it. As my little readers

3.11.8

Broadside for Illinois Antislavery Convention, 1837

This broadside announces the September 27, 1837, meeting of the Illinois abolitionist group. Undersigned by 245 individuals from seventeen communities, it gives a comprehensive list of abolitionists in the state of Illinois. It was printed by Elijah Lovejoy in Alton, Illinois, shortly before his death (see Lesson 5).

ALTON OBSERVER.
Extra.

ALTON, SEPTEMBER 28, 1837.

STATE CONVENTION.

The present aspect of the slavery question in this country, and especially in this State, is of commanding interest to us all. No question is, at the present time, exerting so strong an influence upon the public mind as this. The whole land is agitated by it. We cannot, nor would we remain indifferent spectators in the midst of developements so vitally interesting to us all, as those which are daily taking place in relation to the system of American Slavery.— We have duties to perform, as Christians and as Patriots, which call for united wisdom, counsel and energy of action.

The undersigned would, therefore, respectfully call a meeting of the friends of the slave and of free discussion in the State of Illinois, to meet in Convention at UPPER ALTON, ON THE LAST THURSDAY OF OCTOBER. It is intended that this Convention should consist of all those in the State who believe that the system of American Slavery is sinful and ought to be immediately abandoned, however diversified may be their views in other respects. It is desirable that the opponents in this State of Domestic Slavery—all who ardently long and pray to witness its *immediate* abolition, should co-operate together in their efforts to accomplish it. We therefore hope that all such will make it a point of duty to attend the Convention, not thereby feeling that they are pledged to any particular course of action, but that they may receive as well as impart the benefit of mutual counsel and advice.

It is earnestly to be hoped that there will be a full attendance at the Convention. Let all who feel deeply interested in this cause, not only attend themselves, but stir up their neighbors to attend also. And let each one remember that this call cannot be repeated. But for the destruction of the "OBSERVER" press it would have been circulated some time since. It is hoped, that it will have time to circulate in season to bring together a large number of our friends from all parts of the State.

QUINCY.

John Burns
Richard Eells
Levi Stillman
Rufus Brown
Ezra Fisher,
Peter R. Borien,
Charles Burnham
Evan Williams
John R. George,
Henry Thompson
Myron Gaylord,
Jery Platt
Edward Platt
Lucius Kingman
Charles Howland
J. B. Brown
J. T. Holmes,
J. R. Beston
Edward L. Turner
Ross Hood
Joseph Craig, jr.
Andrew Segur
Alvin T. Smith
David Nelson
Levi B. Allen

John Benson
George Westgate
Benjamin Bran
Samuel Winter
Amos Bancroft
Erastus Benton
Edward Turner
Frederick Carrott
Loren Harkness
H. H. Snow
Willard Keyes
H. L. Montandon
Henry Barrett
James Stobie
Henry Maire
George Ogden
Charles Horhman
Francis Pearson
Henry C. Pitkin
E. B. Kimball
Henry H. Hoffman
James M. Flack
Strong Burnell
R. P. Vance
Lewis Faxon
Peter Felt

John E Morey
Peter M'Worthy
Bernard McKenzie
Porter Smith
A. C. Root
Artemas Ward
Charles Brown
Julius Brown
Elijah Ballard
Ebenezer White
Fairfield, Adams co.
J. B. Chittenden
W. H. Hubbard
William Kirby,
D. Bartholomew
Rufus Hubbard
Caleb Smith
Benjamin Baldwin
J. W. Cook
C. Talcott
Anson M. Hubbard
Chatham, Sangamon county.
L. N. Ransom
Josiah Porter
H. T. White
Cornelius Lyman
A. Stockwell
Peoria.
Jeremiah Porter,
Aaron Russell
Joseph Gambell
Alfred Castler
A. S. Castler
Samuel Castler
Wm. E. Castler
Wm. Guilford jr.
Calvin Winslow
James Clark
Joseph Thompson
Abraham Vaueps
John M. Smith
H. W. Reynolds
J. R. Stanton
Nathaniel Warden
John Reynolds
Henry Little
Moses Pettingill
Galesburgh.
Nehemiah H. Long
Thomas Simmons
Luther Gay
Erastus Swift
H. H. May
Hugh Conger
John Kendall
Adoniram Kendall
Patrick Dunn
John McMullin
Wm. Holyoke
Levi Sanderson,
Eli Farnham
Leonard Chappell
C. W. Gilbert
W. P. Hamlin
Nehemiah West
Abraham Tyler
Geo. Avery
John West
Samuel Tompkins
Sylvanus Ferris
James Bunce
Elisha H King
Abel Goodell
Warren Goodell

Henry Ferris
Wm S Gale
James Waters
Samuel Hitchcock
Lucien Mills
George Ferris
Lorentus Conger
Henry Wilcox
Ephraim P Nail
Enos Pomeroy
John Waters
Geo. W. Gale,
Brainard Orton
Miles Smith
Hennepin.
W. M. Stuart
S. D. Laughlin
J. N. Laughlin
James G. Dunlavy
Stephen D. Willis
Springfield.
Erastus Wright
Z. Hallock
E. B. Hawley
R. P. Abel
Roswell Abel
W. M. Cowgill
Isaac Bancroft jr
J. C. Bancroft
Oliver B. Culver
J. B. Watson
J. Stephenson
C. B. Francis
J. G. Rawson
Joseph Taney
Edmund R. Wiley
James Pratt
Josiah Francis
Elisha Taber
Geo. N. Kendall
S. Conant
E. W. Thayer
Farmington, Sangamon county.
Peter Bates
Asahel Stone
Azel Lyman
Alvan Lyman
Harooldus Estabrook
Ezra Lyman
Bishop Seely
B. B. More
Jay Slater
H. P. Lyman
Oliver Bates
Stephen Child
O. L. Stone
A. S. Lyman
Joel Buckman
John Lyman
T. Galt
Waverly, Morgan co.
Dr. Isaac H. Brown

Carlinville, Ill.
J. W. Buchanan
Alton.
C. W. Hunter
Royal Weller
P. B. Whipple
W. H. Chappell
Elijah P. Lovejoy
Owen Lovejoy
George Kimball
E. Beall

Moses Forbes
S. E. Moore
E. Upham
James Mansfield
J. S. Clark
G. Holton
Rev. H. Loomis
J. Carpenter
E. Dennison
John Bates
H. Sterns
J. Thompson
Thomas Lippincott,
T. B. Hurlburt
F. W. Graves
Pleasant Grove, Tazewell co.
Julius Bascom
Washington, Tazewell co.
James P. Scott
F. R Whipple
Romulus Barnes
Sand Prairie, Tazewell co.
Lemuel Holton
Samuel C. Woodrow
Wm. Woodrow
H. D. Chipman
R. Grosvenor
Pekin, Tazewell co.
Nathaniel Bailey
Joseph Booden
David Bailey

Monmouth, Warren co
George H. Wright
Jacksonville.
Wm. Carter
E. Wolcott
Timothy Chamberlain
Thos W. Melendy
Jeremiah Graves
Maro M. L. Reed
C. B. Barton
J. G. Edwards
Martin Hart
C. B. Blood
F. W. Patterson
D. D. Nelson
W. Jones
M Hicks
W. T. Mills
A. B. Hitchcock
S. Wells
J. S. Graves
R. S. Kendall
E. Scofield
Lyman Harkness
George Pyle
Thomas Lawrie
R. M. Pearson
A. W. Estabrook
Ralph Perry
L. Dunham
Thos. C. Kenworthy
Wm. S. Burnett
S. Chandler
Ebenezer Carter
E Beecher

I hope that in view of the fact, that the "Observer" Press has been THREE TIMES destroyed in Alton, in the space of little more than one year, it will not be deemed out of place, for me, in this special manner to call upon the friends of law, of order, of equal rights, and of free discussion, to rally at the proposed Convention in numbers and with a zeal corresponding to the urgency of the crisis. Our dearest rights are at stake—rights, which as American Citizens ought to be dearer to us than our lives. Take away the right of FREE DISCUSSION—the right under the laws, freely to utter and publish such sentiments as duty to God and the fulfilment of a good conscience may require, and we have nothing left to struggle for. Come up then, ye friends of God and man! come up to the rescue, and let it be known whether the spirit of freedom yet presides over the destinies of Illinois, or whether the "dark spirit" of Slavery has already so far diffused itself through our community, as that the discussion of the inalienable rights of man can no longer be tolerated.

ELIJAH P. LOVEJOY.
Alton. September 27, 1837.

3.11.9

Broadside "Slave Market of America," Washington, D.C., 1836

This broadside was issued during the 1835–1836 campaign to have Congress abolish slavery in Washington, D.C. It condemns the sale and ownership of slaves in the nation's capital.

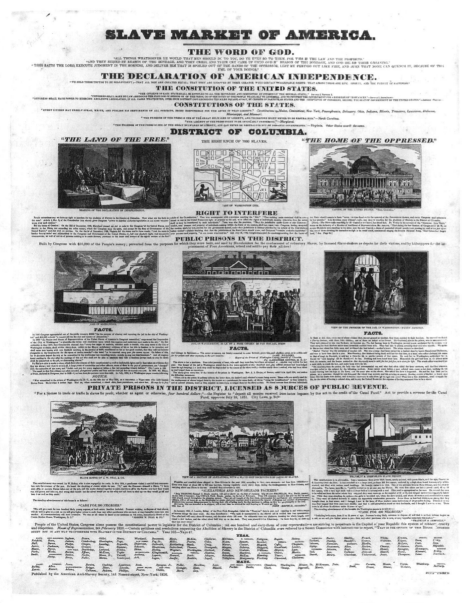

The Black Convention Movement

The Black Convention Movement of the antebellum period was the most significant political activity among free black leaders from 1830 to 1870. The first national convention, in Philadelphia in 1830, drew free black people from nine states, including Virginia, and white people active in the antislavery cause. Here they first determined to establish a national antislavery organization, and two years later, the American Anti-Slavery Society was founded. The national conventions met annually from 1830 to 1835. They were revived in 1840 and met in 1843, 1847, 1848, 1853, 1855, 1864 and 1869. In *Hard Road to Freedom*, James and Lois Horton explain that for the delegates, who came from local, state, and regional societies and conventions, the meetings "provided opportunities for black leaders to discuss and pass public resolutions on issues concerning their communities and to devise strategies for addressing them. The major concerns of these groups were opposition to slavery, the advancement and protection of civil rights, and the advancement of the race, especially through education and moral reform" (p. 131).

Although they agreed on the goals, delegates often disagreed on strategies. One particular area of debate was over whether all-black or integrated organizations and institutions were the most effective means to achieve their agreed-upon goals of black achievement and political and economic equality. Education opportunities for black people were to remain a dominant concern throughout the four decades.

In his introduction to the *Minutes of the Proceedings of the National Negro Conventions 1830–1864*, editor Howard Holman Bell analyzes how the participants, focus, and tone of the conventions changed over the four decades they convened. The national conventions of the 1830s focused on temperance, morality, education, economy, and self-help. A significant number of whites sympathetic to the causes of black civil rights and antislavery attended the initial conventions. Although delegates were strongly opposed to the emigration of free black people to Africa proposed by the African Colonization Society—an organization they saw as largely controlled by slaveowners—there was serious consideration of establishment of settlements in Canada and Haiti.

The conventions of the 1840s were both more militant in their approaches to problems and more independent of white influence. Bell notes "a growing tolerance of, even respect for, violence in freeing those in bondage." Talk was less of moral reform and more of taking direct action to correct wrongs.

In the 1850s delegates explored the possibilities of establishing a black state-within-a-state in the United States or an independent black nation elsewhere in the world. The U.S. Constitution was examined and participants debated whether that founding document was pro- or antislavery. At the 1855 National Convention, delegates decided that "the Constitution was sufficient authority to rid the nation of slavery."

During the decades when the national conventions met, numerous state and local conventions were held as well. The concerns were usually the same as those raised at the national gatherings. Reports of the conventions, local and national, reached a wide audience. Both black and white people heard the speeches in person, and newspapers, especially the black and abolitionist press, gave the conventions extensive coverage.

Organizing Idea

The Black Convention Movement of the antebellum period was yet another significant political activity among free black leaders from 1830 to 1870. These conventions brought together delegates from local, state, and regional societies and conventions to discuss aims and strategies for gaining equality for black people throughout the United States.

Student Objectives

Students will:

❖ learn how, beginning in 1830, free black people organized national and regional conventions to formulate goals and strategies in their fight for equality

❖ understand the range of issues addressed by delegates

Key Questions

❖ What important ideas were expressed and discussed at these national conventions?

❖ How does knowledge of the Black Conventions add to students' understanding of African American agency?

Primary Source Materials

DOCUMENT 3.12.1: Excerpt from "Minutes and Proceedings of the Second Annual Convention," Philadelphia, 1832

DOCUMENT 3.12.2: Several Resolutions passed at the Colored National Convention held in Buffalo, New York, 1843

DOCUMENT 3.12.3: Excerpts from the "Proceedings of the Colored National Convention, held at Cleveland, Ohio, 1848"

DOCUMENT 3.12.4: Excerpts from the "Address of the Colored National Convention, to the People of the United States," Rochester, New York, 1853

DOCUMENT 3.12.5: "An Address To The People of the United States," in the Proceedings of the October 1855 Colored National Convention in Philadelphia

DOCUMENT 3.12.6: "On the Constitution and the Union," *The Liberator*, December 29, 1832

Supplementary Materials

ITEM 3.12.A: Additional vocabulary lists for primary sources

Vocabulary

caste	doctrine	militia
citizenship	expatriation	suffrage

Student Activities

Activity 1   **Reading and Analysis of Convention Proceedings**

The class can be divided into groups, with each group responsible for reading excerpts from the proceedings of one of the national conventions (3.12.1–3.12.5). Much of the text could be challenging to students, and they should familiarize themselves with vocabulary (Item 3.12.A) before beginning to read. The documents are, however, extraordinarily eloquent and well worth students' efforts. Each group should consider:

- ❖ Who is the audience?
- ❖ What is (are) the topic(s)?
- ❖ What point of view is presented?
- ❖ What major points are included?
- ❖ What calls for action are included?

Activity 2   **Creative Extensions—Posters of the Issues**

Each group should design and create a poster that expresses the main points of the excerpt they have read. Suggest that they manipulate the size of the words and their arrangement to make their intentions as clear as possible. The posters can include quotes from the documents and visual images students believe fit their purpose.

When the posters are completed, they should be displayed around the room. Ask students to view the posters and then, as a class, discuss their meaning and connection to each other. What critical issues did free blacks bring to the conventions? What questions do students have?

Comparison and Contrast—Walker, Stewart, and the Colored Conventions

Activity 3

Compare and contrast the writings of David Walker (Lesson 3) and Maria Stewart (Lesson 9) to the views expressed in the black conventions. Consider the audience, the tone, the topics, and the calls for action.

Extended Analysis—The U.S. Constitution

Activity 4

Is the U.S. Constitution a pro- or antislavery document? The October 1855 Colored National Convention affirmed that "the Constitution was sufficient authority to rid the nation of slavery."

Divide the class into two groups, giving each student a copy of the Constitution. Have half of the students read "An Address To The People of the United States" (3.12.5) in the Proceedings (official written record) of the Convention, which were adopted by the delegates as argument for the antislavery character of the Constitution. The balance of the class should read "On the Constitution and the Union," William Lloyd Garrison's argument that the Constitution supported the institution of slavery (3.12.6).

Students should then debate the issue, specifically citing the sections of the Constitution that support their arguments. Remind them that only those Amendments passed *prior* to October 1855 can be included in the debate.

Contemporary Connection

⁙

Working Together

In 1909, the National Association for the Advancement of Colored People (NAACP) was founded by a multiracial group of activists to address issues of social injustice by legal means. Two of its most famous founders were W. E. B. Du Bois and Ida B. Wells-Barnett. In 1913, when President Woodrow Wilson introduced segregation into the federal government and again in 1915 when *Birth of A Nation* appeared in theaters, the NAACP spoke out in protest.

Today, the organization continues proactive initiatives both in and out of the courtroom. The infrastructure of the organization has been strengthened, there are active branches in many cities, and a yearly convention is held. *Crisis* magazine, founded by W. E. B. Du Bois, is published now online. For a history, a time line, and current information about the NAACP, see *www.naacp.org/past_future/index.html*. Students can research the activities and issues of the NAACP in their own communities and can research other black organizations working today on issues of fairness and justice. Which of these organizations exist in your community? What issues are important to their members?

Further Student and Teacher Resources

Bell, Howard Holman, ed. *Minutes of the Proceedings of the National Negro Conventions, 1830–1864.* New York: Arno Press and The New York Times, 1969.

Horton, James Oliver, and Lois E. Horton. *Hard Road To Freedom, The Story of African America.* New Brunswick, NJ: Rudgers University Press, 2001.

Primary Source Material
for Lesson 12

3.12.1

Excerpt from "Minutes and Proceedings of the
Second Annual Convention," Philadelphia, 1832

It will be seen by a reference to our proceedings, that we have again recommended the further prosecution of the contemplated college, proposed by the last Convention, to be established at New Haven, under the rules and regulations then established. A place for its location will be selected in a climate and neighborhood, where its inhabitants are less prejudiced to our rights and privileges. The proceedings of the citizens of New Haven, with regard to the erection of the college, were a disgrace to themselves, and cast a stigma on the reputed fame of New England and the country. We are unwilling that the character of the whole country shall sink by the proceedings of a few. We are determined to present to another portion of the country not far distant, and at no very remote period, the opportunity of gaining for them the character of a truly philanthropic spirit, and of retrieving the character of the country, by the disreputable proceedings of New Haven. We must have Colleges and high schools on the Manual Labor system, where our youth may be instructed in all the arts of civilized life. . . .

The full text of Document 3.12.1 is available on the CD-ROM.

3.12.2

Several Resolutions passed at the Colored National Convention held in Buffalo, New York, 1843

7. *Resolved*, That this Convention recommend and encourage agricultural pursuits among our people generally, as the surest and speadiest road to wealth, influence and respectability.

8. *Resolved*, That this Convention recommend to our people the importance of aspiring to a knowledge of all the Mechanic arts of the age.

9. *Resolved*, That among the various and important measures for the improvement of our people, this Convention view the principles of Temperance as of vital import, and we urge the hearty adoption of them by our whole people. . . .

11. *Resolved*, That it may be possible that the scheme of American Colonization was originally established upon pure motives; but if it were, its subsequent operations show that it has been fostered and sustained by the *murderous spirit of slavery* and prejudice.

12. *Resolved*, That such being the character of the institution, it has neither the confidence or respect of the free people of color of the United States.

13. *Resolved*, That the manner in which the American Colonization Society secures its victims-to wit, by begging slaveholders to emancipate their slaves, only on condition that they will go to Liberia, shows in what low estimation it should be held by common sense, and philanthropy of the nation. . . .

3.12.3

Excerpts from the "Proceedings of the Colored National Convention, held at Cleveland, Ohio, 1848"

Every blow of the sledge-hammer, wielded by a sable arm, is a powerful blow in support of our cause. Every colored mechanic, is by virtue of circumstances, an elevator of his race. Every house built by black men, is a strong tower against the allied hosts of prejudice. It is impossible for us to attach too much importance to this aspect of the subject. Trades are important. Wherever a man may be thrown by misfortune, if he has in his hands a useful trade, he is useful to his fellow-man, and will be esteemed accordingly; and of all men in the world who need trades, we are the most needy.

Understand this, that independence is an essential condition of respectability. To be dependent, is to be degraded. Men may indeed pity us, but they cannot respect us. We do not mean that we can become entirely independent of all men; that would be absurd and impossible, in the social state. But we mean that we must become equally independent with other members of the community. . . .

The full text of Document 3.12.3 is available on the CD-ROM.

3.12.4

Excerpts from the "Address of the Colored National Convention to the People of the United States," Rochester, New York, 1853

We are Americans, and as Americans, we would speak to Americans. We address you not as aliens nor as exiles, humbly asking to be permitted to dwell among you in peace; but we address you as American citizens asserting their rights on their own native soil. Neither do we address you as enemies, (although the recipients of innumerable wrongs;) but in the spirit of patriotic good will. In assembling together as we have done, our object is not to excite pity for ourselves, but to command respect for our cause, and to obtain justice for our people. We are not malefactors imploring mercy; but we trust we are honest men, honestly appealing for righteous judgment, and ready to stand or fall by that judgment. We do not solicit unusual favor, but will be content with rough handed "fair play". We are neither lame or blind, that we should seek to throw off the responsibility of our own existence, or to cast ourselves upon public charity for support. We would not lay our burdens upon other men's shoulders; but we do ask, in the name of all that is just and magnanimous among men, to be freed from all the unnatural burdens and impediments with which American customs and American legislation have hindered our progress and improvement. We ask to be disencumbered of the load of popular reproach heaped upon us—for no better cause than that we wear the complexion given us by our God and our Creator. . . .

The full text of Document 3.12.4 is available on the CD-ROM.

3.12.5

"An Address To The People of the United States," in the Proceedings of the October 1855 Colored National Convention in Philadelphia

Proceedings of the National Colored Convention
Held in Franklin Hall, Sixth Street, Below Arch
Philadelphia, October 16th, 17th, and 18th, 1855

An Address to the People of the United States
Fellow citizens:—In behalf of three million of our brethren, held in Slavery, in the United States:

In behalf of two hundred and fifty thousand, so called, free persons of color, occupying various grades of social and political position, from equal citizenship in most of the New England States, to almost chattel slavery in Indiana and the Southern states:

In behalf of three hundred thousand slave holders, embruted with the lawlessness, and drunken with the blood-guiltiness of slaveholding: . . .

In behalf of the sacred cause of HUMAN FREEDOM, beaten down and paralyzed by the force of American Example-

The undersigned, delegates of a convention of the People of Color, held in the city of Philadelphia, October 18th, 1855, beg leave most respectfully, to address you:-

We claim that we are persons, not things, and we claim that our brethren held in slavery are also, persons not things; and that they are, therefore, so held in slavery in violation of the Constitution, which is the supreme law of the land. For the Constitution expressly declares, that all human beings, described under it, are persons, and afterwards declares, that "No person shall be deprived of liberty without due process of law;" and that the right of the people to be secure in their persons shall not be violated. And as no law has ever been enacted, which reduced our brethren to slavery, we demand their immediate emancipation, and restoration to the rights secured to every person under the constitution, as the instant result of that personality with which the Constitution itself clothes them, and which it was ordained to protect and defend. . . .

The full text of Document 3.12.5 is available on the CD-ROM.

3.12.6

"On the Constitution and the Union," *The Liberator*, December 29, 1832

There is much declamation about the sacredness of the compact which was formed between the free and slave states, on the adoption of the Constitution. A sacred compact, forsooth! We pronounce it the most bloody and heaven-daring arrangement ever made by men for the continuance and protection of a system of the most atrocious villainy [sic] ever exhibited on earth. Yes—we recognize the compact, but with feelings of shame and indignation; and it will be held in everlasting infamy by the friends of justice and humanity throughout the world. It was a compact formed at the sacrifice of the bodies and souls of millions of our race, for the sake of achieving a political object—an unblushing and monstrous coalition to do evil that good might come. Such a compact was, in the nature of things and according to the law of God, null and void from the beginning. No body of men ever had the right to guarantee the holding of human beings in bondage. . . .

The full text of Document 3.12.6 is available on the CD-ROM.

The Underground Railroad

The Underground Railroad (UGRR) was neither a railroad nor underground. Sometimes called the "Liberty Line" or "Lightning Line," it was an informal, relatively secret network of escape routes staffed by free blacks and white sympathizers helping runaway slaves to freedom. In time, those active in the UGRR began to use terms such as "conductors," for those who provided transportation, "stations," for safe havens, and "routes." "Cargoes," "packages," and "passengers" all referred to fugitives.

With or without conductors, slaves fled mainly north of the Mason-Dixon line, via Philadelphia up the coast, or into Ohio, Michigan, and Illinois. Others headed south to the Spanish territories of Florida and Mexico, to the Indian Territory, and even to Europe. Traveling under the cover of night, slaves ran away. They sought swamps and safe houses; they stowed away on boats, disguised themselves, or shipped themselves to the nearest abolitionist. Their goal was singular: freedom by any means necessary.

Harriet Tubman, Frederick Douglass, and Ellen Craft are three African Americans inextricably bound with the UGRR. Each of these figures vividly exemplifies the courage required of anyone involved in resistance to slavery. Harriet Tubman escaped and then returned to the South regularly as a conductor. Douglass dressed as a sailor, borrowed seaman's papers, and traveled by boat and then train to New York. Ellen Craft's daring escape with her husband, William, illustrates the ingenuity that African Americans utilized to obtain their freedom.

In northern cities, Philadelphia, Detroit, New York, and Boston among them, abolitionists established Vigilance Committees. These committees raised money to help fugitives escape the law and to provide food, clothing, and safe places for runaways to live while they adjusted to living as free people. The records of Vigilance Committees are powerful sources of the activities of local communities and their efforts to assist fugitives. Francis Jackson, treasurer of Boston's Vigilance Committee, maintained meticulous records documenting contributors as well as recording the expenses incurred by activists.

William Still, a freeborn black and director of the General Vigilance Committee in Philadelphia, recorded the stories of hundreds of fugitives who crossed into

Pennsylvania. He was among the first to hear the Crafts' story. Published in 1871, Still's *Underground Railroad* is a rich repository documenting the activities and experiences of people connected to the Underground Railroad.

And in Ripley, Ohio, where the Ohio River separates Kentucky—a slave state—from Ohio—where slavery had never been legal—John Parker executed daring rescues of men, women, and children desperately seeking freedom. Parker, born in Norfolk, Virginia, was a slave until he bought his own freedom when he was eighteen. By his own count, he helped more than four hundred slaves to safety, often risking his own life when he snuck back into slave territory to help fugitives. In the 1880s, John Parker's autobiography was transcribed by journalist Frank M. Gregg. Recently, Parker's original manuscript was edited by Stuart Seely Sprague and published as *His Promised Land: The Autobiography of John P. Parker, Former Slave and Conductor on the Underground Railroad*.

"The legend of the Underground Railroad has taken on a life of its own and become a major epic in American history," writes Larry Gara in *Underground Railroad*. "It recalls a time when white and black abolitionists worked unselfishly together in the cause of human freedom. Like all legends it is oversimplified, whereas historical reality is complex."

Organizing Idea

Throughout the history of slavery in this country, resistance on the part of the enslaved as well as free black people and white allies was continuous and, often, well organized. The work of uncovering stories of individuals and groups active in helping people reach freedom has accelerated over the past few years. Now, all of us are able to learn about a period of our history more complex and fascinating than most of us ever knew.

Student Objectives

Students will:

- ❖ develop a broader view of the Underground Railroad (UGRR) and individuals who were part of this story
- ❖ continue their use of primary sources as a source of information and begin more extensive research projects

Key Questions

- ❖ What is "agency" and what can be learned about agency through the stories of people, black and white, who were active in the antislavery movement?
- ❖ How broad was the network of the Underground Railroad?
- ❖ How can original documents expand our understanding of a particular movement in American history?

❖ Who were important participants in the Underground Railroad? What did they accomplish?

❖ What have you learned about agency in the African American community through studying about the UGRR?

Primary Source Materials

DOCUMENT 3.13.1: Excerpt from the Preface to *The Underground Railroad* by William Still, 1873

DOCUMENT 3.13.2: Reynold's Political Map of the United States, 1856

DOCUMENT 3.13.3: Excerpts (part 1) from *The Underground Railroad* by William Still, 1873

DOCUMENT 3.13.4: Excerpt (part 2) from *The Underground Railroad* by William Still, 1873

DOCUMENT 3.13.5(A–E): The Boston Vigilance Committee, Treasurer's Account, excerpts from 1851 and 1854

DOCUMENT 3.13.6: "Rev. John Cross, of Illinois," *The Liberator*, August 23, 1344

DOCUMENT 3.13.7: Excerpt 1 from *His Promised Land: The Autobiography of John P. Parker, Former Slave and Conductor on the Underground Railroad*

DOCUMENT 3.13.8: Excerpt 2 from *His Promised Land: The Autobiography of John P. Parker, Former Slave and Conductor on the Underground Railroad*

Supplementary Materials

ITEM 3.13.A: Additional vocabulary lists for primary sources

ITEM 3.13.B: Map showing UGRR escape routes, National Park Service

ITEM 3.13.C: Outline map of the United States

ITEM 3.13.D: Outline map of Massachusetts

Vocabulary

bondage	fugitive	schooner	skiff
bondsmen	"hire his time"	services rendered	vigilance
Borderland	humane	servitude	

Student Activities

Reading—Overview of Underground Railroad

Activity 1

Students should read William Still's preface to *The Underground Railroad* (3.13.1) and then list the many ways enslaved African Americans escaped. What is their overall impression after reading Still's description?

Activity 2   **Mapping—Setting for Underground Railroad**

Use the Reynold's Political Map of the United States (3.13.2) and the map published by the National Park Service (Item 3.13.B) for reference. Students can create a Big Map as a class, in small groups, or individually. The goal is for everyone to have a sound geographic context before reading additional documents. On an outline map (Item 3.13.C), identify slave states and states where slavery was illegal. Identify major rivers that run north-south or that flow between "slave" and "free" states. Also note mountain ranges that run north-south. Mark the major escape routes. As students read additional primary source documents in this and the fugitive slave law lesson, they should continue to add information to their maps.

Activity 3   **Reading and Discussion—Ways to Freedom**

Document 3.13.3 includes three accounts of how slaves escaped and letters the freemen wrote to William Still sometime later.

- ❖ What do you learn from reading these accounts?
- ❖ Consider the reasons why and the ways that African Americans ran from slavery.
- ❖ What can you tell from the freemen's letters?
- ❖ Identify their destinations on your maps.
- ❖ Why might Jeremiah Colburn and Solomon Brown be using an alias, but not Freeland?
- ❖ What do you learn about William Still from his writing?

Activity 4   **Discussion—Captain F., Underground Railroad Conductor**

Still's account of "Captain F. and the Mayor of Norfolk" (3.13.4) may best be read aloud. The class should then address these questions:

- ❖ Who was Captain F.?
- ❖ Describe his appearance, behavior, and beliefs.
- ❖ What happened at the wharf in Norfolk?
- ❖ Does it sound legal? Was it? How can you find out?
- ❖ What risks did Captain F. face when he took on runaways?
- ❖ Where do you think he may have hidden twenty-one people on his schooner?

Activity 5   **Analysis of Treasurer's Account**

Using pages 18, 19, 30, and 37 of the Treasurer's Account Book (3.13.5A–E), students can answer the following questions:

- ❖ Identify the various ways the Vigilance Committee used donations.

❖ Who seem to be the primary contributors to the Vigilance Committee?

❖ Why is Samuel Clemens listed on page 30 of the account book?

Have students conduct further research to learn more about the activities of Boston's Vigilance Committee and Vigilance Committees in other northern cities.

Mapping the Source of Contributions

Activity 6

Using a map of Massachusetts (3.13.D) and a reference map from an atlas, have students circle the towns from which contributions came to the Vigilance Committee. How widespread was the area? How would contributors have known about the Vigilance Committee and its needs?

Analysis of *The Liberator* Article

Activity 7

Students should read "Rev. John Cross, of Illinois" (3.13.6). Then have them address the following points:

❖ Write a short summary explaining what happened to the Rev. Cross.

❖ What is this document really saying? How does the second half help explain the first?

❖ Who might Lundy and Clarkson have been?

❖ What place are they talking about? Where is the Patriarchal Dominion? Is this a real place? Is Libertyville, Upper Canada, a real place?

❖ Is this a joke or is it serious? Is this a coded message?

❖ If, as the article states, the "Liberty Line" was printed as a handbill, where would it have been distributed? How effective might the handbill have been?

❖ Why is contextual information important to understanding news stories and history? What more would we need to know to fully understand this short piece?

Reading and Discussion—John Parker's Autobiography

Activity 8

The class can be divided in half, each group responsible for one of the two Parker accounts (3.13.7 and 3.13.8). After reading the document, the group should summarize the content for the rest of the class. Discuss:

❖ How did individuals get word about fugitives in need of help?

❖ List the individuals who provided help.

❖ What risks did these individuals face?

❖ Describe the type of personality who might engage in this work.

❖ How does Parker's writing differ from Still's?

Activity 9   **Documents—The Editing Process**

John Parker's autobiography was first transcribed from a barely legible original manuscript by journalist Frank Moody Gregg in the 1880s. Stuart Seely Sprague used the same original manuscript to prepare the book published in 1996. Compare documents 3.13.7 and 3.13.8. When someone like Gregg or Sprague works with an original document, they make decisions about how to present it. Two or three students should work on each paragraph of Document 3.13.8. Each student must work independently rather than collaborate with other students working with the same paragraph. Edit the paragraph, fixing the problems so it reads smoothly. Students may want to work with the original manuscript from the Duke University website *(www.duke.edu/~njb2/history391/parker/New.html)*. Now compare the versions. Are they identical? What does this tell you about any document that has been edited, especially if the original is of poor quality?

Activity 10   **Creative Extensions—Ways to Freedom**

Students can use the narratives in this lesson or find the runaway stories of Harriet Tubman, Ellen and William Craft, Lewis Hayden, Frederick Douglass, and others to write and illustrate a book telling the tale for younger readers. Alternatively, students can create a collage or a poster that captures the experience of one of the fugitive slaves.

Music Connection

→❊←

"Steal Away" (on the accompanying CD-ROM) is one of many songs with double meaning. It speaks of going to heaven upon death but at the same time encourages enslaved people to "steal away" to freedom on earth. The words of "Gospel Train" also speak directly to the Underground Railroad movement.

Get on board, little children
Get on board, little children
Get on board, little children,
There's room for many a more.

The gospel train's a-comin',
I hear it just at hand,_

I hear the car wheels mov-in'
An' rumb-lin' tro the land.

Get on board, little children,
Get on board, little children,
Get on board, little children,
There's room for many a more.

The fare is cheap, an' all can go,
The rich an' poor are there,_
No second class a-board this train,
No diff'-rence in the fare.

Get on board, little children,
Get on board, little children,
Get on board, little children,
There's room for many a more.

Further Student and Teacher Resources

Blockson, Charles L. *The Underground Railroad: Dramatic First Hand Accounts of Daring Escapes to Freedom*. New York: Prentice Hall, 1987.

Brown, Henry. *The Narrative of the Life of Henry Box Brown*. Forward by Henry Louis Gates, Jr. Introduction by Richard Newman. New York: Oxford University Press, 2002.

Fradin, Brindell. *Bound for the North Star: True Stories of Fugitive Slaves*. New York: Clarion, 2000.

Hagedorn, Ann. *Beyond the River, the Untold Story of the Heroes of the Underground Railroad*. New York: Simon and Schuster, 2002.

Hamilton, Virginia. *Many Thousand Gone: African Americans from Slavery to Freedom*. New York: Knopf, 1993.

Hansen, Ellen, ed. *The Underground Railroad: Life on the Road to Freedom*. Lowell, MA: Discovery Enterprises, 1993.

Hansen, Joyce, and Gary McGowan. *Freedom Roads: Searching for the Underground Railroad*. Chicago: Cricket Books, 2003.

Haskins, Jim. *Get on Board: The Story of the Underground Railroad*. New York: Scholastic, 1993.

Jeffrey, Julie Roy. *The Great Silent Army of Abolitionism*. Chapel Hill: The University of North Carolina Press, 1998.

Ringgold, Faith. *Aunt Harriet's Underground Railroad in the Sky*. New York: Crown, 1992.

Sprague, Stuart Seely, ed. *His Promised Land: The Autobiography of John P. Parker, Former Slave and Conductor on the Underground Railroad*. New York: W. W. Norton & Company, 1998.

Tobin, Jacqueline. *Hidden in Plain View: A Secret Story of Quilts and the Underground Railroad*. New York: Doubleday, 1999.

"Underground Railroad." *Footsteps*. 5:1 (January/February 2003).

"The Underground Railroad and the Antislavery Movement." *Cobblestone*. 24:2 (February 2003)

The Underground Railroad. Washington, DC: U.S. Department of the Interior, 1998. The official National Park Service Handbook.

Websites

The Autobiography of John Parker. Duke University, Durham, NC
www.duke.edu/~njb2/history391/parker/New.html

Harriet, the Moses of her People, electronic edition; documenting the American South. University of North Carolina, Chapel Hill, NC
http://docsouth.unc.edu/harriet/harriet.html

Links to Underground Railroad Sites
www.undergroundrr.com/index2.html
In addition to the specific sites listed here, many states provide their own specific information, for example:
Ohio: www.ohioundergroundrailroad.org
New Jersey: www.historiccamdencounty.com/ccnews16.shtml
Vermont: www.vermonthistory.org/educate/ugrr.htm
New York: www.nyhistory.com/ugrr/
Wisconsin: www.wlhn.org/wnf/about.htm

National Underground Railroad Freedom Center, Cincinnati, OH
www.freedomcenter.org
The Underground Railroad will be the subject of one exhibit at the Freedom Center, due to open in the summer of 2004. The website offers resources for educators and students.

National Underground Railroad Network to Freedom. National Park Service, Washington, DC
www.cr.nps.gov/ugrr
The National Park Service maintains an extensive website of materials on and about the Underground Railroad, including information about specific sites
www.cr.nps.gov/nr/travel/underground/states.htm, *teacher resources, and the Underground Railroad Special Resource Study*
www.nps.gov/undergroundrr/contents.htm

The Underground Railroad. The History Channel
www.historychannel.com/exhibits/undergroundrr/

The Underground Railroad. National Geographic Society, Washington, DC
www.nationalgeographic.com/railroad

William Still Underground Railroad Foundation
www.undergroundrr.com
www.undergroundrr.com/index2.html

Video

The Underground Railroad. Videocassette. The History Channel, A&E Television, 1999.

Contemporary Connections

⤝✖⤞

Legacy of the Underground Railroad

In the fall of 1990, Congress enacted a law requiring the Interior Department to initiate a study of the Underground Railroad. An advisory group of historians of African American history, museum staff, and those with experience in public programming came together to work with the National Park Service on this initiative. By 1995, a report was prepared and, in 1998, Congress passed the National Underground Railroad Network to Freedom Act. A handbook has been published with many resources for classroom use. The National Park Service has created a network of UGRR sites around the country with regional offices for each geographic area. "The National Park Service is implementing a national UGRR program to coordinate preservation and education efforts nationwide and integrate local historical places, museums, and interpretive programs associated with the UGRR into a mosaic of community, regional, and national stories" (*www.cr.nps.gov/ugrr*). The Network to Freedom database is accessible to the general public.

Also scheduled to open in 2004 in Cincinnati, Ohio, is the National Underground Railroad Freedom Center. The Center currently has a website and invites ideas and donations for this ambitious project. The Executive Director is Spencer Crew, formerly the director of the National Museum of American History of the Smithsonian Institution in Washington, D.C. For more information see *www.undergroundrailroad.org*.

Ask students to research Underground Railroad sites in the community. Are they on the national list? Students might respond to the request for ideas found on the NURR Freedom Center website.

Still Connected

In June 2003, the William Still Underground Railroad Foundation, which includes descendants of William Still, sponsored a Family Reunion Festival in Philadelphia. Descendants of the men and women Still helped to freedom, descendants of UGRR conductors, such as Harriet Tubman, historians, and educators gathered for three days to contribute oral history stories, participate in workshops, tour UGRR sites in the city, and participate in a service at the Mother Bethel A. M. E Church. For information on the work of the foundation, including their efforts to have a statue of William Still placed in Independence National Historical Park, visit *www.undergroundrr.com*.

Primary Source Materials
for Lesson 13

3.13.1

Excerpt from the Preface to *The Underground Railroad*
by William Still, 1873

William Still was born in New Jersey in 1821 to parents who had gained their own freedom, one by escaping and the other through self-purchase. In 1844, Still moved to Philadelphia and quickly taught himself to read and write. He joined the Philadelphia Vigilance Committee. By 1851 he was chairman of the Pennsylvania Abolition Society. For fourteen years he worked with the Underground Railroad and aided hundreds of fugitive slaves. He interviewed them while they sought refuge in Philadelphia and published his material in book form in 1873.

In these Records will be found interesting narratives of the escapes of many men, women and children, from the prisonhouse of bondage; from cities and plantations; from rice swamps and cotton fields; from kitchens and mechanic shops; from Border States and Gulf States; from cruel masters and mild masters;—some guided by the north star alone, penniless, braving the perils of land and sea, eluding the keen scent of the blood-hound as well as the more dangerous pursuit of the savage slave-hunter; some from secluded dens and caves of the earth, where for months and years they had been hidden away waiting for the chance to escape from mountains and swamps, where indescribable suffering from hunger and other privations had patiently been endured. Occasionally fugitives came in boxes and chests, and not infrequently some were secreted in steamers and vessels, and in some instances journeyed hundreds of miles in skiffs. Men disguised in female attire and women dressed in the garb of men have under very trying circumstances triumphed in thus making their way to freedom. . . .

The full text of Document 3.13.1 is available on the CD-ROM.

3.13.2

Reynold's Political Map of the United States, 1856

Issued during the presidential election campaign of 1856, this map compares statistics on free and slave states.

Library of Congress

3.13.3

Excerpts (part 1) from *The Underground Railroad* by William Still, 1873

SOLOMON BROWN
Arrived per *City of Richmond*

This candidate for Canada managed to secure a private berth on the steamship *City of Richmond*. He was thus enabled to leave his old mistress, Mary A. Ely, in Norfolk, the place of her abode, and the field of his servitude. Solomon was only twenty-two years of age, rather under the medium size, dark color, and of much natural ability.

He viewed Slavery as a great hardship, and for a length of time had been watching for an opportunity to free himself. He had been in the habit of hiring his time of his mistress, for which he paid ten dollars a month. This amount failed to satisfy the mistress, as she was inclined to sell him to North Carolina, where Slave stock, at that time, was commanding high prices. The idea of North Carolina and a new master made Solomon rather nervous, and he was thereby prompted to escape. On reaching the Committee he manifested very high appreciation of the attention paid him, and after duly resting for a day, he was sent on his way rejoicing. Seven days after leaving Philadelphia, he wrote back from Canada as follows:

St. Catherines, Feb 20th, 1854.

Mr. Still—Dear Sir:—It is with great pleasure that I have to inform you, that I have arrived safe in a land of freedom. Thanks to kind friends that helped me here. Thank God that I am treading on free soil. I expect to go to work tomorrow in a steam factory. I would like to have you, if it is not too much trouble, see Mr. Minhett, the steward on the boat that I came out on, when he gets to Norfolk, to go to the place where my clothes are, and bring them to you, and you direct them to the care of Rev. Hiram Wilson, St. Catherines, Niagara District, Canada West, by rail-road via Suspension Bridge. You mentioned if I saw Mr. Foreman, I was to deliver a message— he is not here. I saw two yesterday in church, from Norfolk, that I had known there. You will send my name, James Henry, as you knew me by that name; direct my things to James Henry. My love to your wife and children.

The full text of Document 3.13.3 is available on the CD-ROM.

3.13.4

Excerpt (part 2) from *The Underground Railroad* by William Still, 1873

The way is now clear to present Captain F. with his schooner lying at the wharf in Norfolk, loading with wheat, and at the same time with twenty-one fugitives secreted therein. While the boat was thus lying at her mooring, the rumor was flying all over town that a number or slaves had escaped, which created a general excitement a degree less, perhaps, than if the citizens had been visited by an earthquake. The mayor of the city with a posse of officers with axes and long spears repaired to Captain F.'s boat. The fearless commander received his Honor very coolly, and as gracefully as the circumstances would admit. The mayor gave him to understand who he was, and by what authority he appeared on the boat, and what he meant to do. "Very well," replied Captain F., "here I am and this is my boat, go ahead and search." . . .

The full text of Document 3.13.4 is available on the CD-ROM.

<u>3.13.5</u>

The Boston Vigilance Committee, Treasurers Account,
excerpts from 1851 and 1854

18

The Vigilance Committee Dr.

1851					
April		Am't bro't forward		653	59
"	20	James Scott fugitive passage to Canada		11	
"	"	Prentiss & Sawyer Printing 500 Billets *Brown for Thos. Sims*		3	
"	"	Austin Bearse Sundries for the Committee		10	42
"	24	Benj. F Roberts Printing 1000 Placards & Posting *caution to Colored People*		6	50
"	26	Rev Nath Colver expenses in Canada for Committee		21	—
"	28	Austin Bearse boat in the Harbor		7	
"	"	Joseph K Hayes use of Tremont Temple *Apr 8 & 11th*		50	
"	"	Lewis E Caswell for sending a wounded Fugitive *John Hatten to Canada* {		15	
"	30	John M Spear Horse & chaise case of Thos. Sims		10	
May	1	George Latimer 6 days watching Mr. Caphart		9	
"	3	I B Smith for Joseph Russetts fare to Canada		7	50
"	"	Lewis E Caswell passage of 3 Fugitives to Canada H & Sons J Brown & Wife }		21	7
"	15	Dr. M P Hanson assisting Andrew J Burton & family		20	
"	16	Austin Bearse fare of Sam Ward to Plymouth		7	72
"	"	F W Bird rent of Committee room *& sundries*		25	
"	"	Wm C Nell services for Johnson, Truett, Barnard & *Eliz.th Dorsey*		1	32
"	20	Loring Moody expenses to Fall River		5	
"	21	Amos Baker use of Chapman Hall		12	50
"	24	Prentiss & Sawyer Printing Petitions &c		19	
"	26	Lewis Hayden clothes for S Ward fugitive		7	87
"	"	Austin Bearse services rendered to the Committee		60	
"	"	Samuel May Jr passage to Canada of Priscilla Hatton		10	
June	2	Wm R Stacy use of Washingtonian Hall		10	
"	3	Austin Bearse services		4	25
"		also for aid to Samuel Jones a fugitive {		10	
"	11	Lewis E Caswell for Hatton & Ringle *fugitives*		17	
		Am't carried forward		1034	84

Bostonian Society

The cover and pages 19, 30, and 37 are available on the CD-ROM.

<u>3.13.6</u>

"Rev. John Cross, of Illinois," *The Liberator,* August 23, 1844

Rev. John Cross, of Illinois.

This gentleman was arrested, indicted and imprisoned in Knox county jail, charged with having assisted a runaway slave—having, in fact, given shelter and food to a poor old negro woman. The jailor put him into the 'inner prison'—the judge appeared anxious to do justice to so deserving a criminal—the attorney-general moved a continuance of the case till the next term, as the material witness was absent, and the Court admitted the motion. But Mr. Cross, wishing to come to trial, agreed to admit all this witness would testify. This was a stumper. The prosecutors made as graceful a retreat as the dignity of their position would admit, and Mr. Cross was discharged without the form of a trial. Mr. Cross, as soon as out of jail, published a flaring handbill, headed with a large engraving, representing an under-ground rail-road, with the train just plunging under the earth, loaded with passengers, while in the corner is seen a heavy wagon, with kidnappers stowed in bulk, and bound 'for Texas.'

Appended to this is the following notice:

LIBERTY LINE
New Arrangement—Night and Day

The improved and splendid locomotives, Clarkson and Lundy, with their trains fitted up in the best style of accommodation for passengers will run their regular trips during the present season, between the borders of the Patriarchal Dominion and Libertyville, Upper Canada. Gentlemen or ladies who may wish to improve their health or circumstances by a northern tour, are respectfully invited to give us their patronage.

SEATS FREE, irrespective of color.

Necessary clothing furnished gratuitously to such as have 'fallen among thieves.' 'Hide the outcasts—let the oppressed go free.'—Bible

For seats, apply to any of the trap doors, or to the conductor of the train.

J. CROSS, Proprietor

3.13.7

Excerpt 1 from *His Promised Land: The Autobiography of John P. Parker, Former Slave and Conductor on the Underground Railroad*

Born into slavery in Norfolk, Virginia, John Parker bought his freedom in 1845 with money he had earned from his apprenticeship. He moved to southern Ohio and began a successful business. Parker was one of only a few blacks to obtain patents in the United States before 1900, for a screw for tobacco presses, the first in 1884, the second a year later. Though busy with his business, Parker was very active in the Underground Railroad.

Amidst this commercial activity [in Ripley, Ohio] lived and moved the little group of old-time abolitionists. They were by name Dr. Alexander Campbell, Rev. John Rankin, Theodore, Tom, and Eli Collins, Tom McCague, Dr. Beasley, [and] Rev. James Gilliland. The undoubted leader was Rev. John Rankin.

While the businessmen were not abolitionists, they were antislavery. But the town itself was proslavery as well as the country around it. In fact, the country was so antagonistic to abolitionism at this time, we could only take the fugitives out of town and through the country along definite and limited routes.

There was also very active a certain group of men who made a living by capturing the runaway slaves and returning them to their masters. These men were on watch day and night along the riverbank the year round. While they captured quite a few it was remarkable how many slaves we got through the line successfully. The feeling grew so tense Rev. John Rankin and his followers left the Presbyterian church forming a new congregation who were given over to the antislavery movement. . . .

After the passage of the Fugitive Slave Law [in 1850], the attitude of the town's people grew even more critical of our group. We had to be more secretive than ever, for it meant confiscation of property, a fine, and [a] jail sentence. . . .

The full text of Document 3.13.7 is available on the CD-ROM.

3.13.8

Excerpt 2 from *His Promised Land: The Autobiography of John P. Parker, Former Slave and Conductor on the Underground Railroad*

John Parker's autobiography was first transcribed by journalist Frank Moody Gregg in the 1880s. Parker's original manuscript is barely legible. Excerpt 2 is a print out of the original manuscript with no editorial changes.

One of the most serious encounters, which involved practically every friend of the slave in Ripley, came out of a clear sky figuratively speaking, but actually out of a black sky. It was thus wise. One of the colored freemen came knocking at my door—very—so much excited he could hardly talk. What I got out of him was that there [were] eight run aways—on the—on the Kentucky side immediately opposite the town.—How he knew—He had been scouting along the shore and through sheer luck had come on to the crowd. He was perfectly willing to take on as many as his skiff would hold, but the runaways could not or would not agree as to who should go first.—The—As the night was passing and the clamor of the crowd was growing louder he determined to—come to—go to Rev John Rankin,—the—an old abolition presbyterian minister who lived on the hill above the town. He sent the man to me. By this time is was so near day break I decided to hold a conference with Tom Collins as what was best to be done in this desperate situation. . . .

The full text of Document 3.13.8 is available on the CD-ROM.

The Fugitive Slave Act of 1850

As a result of the Mexican War, the United States had acquired large tracts of land in the west, and controversy erupted over whether the new states would permit slavery. The Compromise of 1850 admitted California to the union as a free state and abolished the slave trade in the District of Columbia. New Mexico and Utah territories were to decide the issue for themselves upon admission to the Union. In addition, Congress voted to significantly tighten the Fugitive Slave Act, first passed in 1793.

The Fugitive Slave Act of 1850, part of this larger compromise, was intended to placate slave states and antislavery activists alike. In hindsight, the compromise appears as an attempt to delay the looming national crisis over the enslavement of more than two million African Americans. The compromise, the Fugitive Slave Act in particular, actually deepened the divisions separating North from South and significantly increased abolitionist protest.

The Fugitive Slave Act of 1850 stipulated that new federal commissioners, rather than established state courts of law, would hear fugitive slave cases. Should a commissioner decide in favor of the slave-catcher's claim, he received $10 in payment. If the African American was released, on the other hand, the payment was $5. The law also required residents in free states to aid in the capture of runaways.

Furthermore, those who assisted escaping African Americans committed a federal crime. They risked huge fines of $1,000, a jail sentence, and additional civil penalties. For enslaved African Americans, the law made escape even more perilous and the journey to freedom far longer. No longer were northern states a relatively safe haven. Now fugitives needed to reach Canada.

White bounty hunters initiated raids into northern states. They didn't limit their captures to fugitives; free black people were also at risk of being kidnapped into slavery. Harriet Jacobs, an escaped slave and author of *Incidents in the Life of a Slave Girl*, called the law the "beginning of a reign of terror to the colored population."

Opponents of the Fugitive Slave Act of 1850 claimed it violated personal liberties and constitutional guarantees and threatened state rights. Protests began immediately. Free black people in several northern cities gathered in Colored Conventions. In October 1850, a meeting of free African Americans in Philadelphia wrote the following resolution:

> [We] deem this law so wicked, so **atrocious**, so utterly at variance with the principles of the Constitution; so **subversive** of the objects of the law, the protection of the lives, liberty, and property of the governed; so **repugnant** to the highest attributes of God, justice, and mercy; and so horribly cruel . . . that we deem it our sacred duty . . . to resist this law at any cost.

White abolitionists such as Ralph Waldo Emerson echoed this sentiment. In 1851, he wrote in his journal: "And this filthy enactment was made in the 19th Century, by people who could read and write. I will not obey it, by God."

Contributions to Vigilance Committees increased. More white people joined the Underground Railroad. Protests quickly went beyond words when African Americans and white sympathizers defied the law. In 1851, they burst through the door of a Boston courthouse and carried out fugitive slave Shadrach Minkins. Within hours, he was out of the city and on his way to Canada. This determined response was repeated in cities throughout the North. Not all rescues of captured fugitives were successful, and in many cases activists were arrested. The line between civil disobedience and civil disorder became increasingly blurred.

Organizing Idea

The Fugitive Slave Act that was part of the Compromise of 1850 galvanized antislavery sentiment throughout the North.

Student Objectives

Students will:

- ❖ be able to explain key provisions of the Fugitive Slave Act of 1850
- ❖ understand the risks activists took and the consequences some faced
- ❖ understand why the Fugitive Slave Act became pivotal in the struggle to abolish slavery
- ❖ recognize how the Act endangered the lives of all African Americans

Key Questions

- ❖ What is civil disobedience?
- ❖ Why did the Fugitive Slave Act of 1850 enrage many Northerners?
- ❖ Why did the work of slave-catchers result in increased antislavery activity?
- ❖ How did the Act increase fear among all African Americans?

Primary Source Materials

DOCUMENT 3.14.1: Excerpts from the Fugitive Slave Act of 1350

DOCUMENT 3.14.2: "High-Handed Outrage," *Daily Morning Advocate,* Racine, Wisconsin, March 13, 1854

DOCUMENT 3.14.3: "Great Excitement! Arrest of Fugitive Slave!" *Milwaukee Daily Sentinel,* March 13, 1854

DOCUMENT 3.14.4: Letter from Charles Sumner to Byron Paine, August 8, 1854

DOCUMENT 3.14.5: Satirical illustration in opposition to the Fugitive Slave Act, 1851

DOCUMENT 3.14.6: Broadside published in Boston, Massachusetts, 1851

DOCUMENT 3.14.7: "Anthony Burns" broadside, Boston, Massachusetts, 1855

DOCUMENT 3.14.8: Excerpt from "The Oberlin-Wellington Rescue," *New Englander and Yale Review,* August 1859

DOCUMENT 3.14.9: Excerpt from Grand Jury indictment of Simeon Bushnell, November 1858

DOCUMENT 3.14.10: Excerpts from testimony of slave-catcher Anderson Jennings at the trial of Simeon Bushnell, April 1859

DOCUMENT 3.14.11: Excerpts from Charles Langston's address to the court prior to sentencing, May 1859

Supplementary Materials

ITEM 3.14.A: Additional vocabulary lists for primary sources

Vocabulary

affidavit	*nolo contendere*	prosecution	writ of *habeas*
indict	Old Dominion	warrant	*corpus*
marshal	prejudiced		

Student Activities

Definition of Civil Disobedience

Activity 1

As a class, write a definition of "civil disobedience." It should be prominently displayed in the classroom, so that students can refer to it as they reflect on the events described in this and Lesson 16 on John Brown. Students can refer back to Martin Luther King's "Letter from a Birmingham Jail" (3.3.7) for his explanation of civil disobedience.

After completing Activities 2–5, have students reconsider their initial definition of civil disobedience. Do the rescues documented here fit their definition? Ask students to consider whether civil disobedience includes the use of violence and efforts by those who defy the law to escape detection and punishment. Compare these instances with civil disobedience as defined and practiced by Henry David Thoreau, Mohandas Gandhi, and Martin Luther King Jr.

Activity 2   Analysis of Fugitive Slave Act

The language in the Fugitive Slave Act (3.14.1) is very formal. Teachers may choose to read the selected sections aloud and discuss the meaning sentence by sentence, or critical sentences can be underlined for students in advance. In small groups and later as a class, students need to identify key aspects of the law. These can be paraphrased and then posted in the classroom for future reference.

Activity 3   Reading, Discussion and Creative Extensions—The Capture and Rescue of Joshua Glover

Students should read the contemporary accounts of Joshua Glover's capture and rescue (3.14.2 and 3.14.3) and discuss what happened. What else would they like to know about this event? How can they find out? Students should respond to the event with a piece of art—a sculpture, a collage, a sketch or painting, or a broadside. The work should reflect the events of March 1854 and what the student thinks and feels about what occurred.

Activity 4   Analysis, Discussion and Essay Writing—Fanning the Flames of Outrage

Students should read the letter from Charles Sumner (3.14.4). To what material does Sumner refer, and how would that have been useful in communications between activists? Next, analyze carefully the three images (3.14.5, 3.14.6, and 3.14.7). Identify words and phrases used in the letter and images that reflect the depth of anger felt by antislavery activists. How were the images used? Who saw them and where? What technology was available to mid-nineteenth century activists? Discuss the ways abolitionists spread their message.

Have students write a one-page essay expressing their thoughts about the Fugitive Slave Act or the Glover or Burns captures. The intent is to sway others to agree with their point of view. They should pay special attention to the words they choose. Listen to several essays read out loud. Which are the most convincing? Why? (*Note:* Teachers may wish to refer to Lesson 7 for further information on Charles Sumner and Robert Morris.)

Activity 5   The Oberlin-Wellington Rescue—Repercussions

The class can be divided into four groups, each responsible for one document (3.14.8–3.14.11). The group should answer the questions pertaining to the assigned document and then prepare a short summary to share with the class.

Document 3.14.8 "The Oberlin-Wellington Rescue"

❖ When did the rescue take place?

❖ Where and when was this account published? What does that tell you?

❖ What happened in Oberlin and then in Wellington?

❖ Who was involved and approximately how many people participated in the rescue?

❖ How did others in the state react?

Document 3.14.9 Indictment of Simeon Bushnell

❖ Define "indictment."

❖ Identify John, Anderson Jennings, John G. Bacon, and Simeon Bushnell.

❖ What law is Simeon Bushnell accused of breaking? How?

❖ How many people were involved in the rescue?

Document 3.14.10 Testimony of Anderson Jennings at the Trial of Simeon Bushnell

❖ Who is Anderson Jennings and what is his relationship to fugitive slave John Price?

❖ Where, specifically, did the rescue take place?

❖ How many people were in the crowd outside?

❖ What happened in Wellington, according to Anderson Jennings?

❖ What is your impression of Jennings? Identify the words and phrases in his testimony that inform your opinion.

Document 3.14.11 Charles Langston's Address to the Court Prior to Sentencing

❖ According to Langston, what was he trying to do in Wellington?

❖ Why should he not be sentenced?

❖ What does Langston say about the rights of black men in the United States?

❖ Paraphrase what Langston says in the final paragraph.

❖ Extract from Langston's speech the statements you consider most powerful, and include them in your presentation to the class.

Music Connection
✠

It is impossible to date accurately many of the songs that enslaved African Americans created. The early protest song "Many Thousand Gone" (available on accompanying CD-ROM) endures as a signature song of resistance. In this song African Americans no longer used any type of code. Emphatically, they sang, "No more auction block for me, No more, No more." Students should discuss whether the words refer to the anticipated end to slavery or to pending escape. Notice what the list includes and how the song reflects on the quality of life as a slave.

Activity 6   **Research—Beyond Each Event**

The cases introduced in this lesson extended beyond the fugitive slave being rescued or, in the case of Anthony Burns, being returned to slavery. Working in pairs, students can learn more about the impact of the Fugitive Slave Act by conducting further research on the people involved and events that followed. Each team can summarize its findings in a one-page paper or a broadside, such as the one of Anthony Burns. The papers can then be compiled into a booklet that every member of the class receives and reads before the class reflects on the lesson as a whole.

Possible topics to research include: trials of Simeon Bushnell and Charles Langston (Ohio); jailing of the rescuers (Ohio); life of John Mercer Langston (Oberlin, Ohio); connections between the Oberlin rescuers and John Brown; Robert Morris (Boston, Mass.); Anthony Burns (Boston, Mass); the Jerry Rescue (Syracuse, N.Y.); the Christiana Riot (Penn.); Sherman M. Booth (Wis.); Byron Paine (Wis.); Margaret Garner (Cincinnati); legal challenges in Wisconsin; ways in which opponents spread the word; Lewis Hayden (Boston, Mass.).

Further Student and Teacher Resources

Brandt, Nat. *The Town that Started the Civil War.* Syracuse, NY: Syracuse University Press, 1990.

Collison, Gary. *Shadrach Minkins.* Cambridge, MA: Harvard University, 1997.

Paulson, Timothy J. *Days of Sorrow, Years of Glory, 1831–1850 : From the Nat Turner Revolt to the Fugitive Slave Law.* New York: Chelsea House, 1994.

Von Frank, Albert. *The Trials of Anthony Burns.* Cambridge, MA: Harvard University Press, 1998.

Websites

The Compromise of 1850. CongressLink
www.congresslink.org/lessonplans//CK1850.html

Eric Foner on the Fugitive Slave Act. *Africans in America,* Part 4, PBS Online, WGBH, Boston, MA
www.pbs.org/wgbh/aia/part4/4i3094.html

Equality before the Law speech by Charles Sumner, African American Pamphlet Collection, American Memory Project, Library of Congress, Washington, DC
http://memory.loc.gov/cgibin/query/r?ammem/rbaapc:@field(DOCID+@lit(rbaapc28400div1))

The Fugitive Slave Act of 1850. The Avalon Project at Yale Law School, New Haven, CT
www.yale.edu/lawweb/avalon/fugitive.htm

Contemporary Connection

✦⧓✦

Protesting Injustice Today

Civil disobedience to protest laws and government actions that people feel are unjust occurs in the United States today. In response to the 2003 war in Iraq there were many examples of civil disobedience. People were arrested at protests from Washington, D.C., to Washington State because they blocked intersections, protested without a permit, or broke through police lines. In the name of peace and a desire to end what they believed to be an unjust war, protesters chained themselves together or staged "die-ins," where they simulated corpses and blocked traffic. These people risked fines and perhaps even jail time because they believed so strongly in their cause. Like the opponents of the Fugitive Slave Act, they consciously broke laws in order to support their convictions and beliefs. Compare these protests, which followed Martin Luther King Jr.'s definition of nonviolent action, with the rescue of fugitive slaves in the 1850s. Are there any protests today that more closely resemble the physical rescue of slaves?

Fugitive Slave Law. Long Road to Justice, Boston, MA
www.atsweb.neu.edu/longroad/01slavery/fsl.htm

John Mercer Langston and Oberlin's Antebellum African American Heritage. Oberlin College Archives, Oberlin, OH
www.oberlin.edu/external/EOG/Langston/Cheek2.html

The Life of Justice Byron Paine. Wisconsin Lawyer, State Bar of Wisconsin
www.wisbar.org/wislawmag/2002/11/ranney.html

Ripon's Booth War, 1860: Aftermath of the Fugitive Slave Act in Wisconsin. Bob Schuster, Monona, WI
www.wlhn.org/topics/boothwar/milwaukee_news.htm

Runaway Slave in Oberlin: A Short Middle School Reading Play Based on a True Story of Civil Disobedience. Oberlin College, Oberlin, OH
www.oberlin.edu/external/EOG/OWRescuePlay/play.html

Sample Lesson: Trial Simulation of Simeon Bushnell for Violation of the Fugitive Slave Act of 1850. Johns Hopkins University, Baltimore, MD
www.jhu.edu/gifted/teaching/lphumanities.html

Samuel J. May Anti-Slavery Collection. Cornell University Library Digital Collections, Ithaca, NY
http://cdl.library.cornell.edu

Primary Source Materials for Lesson 14

3.14.1

Excerpts from the Fugitive Slave Act of 1850

SEC. 7. And be it further enacted, That any person who shall knowingly and willingly obstruct, hinder, or prevent such claimant, his agent or attorney, or any person or persons lawfully assisting him, her, or them, from arresting such a fugitive from service or labor, either with or without process as aforesaid, or shall rescue, or attempt to rescue, such fugitive from service or labor, from the custody of such claimant, his or her agent or attorney, or other person or persons lawfully assisting as aforesaid, when so arrested, pursuant to the authority herein given and declared; or shall aid, abet, or assist such person so owing service or labor as aforesaid, directly or indirectly, to escape from such claimant, his agent or attorney, or other person or persons legally authorized as aforesaid; or shall harbor or conceal such fugitive, so as to prevent the discovery and arrest of such person, after notice or knowledge of the fact that such person was a fugitive from service or labor as aforesaid, shall, for either of said offences, be subject to a fine not exceeding one thousand dollars, and imprisonment not exceeding six months, by indictment and conviction before the District Court of the United States. . .

The full text of Document 3.14.1 is available on the CD-ROM.

3.14.2

"High-Handed Outrage," *Daily Morning Advocate,* Racine, Wisconsin, March 13, 1854

High-Handed Outrage
Attempt to Kidnap A Citizen of Racine by Slave-Catchers!

On Thursday two men came to Glover's house and endeavored to gain admittance, but finding the door locked, went away. This awakened suspicions and a woman, whom it was supposed they were after, left the premises. Just before dark on Friday evening, Chas. Cotton, Kearney, Houghton, the slave-owner, and four others, started from the city with two teams, and drove to within twenty rods of Glover's house, where they left the wagons and proceeded on foot.—Within the house were Glover, Nelson Turner, and William Alby, all colored, seated at a table playing cards. When the knock was heard at the door Glover cried out "don't open it till we know who they are;" but Turner immediately went to the door and unbolted it. Kearney rushed into the room, with a bludgeon, dealing Glover a blow upon the head, which brought him down. A desperate struggle ensued—three men were unable to put irons upon Glover, and even when, with the help of the others, they had succeeded, he broke the manacles from his wrists. Alby fled. Turner was placed with out resistance in the wagon with Glover, and brought two miles towards the city when he got out. . . .

The full text of Document 3.14.2 is available on the CD-ROM.

3.14.3

"Great Excitement! Arrest of Fugitive Slave!" *Milwaukee Daily Sentinel,* March 13, 1854

Resolved, as citizens of Milwaukee, that every person has an indefensible right to a fair and impartial trial by jury on all questions involving personal liberty.

Resolved, That the Writ of *Habeas Corpus* is the great defense of Freedom, and that we demand for this prisoner, as well as for our own protection, that this Writ shall be obeyed.

Resolved, That we pledge ourselves to stand by this prisoner, and do our utmost to secure for him a fair and impartial Trial by Jury.

Soon after the resolutions had been read and passed, a Vigilance Committee of twenty-five was appointed to watch that the fugitive was not secretly taken away, or tried except in an open manner. We understand that the Committee was instructed to ring the bells, and call the city to their aid in case any attempt should be made to get the fugitive away from the jail. . . .

The full text of Document 3.14.3 is available on the CD-ROM.

3.14.4

Letter from Charles Sumner to Byron Paine, August 8, 1854

Byron Paine studied law with his father in Milwaukee, Wisconsin, and was admitted to the bar in 1854. His friend Sherman Booth, founder of the abolitionist paper Free Democrat, *was arrested and charged with organizing the protest rally that culminated with the rescue of Joshua Glover. Paine agreed to act as his lawyer. He applied to the Wisconsin Supreme Court for a writ to release Booth from federal custody. As Booth's counsel, Byron Paine was the first and only lawyer to successfully challenge the constitutionality of the Fugitive Slave Act. As a result, he catapulted to national attention. Among the letters of congratulations he received were ones from Wendell Phillips and Charles Sumner. With the latter, he carried on a correspondence for a number of years.*

Washington. 8th August '54

My Dear Sir: I was about to suggest to you to have the opinions of the court and the arguments of counsel in the Booth case collected and published in a pamphlet when I observed that there was a pamphlet containing the most valuable portions of them. Let me ask you to do me the favor of sending me a copy of the pamphlet to my address in Boston. I congratulate you my dear sir upon your magnificent effort which does honor not only to your state but to your country. The argument will live in the history of this controversy. God grant that Wisconsin may not fail to protect her own rights and the rights of her citizens in the emergency now before her. To her belongs the lead which Massachusetts should have taken. Believe me, my dear sir.

With high esteem
faithfully yours
Charles Sumner

3.14.5

Satirical illustration in opposition to the Fugitive Slave Act, 1851

The illustration captures the bitter antagonism between northern abolitionists and supporters of enforcement of the Fugitive Slave Act, in this case Secretary of State Daniel Webster. The print was probably produced in Boston.

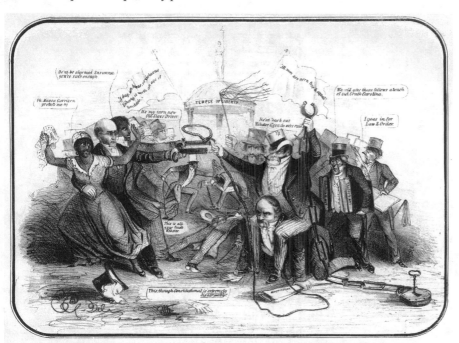

PRACTICAL ILLUSTRATION OF THE FUGITIVE SLAVE LAW.

Library of Congress

3.14.6

Broadside published in Boston, Massachusetts, 1851

Benjamin Roberts printed this broadside. In the late 1840s, Roberts had brought the anti-segregation case before the Massachusetts courts (see Lesson 7). The Boston Vigilance Committee made a record of payment to Roberts in its accounting book (see line item on Document 3.13.5b).

CAUTION!!

COLORED PEOPLE

OF BOSTON, ONE & ALL,

You are hereby respectfully CAUTIONED and advised, to avoid conversing with the

Watchmen and Police Officers of Boston,

For since the recent ORDER OF THE MAYOR & ALDERMEN, they are empowered to act as

KIDNAPPERS

AND

Slave Catchers,

And they have already been actually employed in KIDNAPPING, CATCHING, AND KEEPING SLAVES. Therefore, if you value your LIBERTY, and the *Welfare of the Fugitives* among you, *Shun* them in every possible manner, as so many *HOUNDS* on the track of the most unfortunate of your race.

Keep a Sharp Look Out for KIDNAPPERS, and have TOP EYE open.

APRIL 24, 1851.

3.14.7

"Anthony Burns" broadside, Boston, Massachusetts, 1855

Anthony Burns escaped from slavery in Virginia and made his way to Massachusetts. On May 24, 1854, about two months after he arrived in Boston, federal authorities arrested him. Boston activists were furious and stormed the federal court house. The attack ended with one U.S. Marshal dead and thirteen people arrested. The next week Anthony Burns was the subject of a hearing in which he was represented by Richard Henry Dana and African American attorney Robert Morris. Upholding the Fugitive Slave Act, the judge ruled in favor of Burns' owner. Outraged crowds lined the streets as Burns was taken to a ship that would return him to Virginia. It took 2,000 federal troops and cost $40,000 to get Burns "safely" on board. No other fugitive slave was ever again returned from Boston to the South.

Library of Congress

3.14.8

Excerpt from "The Oberlin-Wellington Rescue,"
New Englander and Yale Review,
August 1859

TIIE OBERLIN-WELLINGTON RESCUE.

The story is as follows. On the fifteenth day of September last, two slave catchers from Kentucky, having been for a few days previous at Oberlin, Ohio, induced a lad of about thirteen years of age, by the gift of twenty dollars, to entice a negro away from his residence in that town, under the false pretense of giving him work, to a place where they could conveniently seize him and carry him off. Some citizens of Oberlin, who had been aware of the presence of these southern slave hunters in their neighborhood, and who had been apprehensive that an attempt would be made to kidnap some of the colored persons living in that vicinity, hearing what had been done, followed after and overtaking the captors and the captive at Wellington, some ten miles distant, rescued the captive from those who had seized him, and he is now free. Thirty-seven of the citizens of Oberlin and Wellington were indicted, for a violation of the fugitive slave act of 1850, in the United States District Court for the northern district of Ohio. . . .

The full text of Document 3.14.8 is available on the CD-ROM.

3.14.9

Excerpt from Grand Jury indictment of
Simeon Bushnell, November 1858

Twenty-nine-year-old Simeon Bushnell worked as a clerk in an Oberlin bookstore. He was a known member of the Underground Railroad. Bushnell drove the "escape wagon," taking John Price from his captors in Wellington back to Oberlin.

The jurors aforesaid do further present and find that Simeon Bushnell, late of the District aforesaid, together with divers, to wit, two hundred other persons, to the jurors aforesaid unknown, heretofore, to wit, on the first day of October, in the year of our Lord one thousand eight hundred and fifty-eight, at the District aforesaid, and within the jurisdiction of this Court, with force and arms, unlawfully, knowingly, and willingly, did rescue the said negro slave called John, then and there being pursued and reclaimed, seized and arrested, and in the custody and control aforesaid, he, the said negro slave called John, being then and there a fugitive from, and held to service and labor as aforesaid, from the custody of the said Anderson Jennings, then and there the authorized agent of the said John G. Bacon as aforesaid, . .

The full text of Document 3.14.9 is available on the CD-ROM.

3.14.10

Excerpts from testimony of slave-catcher Anderson Jennings at the trial of Simeon Bushnell, April 1859

This was the first time I had seen [John Price] since I saw him in Kentucky before he was missing in January, 1856. Met him first in a room below stairs. Didn't like the looks of the room, because it was large, and there was folding doors, and there was no fastening to the door, and the people began to gather in with their guns. Found the landlord, and got him to give us a better room up stairs, in the top story. Lowe, Mitchell, and Davis were helping me, and went up stairs with us. Meant to take the nigger before United States Commissioner Chittenden, at Columbus. Didn't take him there, however. [Laughter.] Don't know the defendant. There was, I thought, as much as a thousand people around and in the house. [Great laughter.] A great many of them had arms;—rifles, shotguns, etc. Should think there were five hundred guns in the crowd. . . .

The full text of Document 3.14.10 is available on the CD-ROM.

3.14.11

Excerpts from Charles Langston's address to the court prior to sentencing, May 1859

Charles Langston, a teacher, was Oberlin Institute's first black student. Very active in the antislavery movement, he was the executive secretary of the Ohio State Anti-Slavery Society. Charles was visiting his brother, John Mercer Langston, when fugitive slave John Price was taken by slave-catchers. Charles Langston was one of two individuals brought to trial after the rescue of John Price. As a result of his impassioned speech, his sentence was reduced to twenty days.

Being identified with that man by color, by race, by manhood, by sympathies, such as God has implanted in us all, I felt it my duty to go and do what I could toward liberating him. I had been taught by my revolutionary father, that the fundamental doctrine of this government was that all men have a right to life and liberty, and coming from the Old Dominion I brought into Ohio these sentiments deeply impressed upon my heart. I went to Wellington, and hearing from the parties themselves by what authority the boy was held in custody, I conceived, from what little knowledge I had of law, that they had no right to hold him. And as your Honor has repeatedly laid down the law in this Court, a man is free until he is proven to be legally restrained of his liberty, and I believe that upon that principle of law, those men were bound to take their prisoner before the very first magistrate they found, and there establish the facts set forth in their warrant and that until they did this every man should presume that their claim was unfounded, and to institute such proceedings for the purpose of securing an investigation as they might find warranted by the laws of this State. . . .

The full text of Document 3.14.11 is available on the CD-ROM.

The Dred Scott Decision—A Case That Led to the Civil War

In 1857, the United States Supreme Court ruled against Dred Scott, who had sued for his freedom and that of his wife and children. The Chief Justice's majority opinion declared that: (a) no slave, or free person whose ancestors were enslaved, was a citizen of the United States; and (b) Congress had no power to prohibit slavery in the territories as it had done in the Missouri Compromise of 1820.

Dred Scott and his wife, Harriet Robinson Scott, first sued to gain their freedom in the State of Missouri in 1846. The case was based on their many years of residence in a free territory and in a free state, arguing that they could no longer be held in slavery in Missouri when they returned to that state where slavery was legal. However, in 1846, the court's decision denied their claim on both points: they had no right to bring a suit in court, and, even if they had, they could not gain their freedom by having lived in a place where slavery was illegal.

When the Scotts' case reached the Supreme Court, the Chief Justice's majority opinion went far beyond the question of the Scotts' status and stated that the Missouri Compromise was unconstitutional. The political consequences of this decision were immediate and far-reaching. The decision strengthened the legal standing of slavery and the political position of slaveholders. In addition, it further intensified the conflict between free and slave states by invalidating long-standing compromises between sections of the country. The decision also strengthened the Republican Party by cementing the alliance between abolitionists and people opposed to the expansion of slavery into the western territories. By sharpening the issues of race, property, and power, the case contributed significantly to the coming of the Civil War.

Who were the Scotts and why did they sue for their freedom? Dred, the plaintiff for whom the case is named, was born in Southampton, Virginia, around 1799. He and his parents were the property of Peter Blow. Dred moved west with his master's family, first to Alabama and then, in 1830, to St. Louis, Missouri. After Peter Blow's death in 1832, Dred Scott was sold to Dr. John Emerson, a surgeon in the United States Army. Dred accompanied Dr. Emerson to the free state of Illinois, where he lived until 1836, and then to the free territory of Wisconsin (which included the area that is now the state of Minnesota), where he stayed until 1840. Dred Scott thus spent at least eight years living with his master in places where slavery was illegal. He apparently spent another year or so living in the Wisconsin Territory without a master. Dr. Emerson was transferred to Louisiana and then to St. Louis, but he waited until 1842 before summoning Scott and his wife to return to St. Louis.

Dred Scott had married Harriet Robinson in 1836 while both were living in Ft. Snelling (near present-day Minneapolis). Harriet was owned by Major Lawrence Taliaferro, the United States Indian Agent for the Upper Mississippi River region. Harriet was probably born in Virginia about 1819 and spent her childhood in Pennsylvania. She was seventeen when she married Dred Scott, who was about twenty years her senior. Major Taliaferro presided over the civil ceremony, and he transferred ownership of Harriet to Dr. Emerson, then Dred Scott's owner.

Dred and Harriet Scott did not seek legal freedom while they were living in free territory but filed suit after their return to Missouri and the death of Dr. Emerson. The doctor had married in 1840 and died in 1843, and his widow, Irene, eventually returned to her native Massachusetts. Her second husband, Calvin C. Chaffee, was a northern congressman opposed to slavery. So, Irene transferred legal ownership of the Scotts to John F. A. Sanford, her brother who lived in New York State.

What prompted Dred and Harriet Scott to sue for their freedom in 1846? Evidence suggests that Irene Emerson was more difficult to deal with than Dr. John Emerson had been. After Dr. Emerson's death, Mrs. Emerson hired Dred out to an army captain. Hiring out was relatively common in St. Louis and other cities in slave states. Slaves would work for someone other then their owner and turn over a fixed sum to their owner each week or month. If they could earn more than that amount, they could keep the extra money for themselves. Many slaves who were hired out saved their earnings to buy themselves from their owners. Dred Scott tried to buy his freedom from Irene Emerson, offering her $300—a fair price because he was not a young man. She refused his offer.

There is also testimony that on at least one occasion, she beat him. It was not uncommon for women as well as men to inflict physical punishment on slaves who challenged an owner's authority. The Scotts' suit was probably also motivated by their concern for their two daughters, Eliza, age fourteen, and Lizzie, age seven. Enslaved families were often separated by sale when their owner died or needed money.

The Scotts were aware that a number of slaves living in Missouri had successfully sued for their freedom on the grounds of their previous residence in a free state or territory. In 1824, the Missouri Supreme Court had ruled in *Winney v. Whiteside* that if a master took his slave just north of Missouri, the slave was free even if later returned to the slave state. Harriet Robinson Scott's friend Rachel, whom she met at Ft. Snelling, had already attained her freedom by bringing suit in Missouri. So the Scotts had good reason to be optimistic that the state court would rule in their favor.

Unfortunately, judges who had recently been appointed to the Missouri State courts were not willing to follow the precedent set by the 1824 case. Two decades after the Missouri Compromise, as sectional conflict increased, states were less willing to uphold the laws of other states when the enslavement or freedom of African Americans was at stake.

When the Scotts filed suit in 1846, they had moral support and financial backing from the sons of Peter Blow, Dred's former owner; apparently the Blow sons and Dred Scott had been friends since childhood. The Scotts also were supported by the Reverend John Anderson, their minister in St. Louis. After several years and many twists and turns at the state level, in 1853–1854, the Scotts' case was filed in the U.S. District Court in St. Louis. John Sanford, who had become the Scott family's legal owner, was resident of New York state, thus allowing the case to be heard at the federal level. The U.S. District Court ruled against Scott, as the state courts had done. The Scotts then appealed to the United States Supreme Court, where they were represented by Roswell Martin Field, a nationally prominent lawyer. By this time, the Scotts' suit for freedom had attracted national attention.

After the U.S. District Court ruled that Sanford could continue to hold the Scotts in slavery, their friends, the Blows, purchased their freedom by paying Sanford and then manumitted the family. Dred Scott, who had long suffered from tuberculosis, died in 1858. Harriet continued to work as a washerwoman, a common occupation for African American women, and lived to see the end of slavery. The date and place of her death is unknown. In 1957, a monument was erected near Dred Scott's grave. The inscription reads, "In memory of a simple man who wanted to be free."

Organizing Idea

By suing for their freedom in state and then federal courts, Dred and Harriet Scott forced the nation to face the fundamental questions of race, property, and power. The 1857 U.S. Supreme Court decision declaring that slaves and even their free descendants were not citizens and that Congress had no power to prohibit slavery from the western territories intensified the conflicts that culminated in the Civil War.

Student Objectives

Students will:

- ❖ understand the U.S. Supreme Court case: the arguments of the plaintiff and defendant and the opinions of the Chief Justice
- ❖ relate the questions raised by the Dred Scott case to the Constitution and other founding documents and their contested interpretation over time
- ❖ place the Dred Scott case in the context of (1) sectional divisions since the 1820 Missouri Compromise, (2) the 1860 presidential election, and (3) the onset of the Civil War
- ❖ begin to relate the Dred Scott suit for freedom to other legal and extra-legal efforts slaves made to secure their freedom

Key Questions

- ❖ Who were Dred Scott and Harriet Robinson Scott, and why did they sue for their freedom from 1846 on?

❖ What fundamental legal and political issues did the Dred Scott case raise?

❖ How did the Chief Justice's opinion affect national politics in and after 1857?

❖ In what way do you think this case may have influenced the language in the post–Civil War amendments (Thirteenth and Fifteenth), which declare specifically that all persons born in the United States are citizens and that no state can abridge that right regardless of a person's previous servitude?

Primary Source Materials

DOCUMENT 3.15.1: Illustration of Dred Scott and his family from *Frank Lesley's Illustrated Newspaper,* June 27, 1857

DOCUMENT 3.15.2: Excerpts from text accompanying illustration from *Frank Lesley's Illustrated Newspaper,* June 27, 1857

DOCUMENT 3.15.3: Excerpts from the Dred Scott decision written by Chief Justice Roger B. Taney of the United States Supreme Court, March 1857

DOCUMENT 3.15.4: Excerpt from dissenting opinion written by Justice Benjamin Robbins Curtis of the United States Supreme Court, March 1857

DOCUMENT 3.15.5: Excerpt from notes Abraham Lincoln wrote in 1858 in advance of his "house divided" speech

DOCUMENT 3.15.6: "The Political Quadrille. Music by Dred Scott," a cartoon, 1860

DOCUMENT 3.15.7: Excerpts from the *Pittsburgh Gazette*, 7 March 1857

DOCUMENT 3.15.8: Excerpts from "The Question Settled," *New Hampshire Patriot,* 18 March 1857

Supplementary Materials

ITEM 3.15.A: Additional vocabulary lists for primary sources

Vocabulary

appeal	Free-soiler	majority opinion	*obiter dictum*
defendant	judicial review	manumission	treason
dissenting opinion	jurisdiction	nullity	
	locofoco		

Student Activities

Activity 1   **Analysis of Bias**

Document 3.15.1, from *Frank Lesley's Illustrated Newspaper*, presents portraits of Dred and Harriet Scott and their two daughters, Eliza and Lizzie. Ask students to look closely at these images. In what ways do these portraits resemble portraits of white Americans in the 1850s? In what ways do they differ? Is this what you expected the Scott family to look like? If not, why not?

The text that accompanies the portraits purports to tell how the Scotts were persuaded to have their "likeness" taken for publication in the paper. Ask students to read the news story carefully. What attitude does the author of the article express toward the Scotts? Note that the author is not identified but speaks in the first person plural as "we." Consider the text's descriptions of the Scotts: Dred "made a rude obeisance to our recognition"; he looked like "a pure-blooded African"; "he had a shrewd, intelligent, good-natured face."

- ❖ In what ways do these descriptions reinforce or contradict prevailing stereotypes of African Americans?

- ❖ Why might Dred Scott have been reluctant to be photographed and have an engraved portrait published in a weekly newspaper with a national circulation?

- ❖ Why does the author ascribe his reluctance to "superstitious feeling"?

- ❖ Why would Dred agree only after hearing from his lawyer?

- ❖ What part of town do they live in?

- ❖ Consider the description of Harriet Scott and her daughters: "a smart, tidy-looking negress . . . who, with two female assistants, was busy ironing." Is this a positive and/or stereotypical description?

- ❖ Then read the final paragraph out loud. Why did the author put her words into what he thought was "negro dialect" even though Harriet Scott spoke standard English?

- ❖ Why did Harriet refuse to say whether Dred was home? Was her concern reasonable in the context of St. Louis in 1857?

Analysis of the U.S. Supreme Court Dred Scott Decision

Activity 2

Roger B. Taney, who wrote the decisive opinion in the Dred Scott case, followed John Marshall as Chief Justice of the U.S. Supreme Court. He was born in Calvert County, Maryland, where his ancestors had arrived in the seventeenth century as indentured servants. His family then owned slaves who worked the tobacco fields. They were Catholic, as was the colony's original proprietor. The Taneys' historical experience—from indentured servitude to slave ownership—was typical of many white Marylanders in the colonial period. However, Taney did not regard slavery as a beneficial institution. Like Thomas Jefferson, he was concerned that slavery was incompatible with American ideals. Taney once said: "Slavery is a blot on our national character and every lover of freedom confidently hopes that it will be effectively, though it must be gradually, wiped away." Unlike Jefferson, Taney freed his own slaves.

Have each student read the (condensed) opinion of Chief Justice Roger B. Taney (3.15.3). Seven of the nine justices agreed that Scott was not free because slaves were not citizens. Taney's opinion was the most far-reaching, also ruling on the power of Congress to regulate slavery in the territories. Here Taney was exercising the Supreme Court's power of judicial review—to decide whether or not an Act of Congress is compatible with the Constitution.

Divide the students into four groups. Each group should assume responsibility for analyzing a portion of Taney's opinion and should be prepared to share their findings and their ideas with the rest of the class. Copies of the Constitution should be readily available.

First Group

❖ How does Taney approach the interpretation of the Constitution?

❖ Does he try to follow what he thinks is the "original intent" of the "framers"?

❖ Consider Taney's claim that, at the time the Declaration of Independence was written, the founding fathers did not include African and African American slaves among "men" who were "created equal and endowed by their Creator with . . . inalienable rights." Is that an accurate assessment of the framers' intent?

❖ How might this approach to constitutional interpretation respond to society's change over time?

Second Group

❖ On what grounds does Taney base his ruling that slaves and their descendants were not citizens?

❖ Consider the characterization of African Americans as "beings of an inferior order" with "no rights which the white man was bound to respect." Whose attitudes is he describing? Of most white Americans in 1857? Are these attitudes his own?

❖ Why did Taney refer to African Americans as an "unfortunate race"?

Third Group

Taney asserts that the Constitution is explicitly a proslavery document.

❖ Is his opinion correct in this matter?

❖ What, if any, sections of the Constitution limited slavery or the rights of slaveowners?

Fourth Group

Taney rests his case for the perpetuation and expansion of slavery upon the constitutional right to property. Governments are formed to protect property, Taney argues, and the Constitution guarantees in the Bill of Rights that no property holder can be deprived of his property without due process of law. Slaves were simply one form of property (land was the other major form of property in the mid-nineteenth century), and if the court granted slaves their freedom, it would undermine the fundamental rights of all property owners. This concern about property in all its forms was a major theme in nineteenth-century American politics.

❖ Why did most Northern states adopt gradual rather than immediate emancipation of slaves after the adoption of the Constitution?

❖ How did the abolitionists counter this argument about property rights?

Analysis of Dissenting Opinion

Activity 3

As a class (perhaps as a read-aloud), read the dissenting opinion (3.15.4) by Justice Benjamin Robbins Curtis, a native of Massachusetts.

❖ What is his argument?

❖ Do you think his statement that free, native-born, African Americans were recognized as citizens by the New England states and by North Carolina at the time the Constitution was adopted was correct? Why or why not?

❖ Were there also restrictions of the rights of free African Americans? Looking back at the lesson in Sourcebook 2 on Quok Walker, consider how the Supreme Judicial Court of Massachusetts (in 1783) interpreted the state constitution's first article.

Curtis also asserts that the U.S. Constitution grants Congress the right to regulate slavery in the territories. Can you find this language in the Constitution? Is there anything about this issue in the Articles of Confederation and the Northwest Ordinance?

Essay Writing—Abraham Lincoln's Notes

Activity 4

Read Abraham Lincoln's notes (3.15.5) made for preparing his acceptance speech for the Republican Party's nomination for President of the United States in 1858. Write a reflective essay addressing some of the following questions: What did Lincoln mean when he said, "A house divided against itself cannot stand"? Why did Lincoln refer to Kansas? What does Lincoln see as the fundamental or "real question"? Do you agree with his statement that, given the situation in 1858, slavery was bound to become legal everywhere or nowhere? What three points does Lincoln believe the Dred Scott decision made? How did the decision affect the Republican Party's political strategy for preventing the expansion of slavery?

A Political Cartoon—What Does It Mean?

Activity 5

"The Political Quadrille. Music by Dred Scott" (3.15.6), an editorial cartoon, satirized all four candidates for the presidency in the 1860 election. Have students examine the caricatures in this cartoon. For discussion: Can you identify the candidates and their positions on the question of the day—whether free African Americans were citizens and whether slavery should be expanded into the western territories? What does the cartoon suggest is wrong with each candidate?

After students have had a chance to study and discuss the cartoon, teachers share with students the following information and questions:

❖ Southern Democrat John C. Breckinridge is dancing with incumbent President James Buchanan, who was rumored to have influenced Taney's decision in the Dred Scott case.

❖ Illinois Republican Abraham Lincoln is dancing with a black woman. How would this image of racial mixing have struck a white audience at that time?

❖ Is this depiction of Lincoln as a radical abolitionist accurate?

❖ John Bell of the Congressional Union Party is dancing with an Indian "brave." This image of a Native American was a well-known symbol of the Know-Nothing Party, which discouraged immigration and argued that the United States belonged to its native-born residents (and that did not mean American Indians).

❖ Why did the Know-Nothings inspire mistrust among voters?

❖ Stephen A. Douglas of Illinois is dancing with an Irishman. What negative stereotypes of Irish immigrants had been in circulation since the late 1840s?

❖ It was rumored that Douglas himself was a Catholic. Why would that religious affiliation arouse mistrust among Protestants?

❖ Finally, Dred Scott is depicted as the fiddler in the middle; all four candidates are literally "dancing to his tune." Why does the cartoon present this situation as an inversion of the normal social order?

❖ What do you think was the artist's point of view?

Activity 6   Analysis—The Contemporary Press

In the mid-nineteenth century, most daily newspapers openly affiliated with political parties. They made no pretense of separating factual reporting from editorial opinion, and thus they provide good evidence of divergent political viewpoints at the time.

❖ As a class, read the article from the *Pittsburgh Gazette*, March 1857 (3.15.7). This paper, closely aligned with the Republican party, chose to focus on the second part of Taney's decision, the part regarding the expansion of slavery into the territories. Why?

❖ What is the basis of the paper's argument that this ruling has no legal force?

❖ Why does the writer see the decision as part of a conspiracy to impose tyranny on all Americans, including northern white men?

❖ Why might the paper have asserted that the "slave powers" sought to dominate the federal government and infringe on the rights of non-slaveholding white people? (Think of what you know about President Buchanan.)

❖ What did the writer mean by "slave powers"?

❖ Would you infer from this writing that the Republicans favored abolition?

❖ How would you describe the tone of this editorial?

The Concord, *New Hampshire Patriot*, a Democratic paper, also focuses on the second part of the decision (3.15.8).

❖ What is the basis for their argument that the decision settles the question of slavery in the territories once and for all?

❖ Why does the article portray the Republicans as sectionalists seeking to undermine the Union?

❖ What words are used that show us the writer's view that abolitionists sought to dominate the federal government and infringe on the rights of slaveholding white men?

The article refers to the opposing party negatively as "black Republicans," implying that African Americans were influential in the party—and drawing on the other negative connotations of blackness in dominant American culture. How can we find out how many African Americans actually were active in the Republican Party leadership?

Ask students to write two editorials in contemporary language, each defending one of these two positions and referring to the Supreme Court's decision on Dred Scott.

Debate—The Dred Scott Decision: Is It the Law of the Land?

Activity 7

To summarize and pull together knowledge of this complex time, organize students to choose a role, research the political position, move back in time, and conduct a debate on the following question: *Should the decision in the Dred Scott case be accepted as the law of the land, applicable to all the states as well as the western territories?*

Students play the roles of people from different places and with differing political positions in 1857–1860. (*Note:* In the period before the Civil War, the speakers at public meetings and formal debates held at lyceums were almost always white men. African American men and women spoke only at meetings sponsored by abolitionists or at gatherings held in black communities. White women spoke only at meetings sponsored by women's rights advocates or at private gatherings of women held in parlors. Students should understand that a debate in 1858 would have looked quite different than the one they are conducting.)

Key roles include

❖ the lawyer who represents Dred Scott in federal court (Roswell M. Field)

❖ legal counsel for John F. A. Sanford, who, at this time, owned the Scott family

❖ a slaveholder from Missouri

❖ a resident of the free state of Illinois (such as Lincoln and/or Douglas)

❖ a white abolitionist from Massachusetts or New York (such as Calvin C. Chaffee)

❖ a black abolitionist from New England (such as Frederick Douglass, William Cooper Nell, or Charles Remond)

❖ a white woman with views on this subject (such as Elizabeth Blackwell or Lucy Stone)

❖ a black woman who spoke out (such as Charlotte Forten)

❖ a "free soil" supporter from New York or Massachusetts

❖ a person who does not own slaves from the "Old South," such as Virginia

❖ a person who does own slaves, from the "Deep South," such as Alabama

Other roles can include

❖ a person who doesn't own slaves but is from a slave state with a relatively large population of free blacks, such as Maryland

❖ a Quaker from Pennsylvania

❖ a native of Louisiana, which because of its Creole culture has a significant number of free people of color and a history of social contacts between people of color and white people

❖ a person from a state such as South Carolina, where in some places African Americans outnumber white people

❖ a farmer from a free state settling in a new territory, such as Wisconsin

❖ a farmer from a slave state settling in a new territory

❖ a Kansas settler who favors the prohibition of slavery in the new state

❖ a Kansas settler who favors the legalization of slavery in the new state

If students have the necessary background information from prior studies, they might choose to portray

❖ an Irish immigrant raised in a city such as Boston or New York but working on a railroad construction crew

❖ a native-born New Englander who has no land and works in a textile mill but grew up on a farm and hopes to go west and buy a farm in the future

❖ a German immigrant who has been working as a hired hand on a Pennsylvania farm but wants to go west and buy a farm in the future

❖ A Scots-Irish family living on rented land in Kentucky, a slave state

In developing their roles, students should consider how people's backgrounds—their place of origin, religious beliefs and ideas about society and property—shaped their views on the citizenship of African Americans and the expansion of slavery into the territories.

Further Student and Teacher Resources

Fehrenbacher, Don. *Slavery, Law, and Politics: The Dred Scott Case in Historical Perspective.* New York: Oxford University Press, 1981.

Finkelman, Paul. *Dred Scott v. Sandford: a Brief History with Documents.* Boston: Bedford Books, 1997.

Contemporary Connection

※

An Annual Commemoration

Beginning in 1846, Dred and Harriet Scott spent eleven years in litigation as their case wound its way to the United States Supreme Court. In March, the same month that Chief Justice of the Supreme Court, Roger B. Taney, handed down his infamous decision, the National Park Service holds a commemorative program in the St. Louis Old Courthouse, where the Scotts' first two trials were held.

In addition, in the courthouse rotunda, a permanent exhibit, "Dred Scott, Slavery and the Struggle to Be Free," examines the historic case. Photographs, illustrations, and contemporary newspaper articles chronicle the institution of slavery in St. Louis and Missouri. (Visit **www.nps.gov/jeff.**) Students may wish to use the documents from the lesson and to conduct further research to create their own exhibit for the school.

Fleischner, Jennifer. *The Dred Scott Case: Testing the Right to Live Free*. Brookfield, CT: Millbrook Press, 1997.

Gordon-Reed, Annette, ed. *Race on Trial: Law and Justice in American History*. New York: Oxford University Press, 2002.

Herda, D. J. *The Dred Scott Case: Slavery and Citizenship*. Hillside, NJ: Enslow Publishers, 1994.

Websites

The Dred Scott Case. Washington University Libraries, St. Louis, MO
   www.library.wustl.edu/vlib/dredscott/
   www.library.wustl.edu/vlib/dredscott/chronology.html
   http://library.wustl.edu/vlib/dredscott/toc.html

   www.nps.gov/jeff/ocv-dscottd.htm

   www.uiowa.edu/~fyi/oldfyi/issues97-98/022798web/law_022798.html

Video

Abolition: Broken Promises. Films for the Humanities and Sciences, 1998.

Primary Source Materials for Lesson 15

3.15.1

Illustration of Dred Scott and his family from *Frank Lesley's Illustrated Newspaper*, June 27, 1857

3.15.2

Excerpts from text accompanying illustration from
Frank Lesley's Illustrated Newspaper, June 27, 1857

We found [Dred Scott] on examination to be a pure-blooded African, perhaps fifty years of age with a shrewd, intelligent, good-natured face, of rather light frame, being not more than five feet six inches high. After some general remarks we expressed a wish to get his portrait (we had made efforts before, through correspondents, and failed), and asked him if he would not go to Fitzgibbon's gallery and have it taken. The gentleman present explained to Dred that it was proper he should have his likeness in the "great illustrated paper of the country," overruled his many objections, which seemed to grow out of a superstitious feeling, and he promised to be at the gallery the next day. This appointment Dred Scott did not keep. Determined not to be foiled, we sought an interview with Mr. Crane, Dred's lawyer, who promptly gave us a letter of introduction, explaining to Dred that it was to his advantage to have his picture taken to be engraved for our paper, and also directions where we could find his domicile. We found the place with difficulty the streets in Dred's neighborhood being more clearly defined in the plan of the city than on the mother earth; we finally reached a wooden house, however, protected by a balcony that answered the description. Approaching the door, we saw a smart, tidy-looking negress, perhaps thirty years of age, who, with two female assistants, was busy ironing. To our question, "Is this where Dred Scott lives?" we received, rather hesitatingly, the answer, "yes." Upon our asking if he was home, she said, "What white man arter dad nigger for?—why don't white man tend to his own business, and let dat nigger 'lone? Some of dese days dey'll steal dat nigger—dat are a fact.". . .

The full text of Document 3.15.2 is available on the CD-ROM.

3.15.3

Excerpts from the Dred Scott decision written by Chief Justice
Roger B. Taney of the United States Supreme Court, March 1857

Mr. Chief Justice Taney delivered the opinion of the Court. . .

In the opinion of the Court the legislation and histories of the times, and the language used in the Declaration of Independence, show that neither the class of persons who had been imported as slaves nor their descendents, whether they had become free or not, were then acknowledged as a part of the people nor intended to be included in the general words used in that memorable instrument. . .

They had for more than a century before been regarded as beings of an inferior order and altogether unfit to associate with the white race, either in social or political relations; and so far inferior that they had no rights which the white man was bound to respect; and that the Negro might justly and lawfully be reduced to slavery for his benefit. He was bought and sold and treated as an ordinary article of merchandise and traffic whenever a profit could be made by it. This opinion was at that time fixed and universal in the civilized portion of the white race. . .

The full text of Document 3.15.3 is available on the CD-ROM.

3.15.4

Excerpt from dissenting opinion written by Justice Benjamin Robbins Curtis of the United States Supreme Court, March 1857

Justice Benjamin Robbins Curtis of Massachusetts protested Taney's conclusions.

At the time of the ratification of the Articles of Confederation [1781], all free native-born inhabitants of the States of New Hampshire, Massachusetts, New York, New Jersey, and North Carolina, though descended from African slaves, were not only citizens of those states, but such of them as had the other necessary qualifications possessed the franchises of electors, on equal terms with other citizens. . . these colored persons were not only included in the body of 'the people of the United States,' by whom the Constitution was ordained and established, but in at least five of the States they had the power to act, and doubtless did act, by their suffrages, upon the question of adoption. . . . *Curtis also argued that under a* "reasonable interpretation of the language of the Constitution," *Congress had the power to regulate slavery in the federal territories.*

3.15.5

Excerpt from notes Abraham Lincoln wrote in 1858 in advance of his "house divided" speech

Why Kansas is neither the *whole*, nor the *tithe* of the real question.
    "A house divided cannot stand."
    I believe this government can not endure permanently half slave, and half free.
    I expressed this belief a year ago; and subsequent developments have but confirmed me.
    I do not expect the Union to be dissolved. I do not expect the house to fall; but I *do* expect it will cease to be divided. It will become *all* one thing, or *all* the other. Either the opponents of slavery will arrest the further spread of it, and put it in the course of ultimate extinction; or its advocates will push it forward till it shall become

alike lawful in *all* the states, old, as well as new. Do you doubt it? Study the Dred Scott decision, and then see, how little, even now, remains to be done.

That decision may be reduced to three points. The first is, that a Negro can not be a citizen. That point is made in order to deprive the Negro in every possible event, of that provision of the U.S. Constitution which declares that: "The *citizens* of each State shall be entitled to all privileges and immunities of citizens in the several States."

The second point is, that the U.S. Constitution protects slavery, as property, in all the U.S. territories, and that neither congress, nor the people of the territories, nor any other power, can prohibit it, at any time prior to the formation of State constitutions.

This point is made, in order that the territories may safely be filled up with slaves, *before* the formation of State constitutions, and thereby to embarrass the free state [sentiment and enhance the chances of slave constitutions being adopted.]

[The third point decided is that the voluntary bringing of Dred Scott into Illinois by his master, and holding him here a long time as a slave, did not operate his emancipation—and did not make him free.]

3.15.6

"The Political Quadrille. Music by Dred Scott," a cartoon, 1860

The cartoon is a parody of the 1860 presidential election, highlighting the impact of the Dred Scott decision on national politics.

Library of Congress

3.15.7

Excerpts from the *Pittsburgh Gazette*, 7 March 1857

We shall treat the so-called decision of that Court as an utter nullity. . . . Look at the facts in the case. Dred Scott, an alleged Missouri slave, brings a suit against his claimant, for his freedom, upon the ground that his master, having voluntarily removed him from Missouri on to free soil, he thereby became free. The Supreme Court decide that Dred Scott is not a citizen of Missouri or of the United States, and therefore was not entitled to bring a suit in that Court; hence they dismiss his suit for want of jurisdiction. That, then, was the only point for them to decide, and that decided, there was an end of the case. The suit fell because the party bringing it had no rights in that Court.

Beyond this legal point the Court had no power to decide anything. They had no right to go into the merits of a case, when the case itself was dismissed for want of jurisdiction. All that follows is simply extra judicial and is entitled to be regarded only as the unauthorized opinion of so many individuals. . . .

The full text of Document 3.15.7 is available on the CD-ROM.

3.15.8

Excerpts from "The Question Settled," *New Hampshire Patriot*, 18 March 1857

We give in this paper an abstract of the decision of the U.S. Supreme Court in the Dred Scott case, in which it is solemnly adjudged and decided, by the highest judicial tribunal of the Union, that the Missouri Compromise was unconstitutional, and that Congress has no constitutional power or authority to legislate upon the subject of slavery in the Territories. It will be seen that other incidental questions were decided in this case, but this is the one of the most political importance, and interest. It utterly demolishes the whole black republican platform and stamps it as directly antagonistical to the constitution. This is the end of the matter, so far as argument and voting and legislation are concerned. . . .

The full text of Document 3.15.8 is available on the CD-ROM.

John Brown: Action for Freedom—Courage and Sacrifice or Fanaticism and Futility?

The story of John Brown's ill-fated raid on the arsenal at Harpers Ferry, October 16, 1859, began in Kansas more than five years before the event and was filled with intrigue and drama. Brown and a band of free black and white people, including three of his sons, attacked the federal arsenal in Virginia as part of a larger plan to recruit and arm slaves to rise up in rebellion across northern Virginia. The goal was to spark a major uprising that would deliver a fatal blow to the institution of slavery in the United States. After holding the armory briefly, Brown and his followers were overcome by federal militia forces led by Commander Robert E. Lee. Two of Brown's sons and eight others were killed in Lee's assault. Brown and six of his men were captured and hanged in the five months following the raid.

What brought this man of deep convictions and radical action to this point in time and history was a series of circumstances and events starting in Kansas. In 1854, the Kansas-Nebraska Act had passed Congress and opened the new territory to slavery. Whether the new states carved from the new territory would be slave or free would be determined by popular vote. Supporters of slavery and those who opposed it rushed to occupy the land. Each side purposed to have a majority of the residents by the time a vote was taken.

John Brown, born of strong religious roots in Torrington, Connecticut, steeped in Ohio's abolitionist tradition, and an outspoken activist, settled in Kansas with his five sons. They were all involved in efforts to keep Kansas from becoming a slave state. In 1856, Brown and his followers became wanted men after dragging five allegedly proslavery supporters (some evidence suggests they all may not have been) from their homes in the middle of the night and killing them. The Pottawatomie Killings, as the attack became known, a retaliatory act for a proslavery raid on Lawrence, Kansas, shocked the abolitionist community. In 1858, he was involved in another raid, this time to free slaves in Missouri. Brown, fully committed to ending slavery "by any means necessary," now turned his energy toward even bigger targets. This brings us to the events at Harpers Ferry.

The trial and execution of John Brown were events of national proportion. The public's appetite for news of Brown's successes and failures had been insatiable. Readers soaked up articles and illustrations like bread soaks up gravy.

Among the documents included in this lesson is a detailed eyewitness account of John Brown's raid on Harpers Ferry by a Virginia congressman Alexander Boteler, and a response to that account from a close friend of John Brown, Frank B. Sanborn. Both documents were printed in the *Century Magazine* on July 26, 1883, nearly twenty-four years after the event. Both authors, therefore, wrote with the knowledge and hindsight of the future that John Brown and his followers would not live to see but perhaps foreshadowed: Civil War, Reconstruction, and the country's response to both. Even today, John Brown's actions remain a topic of great controversy in the ongoing debate on the institution of slavery in America.

Organizing Idea

To the present day, opinion remains divided regarding abolitionist John Brown and his actions. The raid at Harpers Ferry, however, stands indisputably as a major step that brought the nation closer to civil war.

Student Objectives

Students will:

❖ learn who John Brown was, what he did, and why he did it

❖ begin to explore differing public perspectives on John Brown and his actions

❖ demonstrate the ability to formulate specific questions to help determine the veracity of eyewitness accounts of contemporary events

❖ demonstrate through a written, oral, or visual demonstration to peers and/or the teacher that they understand the meaning, implications, and significance of John Brown's raid on Harpers Ferry and his subsequent execution

Key Questions

❖ What response does aggressive or violent resistance usually get from the government? The public? Is this kind of resistance effective? Why or why not?

❖ Would you interpret the raid at Harpers Ferry as an act of heroic civil disobedience or one of treasonous rebellion?

❖ How can we determine the truth of a retelling of an event—or can we?

Primary Source Materials

DOCUMENT 3.16.1: Excerpts from a letter from John Brown to his father, March 1856

DOCUMENT 3.16.2: Excerpt from "The Pottawatomie Killings," statement by James Townsley, December 1879

DOCUMENT 3.16.3: Excerpts from "Recollections of the John Brown Raid by a Virginian Who Witnessed the Fight" by Alexander Boteler, from *Century Magazine*, July 1883

DOCUMENT 3.16.4: Address of John Brown to the Virginia Court at Charles Town, Virginia, on November 2, 1859 when about to receive the sentence of death

DOCUMENT 3.16.5: Image of John Brown meeting the slave-mother and her child on the steps of Charlestown jail on his way to execution, 1863

DOCUMENT 3.16.6: Image of John Brown ascending the scaffold preparatory to being hanged

DOCUMENT 3.16.7: "Comment by a Radical Abolitionist" by F. B. Sanborn, from *Century Magazine,* July 1883

Supplementary Materials

ITEM 3.16.A: Additional vocabulary lists for primary sources

Vocabulary

abolition	deport	fanatic	martyrdom
armory	despotic	gallows	pickets
arsenal	emancipation	insurgent	scaffold
civil power			

Student Activities

Reading and Discussion—John Brown Prior to Harpers Ferry

Activity 1

Students should read John Brown's letter to his father (3.16.1) and James Townsley's statement regarding the Pottawatomie Killings (3.16.2).

- ❖ What do they learn about John Brown? The class may want to keep a running list of terms that describe him as students work with all the documents.
- ❖ How valid is a statement given more than twenty years after the event?
- ❖ What can be learned about Townsley from his statement?

A Newspaper Article—Harpers Ferry: What Happened?

Activity 2

Alexander Boteler's account of the raid on Harpers Ferry (3.16.3) is detailed and consequently lengthy. After reading the complete document and John Brown's last speech (3.16.4), students should jot down key information that they plan to include in a 250-word article for a newspaper. They need to keep in mind that a reporter is supposed to write as objectively as possible. When students have completed the writing assignment, several articles should be read aloud. How do they differ? Why? Can students explain why they chose to exclude some facts? What can they conclude about media reporting?

Activity 3 — Harpers Ferry—A Skit

Identify the major participants and victims of the attack on Harpers Ferry, according to Boteler's account. Have the class write a script and perform a short skit depicting some event described in the account of the attack. One or more students could act as reporter, interrupting the dialogue at appropriate times, freezing the action, and interviewing the characters with the goal of exploring the thinking and motives of the person being interviewed. Brief character bios developed from the information given in the document and prior knowledge of the time and place should be written by students as part of the assignment and given to the students who portray the characters.

Activity 4 — Discussion of Visual Images—The Message

Students should carefully examine the two images (3.16.5 and 3.16.6).

- ❖ What words come to mind? List them on the board.
- ❖ How is John Brown portrayed?
- ❖ Are the artists sympathetic to John Brown? How do you know?
- ❖ Describe all the other details in the images.
- ❖ In Document 3.16.5 how is the slave-mother shown? The soldier?
- ❖ What is the figure behind Brown?

Activity 5 — Two Essays—Twenty-four Years Later

Students should read Frank Sanborn's perspective of the Harpers Ferry raid (3.16.7). Refer back to Boteler's account, too (3.16.3), and consider these questions:

- ❖ What do the two accounts tell you about the perspective of the authors?
- ❖ Speculate on the prevailing opinion of American society on the issue of slavery and emancipation at the time these pieces were written.
- ❖ Do you think John Brown was a hero or a misguided fanatic? Explain.

Activity 6 — An Interview

Ask students to consider John Brown's letter, last speech, and other quotes of his they've read. They should also conduct some research online to learn as much about him as possible. In small groups, select one person to be John Brown and have someone else act as the interviewer. Others in the group need to assess whether the questions posed are pertinent and the answers are accurate, given what they know about John Brown and the events in which he was involved.

A Debate—Who Was John Brown?

Activity 7

Send students to opposite sides of the room based on whether they think John Brown was an American hero or a villain. Students who are undecided remain in the middle of the room. In an organized fashion, individuals from each side take turns presenting their argument in an effort to convince the undecided to their side of the room. Proponents can also be persuaded to change their positions.

Research—Harpers Ferry: The Reaction

Activity 8

The raid at Harpers Ferry and John Brown's execution sparked intense reaction across the country. Each student should select a topic of most interest to him or her, gather information, and be prepared to share findings with the class. For example, they can check local or regional newspapers (in library archives) to find accounts of either event. Research how *Freedom's Journal*, *The Liberator*, and *The North Star* responded. What happened to Frank Sanborn in Concord, Massachusetts, shortly after the raid? What did Frederick Douglass, Lewis Hayden, John Mercer Langston, Henry David Thoreau, Wendell Phillips, Charles Sumner, or any one of the other men and women they have read about in preceding lessons write or say about the raid and subsequent hangings?

Further Student and Teacher Resources

Cox, Clinton. *Fiery Vision: The Life and Death of John Brown*. New York: Scholastic, 1997.

Du Bois, W. E. B. *John Brown*. Edited and with an introduction by David Roediger. New York : Modern Library, 2001.

Oates, Stephen B. *The Approaching Fury: Voices of the Storm, 1820–1861*. New York: HarperCollins, 1997.

Oates, Stephen B. *To Purge This Land with Blood: A Biography of John Brown*. Amherst: University of Massachusetts, 1984.

Websites

Civil War Newspapers: Coverage of John Brown's Raid. Institute for Advanced Technology in the Humanities, University of Virginia, Charlottesville, VA
www.iath.virginia.edu/vshadow/jbrownnews.html

Harpers Ferry National Historical Park, Harper's Ferry, WV
www.harpersferryhistory.org/

Contemporary Connection

✠

Considering John Brown Today

Debate about John Brown's crusade continues today. A few years ago, as part of *The American Experience* series, WGBH in Boston produced a film, "John Brown's Holy War." The introduction on the PBS website says, "Martyr, madman, murderer, hero—John Brown remains one of history's most controversial and misunderstood figures." The video may be ordered from PBS Video. The PBS website contains further ideas as well as resources for teaching about this controversial figure from a troubled and painful time in America's past (*www.pbs.org/wgbh/amex/brown/filmmore/index.html*). Students might view the video and consider Brown's protest and actions. Are they comparable with anything happening in our world today?

John Brown and Harper's Ferry, National Archives and Records Administration, Washington, DC
www.archives.gov/exhibit_hall/american_originals/civilwar.html#brown

John Brown and the Valley of the Shadow. Institute for Advanced Technology in the Humanities, University of Virginia, Charlottesville, VA
www.iath.virginia.edu/jbrown/master.html

Master List of John Brown Articles. University of Virginia, Charlottesville, VA
http://jefferson.village.virginia.edu/jbrown/news.html

"In Readiness to do Every Duty Assigned," Maryland Historical Society, Baltimore, MD
www.mdarchives.state.md.us/msa/speccol/sc2200/sc2221/000030/html/readiness1.html

Secession Era Editorials Project. Furman University History Department, Greenville, SC
http://history.furman.edu/~benson/docs/jbmenu.htm

Speeches and Other Commentaries prompted by John Brown's Actions, Prosecution, and Death. Assumption College, Worcester, MA
www.assumption.edu/ahc/rhetoric/oratoryjohnbrown.html

Primary Source Materials for Lesson 16

3.16.1

Excerpts from a letter from John Brown to his father, March 1856

John Brown wrote this letter to his father two months before the attack at Pottawatomie Creek.

Dear Father,

Your letter of the 8th of March to Mr. Adair and family came on all right. We are all feeling sensible of your care for us and wish it was in our favor to make you a better return. We all wish you to accept our grateful acknowledgements; and we do not wish you to give yourself unreasonable trouble or anxiety on our account. We are all now able to be about and are learning something in different ways. Some four of us were out a few days since tracing out old boundary lines for an Indian tribe. The Spring is backward but the grass begins to start a little. The horses and cattle belonging to the boys have been got through middling well. I think there is a general disposition on the part of the connection here to help one another. There is great anxiety felt here about the action of Congress. If Congress do not recognize the action of the free state people here there is every reason to expect trouble: as the Missourians will take new courage in that event. Free state people here are generally quite firm and determined to persevere even though Congress do nothing for them. The surveying of government lands runs under divine Providence to derange the plans of the Pro Slavery men here much more than any others. They have been exceedingly greedy of the timbered lands . . . Some slaveholders near us we are informed have become quite discouraged and are about to clear out . . . Wishing you may be continued to witness the triumph of that cause you have laboured to promote.

Your affectionate son,

John Brown

3.16.2

Excerpt from "The Pottawatomie Killings," statement by James Townsley, December 1879

We started, the whole company, in a northerly direction, crossing Mosquito Creek above the residence of the Doyles. Soon after crossing the creek some one of the party knocked at the door of a cabin but received no reply. I have forgotten whose cabin it was if I knew at the time. The next place we came to was the residence of the Doyles. John Brown, three of his sons and son-in-law went to the door, leaving Frederick Brown; Winer and myself a short distance from the house. About this time a large dog attacked us. Frederick Brown struck the dog a blow with his short two-edged sword, after which I dealt him a blow on the head with my sabre and heard no more from him. The old man Doyle and two sons were called out and marched some distance from the house toward Dutch Henry's in the road, where a halt was made. Old John Brown drew his revolver and shot the old man Doyle in the forehead, and the two youngest sons immediately fell upon the younger Doyles with their short two-edged swords. One of the young Doyles was stricken down in an instant, but the other attempted to escape, and was pursued a short distance by his assailant and cut down. The company then proceeded down Mosquito creek to the house of Allen Wilkinson. Here the old man Brown, three of his sons and son-in-law, as at the Doyle residence, went to the door and ordered Wilkinson to come out, leaving Frederick Brown, Winer and myself standing in the road east of the house. Wilkinson was taken, marched some distance south of the house, and slain in the road with a short sword by one of the younger Browns. After he was killed his body was dragged out to one side and left. . . .

The full text of Document 3.16.2 is available on the CD-ROM.

3.16.3

Excerpts from "Recollections of the John Brown Raid by a Virginian Who Witnessed the Fight" by Alexander Boteler, from *Century Magazine*, July 1883

Sunday night, October 16th, was fixed for the foray; and at eight o'clock that evening, Brown said to his companions: "Come, men, get on your arms; we will proceed to the Ferry." They took with them a one-horse wagon, in which were placed a parcel of pikes, torches, and some tools, including a crow-bar and sledge-hammer, and in which also Brown himself rode as far as the Ferry.

Brown's actual force, all told, consisted of only twenty-two men including himself, three of whom never crossed the Potomac. Five of those who did cross were negroes, of whom three were fugitive slaves. Ten of them were killed in Virginia; seven were hanged there, and five are said to have escaped, viz., two of those who crossed the river, and the three who did not cross. Six of the white men were members of Brown's family, or connected with it by marriage, and five of these paid the forfeit of their lives to the Virginians. Owen Brown is the only one of the whole party who now survives. . . .

The full text of Document 3.16.3 is available on the CD-ROM.

3.16.4

Address of John Brown to the Virginia Court at Charles Town, Virginia, on November 2, 1859 when about to receive the sentence of death

I have, may it please the court, a few words to say.

In the first place, I deny everything but what I have all along admitted,—the design on my part to free slaves. I intended certainly to have made a clean thing of that matter, as I did last winter, when I went into Missouri and took slaves without the snapping of a gun on either side, moved them through the country, and finally left them in Canada. I designed to do the same thing again, on a larger scale. That was all I intended. I never did intend murder, or treason, or the destruction of property, or to excite or incite slaves to rebellion, or to make insurrection.

I have another objection; and that is, it is unjust that I should suffer such a penalty. Had I interfered in the manner which I admit, and which I admit has been fairly proved (for I admire the truthfulness and candor of the greater portion of the witnesses who have testified in this case),—had I so interfered in behalf of the rich, the powerful, the intelligent, the so-called great, or in behalf of any of their friends—either father, mother, sister, wife, or children, or any of that class—and suffered and sacrificed what I have in this interference, it would have been all right; and every man in this court would have deemed it an act worthy of reward rather than punishment. . . .

The full text of Document 3.16.4 is available on the CD-ROM.

3.16.5

Image of John Brown meeting the slave-mother and her child on the steps of Charlestown jail on his way to execution, 1863

The original painting was done by Louis Ransom in the North during the Civil War. It depicts John Brown as a martyr to the abolitionist cause.

JOHN BROWN

Meeting the Slave-mother and her Child on the steps of Charlestown jail on his way to execution.
The Artist has represented Capt. Brown regarding with a look of compassion a Slave-mother and Child who obstructed the passage on his way to the Scaffold. Capt. Brown stooped and kissed the Child, then met his fate.

Library of Congress

3.16.6

Image of John Brown ascending the scaffold
preparatory to being hanged

The execution of John Brown enraged abolitionists across the northern states. Many wrote and spoke of the event; others spread the word through visual images. This illustration first appeared in Leslie's Illustrated Newspaper, *Vol. 9, December 17, 1859.*

"JOHN BROWN ASCENDING THE SCAFFOLD PREPARATORY TO BEING HANGED.—FROM A SKETCH BY OUR SPECIAL ARTIST."

North Wind Picture Archives

3.16.7

"Comment by a Radical Abolitionist" by F. B. Sanborn,
from *Century Magazine* July 1883

I knew John Brown well. He was often at my house and at the houses of my friends and I traveled with him for days. He was what all his speeches, letters, and actions avouch him a simple, brave, heroic person incapable of anything selfish or base. . . . [H]e had . . . a certain predestined relation to the political crisis of his time, for which his character fitted him and which, had he striven against it, he could not avoid. . . . [H]e was an unquestioning believer in God's fore-ordination and the divine guidance of human affairs; . . but in this God-appointed, inflexible devotion to his object in life he was inferior to no man, and he rose in fame far above more gifted persons because of this very fixedness and simplicity of character. His renown is secure. . .

Young men never knew, perhaps, and some old men have forgotten, that we once had statesmen (so called) who loudly declared that negro slavery was the basis not only of our national greatness, but of the white man's freedom. This groveling doctrine found favor in Virginia in John Brown's time, and it was his work, as much as any man's, to overthrow it. . . .

The full text of Document 3.16.7 is available on the CD-ROM.

Glossary

abject: of the lowest degree; miserable; wretched.

abolition: an end to an institution, practice or condition.

abolitionist: a person in favor of bringing an end to an institution, law, custom, etc., especially associated with the abolition of slavery.

advocate: one that pleads the cause of another; one that defends or maintains a cause or proposal, to plead in favor of.

affidavit: a sworn statement in writing made under oath.

agent: a person empowered to act for or representing another; in this context for antislave societies.

anarchy: absence of government; a state of lawlessness or political disorder due to the absence of governmental authority.

appeal: to make a request to a higher court to review a case, to request help or sympathy from someone.

armory: a place storing weapons and other munitions.

arsenal: a place for making or storing weapons and other munitions.

avarice: excessive or insatiable desire for wealth or gain; extreme greed.

barbarous: uncivilized; lacking culture or refinement.

benefactor: one that confers a benefit; one that makes a gift or bequest.

betray: to deliver to an enemy by treachery.

bondage: slavery.

bondsman: the person who assumes responsibility for returning an individual for trial.

Borderland: territory at or near a border; in this context between slave and free states.

brethren: a fellow member of the same race, church, profession, organization, etc.; often used as a familiar term of address.

caste: a division of society based on differences of wealth, inherited rank or privilege, profession, or occupation.

chattel: a movable item of personal property; in this context a slave.

citizenship: the status of an individual considered a member of a state or nation; the duties, rights, and privileges of this status.

civil disobedience: refusal to obey what are perceived as unjust laws especially as a nonviolent and usually collective means of forcing concessions from the government.

civil power: power associated with a government chosen by citizens.

defendant: a person sued or accused in a court of law.

deficient: lacking in some necessary quality or element; not up to a normal standard or complement.

degradation: to drag down in rank, status, moral or intellectual character.

deport: to carry or send away; specifically, to force (an alien) to leave a country by official order.

despotic: of or like an absolute ruler; autocratic; tyrannical.

disparagement: to lower in rank or reputation, degrade.

dissenting opinion: a conclusion or judgment that differs from the majority.

doctrine: something taught as the principles or creed of a religion, political party, etc.

eloquent: having or characterized by gracefulness, fluency, and persuasion.

emancipate: to free from restraint, control, or the power of another; to free from slavery.

emancipation: freedom from restraint, control, or power of another; freedom from slavery.

expatriation: the state of being driven or withdrawn from one's native land or from allegiance to it; exile.

fanatic: a person whose extreme zeal, piety, etc., goes beyond what is reasonable.

flogging: a beating with a whip.

Free-soiler: someone opposed to the expansion of slavery in the territories.

fugitive: a person who flees from danger or justice; in this case slavery.

gallows: an upright frame with crossbeam and rope for hanging condemned persons.

habeas corpus, **writ of:** a document issued by a legal authority requiring that a jailed person be brought before a court to decide whether he/she is being held lawfully.

heathen: a person who does not acknowledge the God of the Bible.

"hire his time": the practice of slaves working elsewhere for pay, with the owners keeping most of the earnings.

humane: marked by compassion, sympathy, or consideration for humans.

"inalienable rights": rights that may not be taken away (as stated in the Declaration of Independence).

incumbent: pressing; essential.

indict: to charge with a crime.

inferiority: a sense of being of low or lower degree or rank, of poor quality, of little or less importance, value, or merit.

infringement: a breaking in on; an encroachment or trespassing on.

insurgent: a person who revolts against civil authority or an established government.

insurrection: an act of rebellion against civil authority or an established government.

Jim Crow: traditional discrimination against or segregation of blacks (named for an early black minstrel song).

judicial review: to reexamine a legal case through another court of law.

jurisdiction: the area overseen by a particular law court or system of courts.

lash: a whip; to whip.

locofoco: a negative name for a group of Democrats who supported slavery; it connoted that they were crazy and out of control.

macrocosm: the great world; a large-scale view.

manumission: being freed from slavery; liberation; emancipation.

majority opinion: a certain conclusion or judgment believed by more than half of the total number of people.

marshal: an officer having charge of prisoners.

martyrdom: the act of choosing to be tortured or killed rather than giving up one's beliefs.

melee: a noisy, confused fight or hand-to-hand struggle among a number of people.

militia: an army composed of citizens rather than professional soldiers.

mobocratic: ruled or dominated by the disorderly or lawless masses.

"moral suasion": persuasion by appealing to a person's sense of moral values or civic duty.

nolo contendere: a plea in criminal prosecution whereby a defendant does not admit guilt but can then be convicted and sentenced.

nullity: something that is null and void, with no power.

obiter dictum: any incidental remark or opinion expressed by someone; in this context, suggesting it has no legal force or legitimacy.

oppression: unjust or cruel exercise of authority or power.

oppressor: someone that uses power and authority unjustly and/or cruelly.

orator: someone highly skilled and powerful as a public speaker.

paternalistic: fatherlike; inappropriately controlling.

"peculiar institution": a euphemistic term that southerners used as a pseudonym for slavery; the term came into general use in the 1830s when abolitionists began to attack slavery.

perpetrator: someone who performs an action evil, criminal, or offensive.

perpetuate: to make something continue; to cause to last indefinitely.

persecute: to harass in a manner designed to injure, grieve, or afflict.

persevere: to persist in spite of opposition or discouragement.

petitioner: a person making a request using a formal written document.

physiology: a branch of biology that deals with the functions and activities of life or of living matter.

pickets: protestors stationed outside a factory, store or public building, often carrying signs, demonstrating opposition to certain views or practices.

plaintiff: a person who brings legal action.

precedent: (in this context) an earlier judicial ruling or opinion.

prejudiced: having a bias against someone or something.

prosecution: the conducting of criminal proceedings in court against a person.

rabble-rouser: one that stirs up (as to hatred or violence) the masses of the people.

redress: to correct.

scaffold: a temporary wooden or metal framework to support workmen and materials.

schooner: a two-masted vessel.

secesh: (from secession) colloquial term variously defined as Confederate troops and Southern sympathizers.

sectionalism: concern for the interests of only one area of a country.

sectional conflict: a pattern of political conflict between two or more geographical regions of a nation, in this context the "free" and "slave" states.

segregationist: a person who believes in the separation of the races.

services rendered: work having been completed.

servitude: the condition of a slave; slavery.

skiff: a small boat; especially a flat-bottomed rowboat.

stripes: whipping.

submission: an act of giving in to the authority or control of another.

suffrage: the right to vote, especially in political elections; franchise.

treason: betraying one's country by aiding its enemies or assisting in a war against one's own country.

tribunal: a court of justice.

vigilance: the quality or state of being watchful especially to avoid danger.

vindication: a fact or circumstance that clears someone from criticism, blame, guilt, suspicion, etc.

warrant: a legal document authorizing an officer to make an arrest, a seizure, or a search.